REAL ESTATE PRE-EXAM COURSE
WORKBOOK©

REAL ESTATE TRAINING INSTITUTE
LESLIE CLAUSON, DREI, CDEI

A STUDY GUIDE TO HELP YOU PASS THE REAL ESTATE EXAM.

Main Office

284 Eisenhower Drive

Biloxi, Mississippi 30531

228-354-8585

ISBN-13:
978-0692753255 (Leslie Clauson)

ISBN-10:
0692753257

Online resources available.

Please call the Main Office to receive your password to register at www.goretionline.com

228-354-8585

PROPERTY OWNERSHIP

<u>Home Ownership</u>

Reasons for Home Ownership

Sign of financial stability
Investment—appreciation/ homeowners
Intangible benefits

Real Property versus Personal Property
Real Property

Real Property is any land and things permanently attached to the land. It consists of minerals, oil, mines or quarries. When you own real estate, you own from the center of the earth and up unto infinity. You own air space.

Examples of real property include buildings, fixtures attached to the building, fences, structures, fruit, nut and ornamental trees and bushes. Standing timber and a vineyard are real.

Real property also includes; buildings, standing timber, pear trees, apple trees, orange trees, fences, doors, faucets, plumbing fixtures, washer less faucets, hot water heater, fences, landscape shrubs, an in-ground swimming pool.

Fructus Naturales – fruits created by the nature of the land. No assistance from man. Examples are fruit and nut trees.

Fruit trees once planted are real property. (Fructus Naturales : Latin, literally, natural fruits)

Real Estate is Real Property

The land and all things permanently attached to it by either nature or by man (improvements)

7

The bundle of legal rights/sticks includes the rights of real estate ownership

Possession

Control

Enjoyment

Exclusion

Disposition

Encumbrance

Annexation

Personal property that has been annexed to real property becomes real property. Such as doors, windows, mouldings…

Severance

An item of real property may be changed to personal property. It is severed from the real property.

Personal Property

Personal Property is movable. Things not permanently attached to the land are personal property. Personal property is movable.

All property that does not fit the definition of real property.

Personal property can be called chattel. Chattel is the French word for cattle. Cattle are movable. Some examples of personal property include leases and stock.

Personal – movable – chattels – Conveyed by Bill of Sale

Bricks placed on the driveway before they are built into a patio are personal property.

Fence posts that are put onto a driveway are personal property.

When an orange falls from its tree, it is personal property.

A lease or stock ownership interest in real estate is truly a piece of paper that allows someone to have possession of real property. Both pieces of paper are movable.

Crops that need yearly cultivation are personal property and called emblements. Examples of emblements include, tomato, corn, peas, beans, and cotton plants. Crops you plant every year (cultivate) are personal property.

Fructus Industrials

Crops cultivated yearly are personal property. (corn, peas, tomatoes)

When a tenant farmer gets evicted, he is allowed to cultivate the crops. A farmer is entitled to the fruits of his labor.

Legal tests of a fixture: overall test is intention of the annexor.

(MARIA)

Method of attachment

Agreement between the parties

Relationship of the parties – lessor/lessee

Intention of the annexor

Adaptation of the article to real estate

Fixtures are those things attached to the structure that is attached to the land such as doors, water heaters, built in air conditioners, sinks, faucets and ceiling lamps.

Fixtures include the landlord's personal property that was annexed to his real property such as fences, landscaping bushes, planted apple, pear and orange trees, a built-in pool and a brick patio.

Fixtures are personal property of the real estate owner, which is attached (annexed) to his real property.

Fixtures are the Landlord's property.

The doors, ceiling lights, toilets, sinks, waterless heater, water softener…..
A brick patio is real property.

A fence standing between two properties dividing the properties is real property.

Trade Fixtures

Trade Fixtures are a commercial tenant's personal property that was attached to the landlord's real property for the tenant's use in the course of his business. When the tenant moves out, trade fixtures are to be severed from the real property and any damage is repaired to the landlord's real property. The tenant takes his personal property with him.

A trade fixture will transfer to the real property owner if the tenant leaves it behind after moving out of the leased property.

The method of which the item is transferred to the landlord is called accession. When the landlord takes possession of the trade fixture left behind through accession, it becomes the landlord's real property.

Trade Fixtures are Tenant's Property.

Shelves attached to walls in a bookstore, the lanes in a bowling alley, the TV monitor your professor uses in school....

A bowling alley is the most trade fixture business.

Lets Review
Real vs. Personal

Property

A vineyard is real property.

This standing wood fence is real property.

Emblements

This cornfield is personal property.

It's cultivated yearly.

This olive grove is real property.

It is not cultivated yearly.

Fructus Naturales

A farmer is entitled to the fruits of his labor.

Land, sometimes referred to as dry land, is the solid surface of the Earth that is not permanently covered by water.

Areas where land meets large bodies of water are called coastal zones.1
The earth's surface extending downward to the center of the earth and upward to infinity, including things permanently attached by nature, such as trees and water.

Physical Characteristics of Land	**Economic Characteristics of Land**
Immobility Land cannot be moved. You cannot pick land up and move it to another location. Indestructibility Land cannot be destroyed. It may change on occasion but land goes on forever. Uniqueness (heterogeneity / non-homogeneous) There is no standardized land. All parcels are different in size and shape. No two parcels of land can be place at the same location.	Scarcity There is a limited supply. You cannot make more land. Land is not limitless. Situs - Area Preference Location – Location - Location Permanence Land is long term and relatively stable.

Improvements
Anything manmade added to land.

---

1 .1
..

A City is able to fairly accurately project what their tax base will be in ten years because of immobility. You can't pick up all the homes and businesses and move them out of the city.

A builder built two identical homes. One was on the ocean and the other was six miles inland. The house on the ocean sold for $200,000 more than the home six miles inland because of situs (location / areal preference)

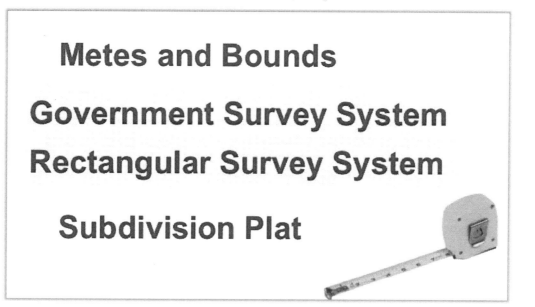

Metes and Bounds

A measurement that tells a story. The most important feature is the Point of Beginning. (POB) A surveyor will begin at a specific point such as a very old oak tree, a large boulder, and a corner of a fence, an intersection and so forth. The surveyor refers to distance and direction to measure the property. An example could be the following.

Beginning at a point (POB) on the South Side of School Street at the very old oak tree, 60 feet east to the Rushing River..........

The surveyor will return to the Point of Beginning. (POB)

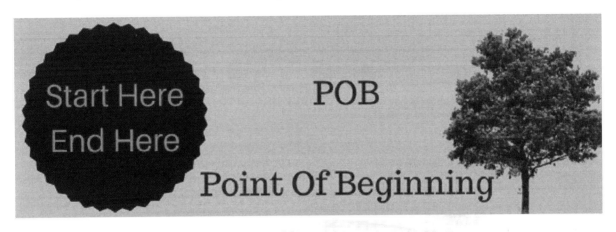

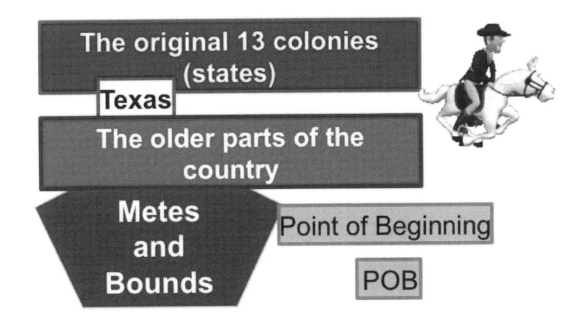

Metes and Bounds

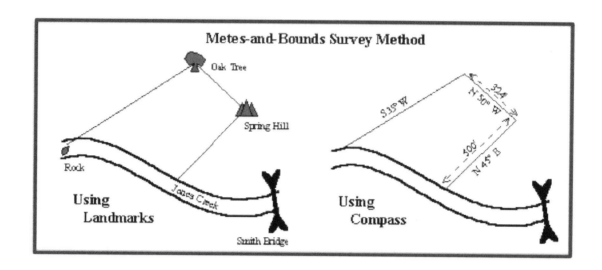

Metes-and-Bounds Survey Method

Oak Tree

Spring Hill

Rock

Tates Creek

Using Landmarks

Smith Bridge

S 35° W

N 50° W

32A

N 45° E

400'

Using Compass

Government Survey System
Rectangular Survey System

Governmental Survey System

Rectangular Survey System

Public Land Survey System (PLSS)

6	5	4	3	2	1
7	8	9	10	11	12
18	17	16	15	14	13
19	20	21	22	23	24
30	29	28	27	26	25
			34	35	36

There are 36 sections

Section 16 is set aside for schools.

6	5	4	3	2	1
7	8	9	10	11	12
18	17	16	15	14	13
19	20	21	22	23	24
30	29	28	27	26	25
31	32	33	34	35	36

Principal Meridian

Township

36 Sections

Baseline

Range Lines

Principal Meridian

6	5	4	3	2	1
7	8	9	10	11	12
18	17	16	15	14	13
19	20	21	22	23	24
30	29	28	27	26	25
31	32	33	34	35	36

Township

36 Sections

Baseline

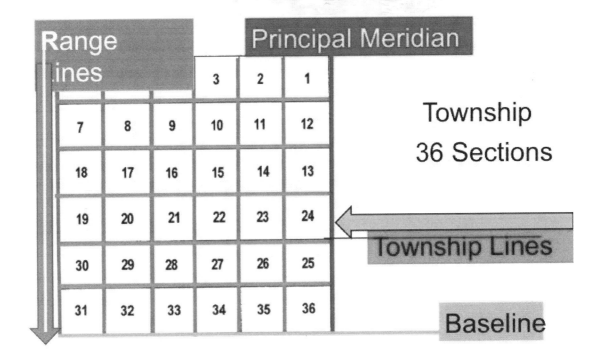

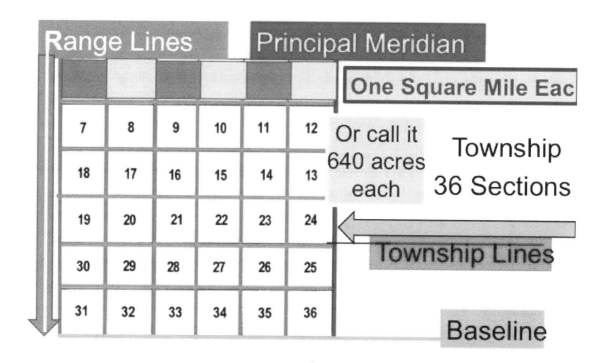

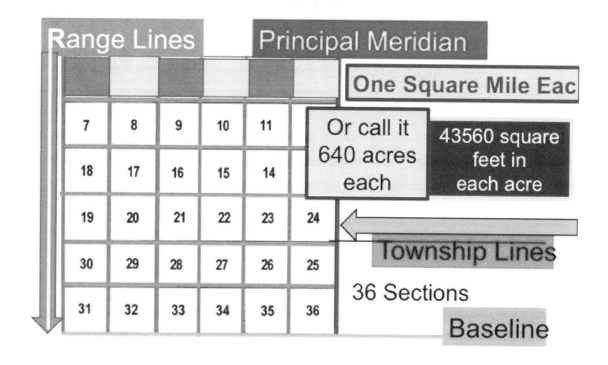

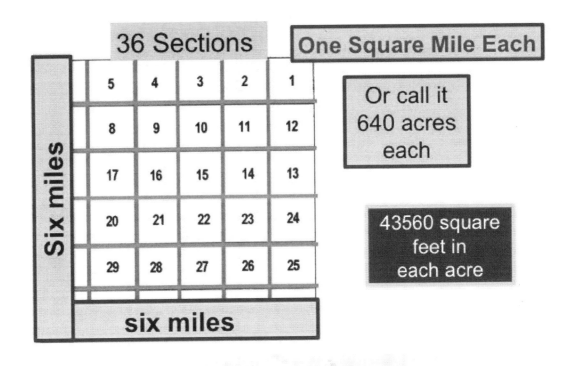

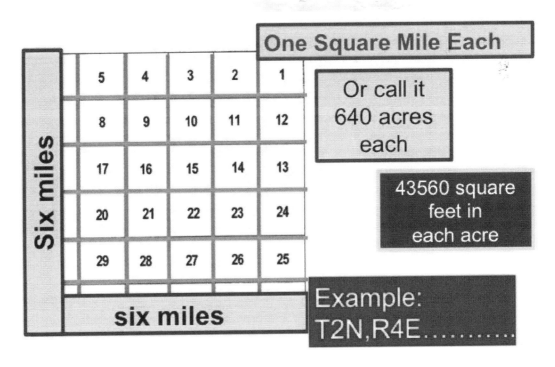

There are 43560 square feet in an acre.

4 old ladies driving 35 in a 60.

For the curvature of the
earth

Correction Line

5	4	3	2	1
8	9	10	11	12

15	14	13	18	17	16	15	14	13	18	17	16	15	14	13
22	23	24	19	20	21	22	23	24	19	20	21	22	23	24
27	26	25	30	29	28	27	26	25	30	29	28	27	26	25
31	32	33	34	35	36	31	32	33	34	35	36	31	32	33	34	35	36

6	5	4	3	2	1	6	5	4	3	2	1	6	5	4	3	2	1
7	8	9	10	11	12	7	8	9	10	11	12	7	8	9	10	11	12
18	17	16	15	14	13	18	17	16	15	14	13	18	17	16	15	14	13
19	20	21	22	23	24	19	20	21	22	23	24	19	20	21	22	23	24
30	29	28	27	26	25	30	29	28	27	26	25	30	29	28	27	26	25
31	32	33	34	35	36	31	32	33	34	35	36	31	32	33	34	35	36

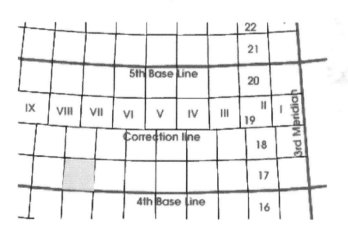

There are four townships in a row. The fifth township shifts over. The line is called the correction line. It is for the curvature of the earth.

Crops in Kansas

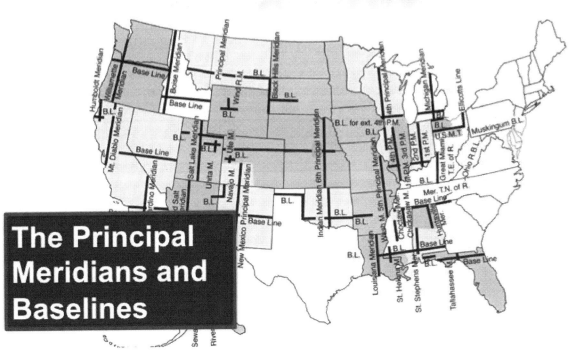

The Principal Meridians and Baselines

The Public Land Survey System (PLSS)

- ⬇ What is the PLSS?
- ⬇ History
- ⬇ Commonly Used Terms
- ⬇ Related Links

What is the PLSS?

States Included in the PLSS

Included

The Public Land Survey System (PLSS) is a way of subdividing and describing land in the United States. All lands in the public domain are subject to subdivision by this **rectangular system** of surveys, which is regulated by the U.S. Department of the Interior, Bureau of Land Management (BLM).

National Atlas of the United States®

The PLSS is used to divide public domain lands, which are lands owned by the Federal government for the benefit of the citizens of the United States. The original public domain included the land ceded to the Federal Government by the thirteen original States, supplemented with acquisitions from native Indians and foreign powers. It encompasses major portions of the land area of 30 southern and western States. Since the original PLSS surveys were completed, much of the land that was originally part of the public domain has been transferred to private ownership and in some areas the PLSS has been extended, following similar rules of division, into non-public domain areas.

PLSS rules of division are explained below.

For areas that were once part of the public domain, legal land descriptions are usually written in terms of PLSS descriptions.

The PLSS typically divides land into 6-mile-square townships, which is the level of information included in the National Atlas.

Townships are subdivided into 36 one-mile- square sections.

Sections can be further subdivided into quarter sections, quarter-quarter sections, or irregular government lots.

Normally, a permanent **monument,** or marker, is placed at each section corner. Monuments are also placed at quarter-section corners and at other important points, such as the corners of government lots.

Today permanent monuments are usually inscribed tablets set on iron rods or in concrete. The original PLSS surveys were often marked by wooden stakes or posts, marked trees, pits, or piles of rock, or other less-permanent markers.

The PLSS actually consists of a series of separate surveys. Most PLSS surveys begin at an initial point, and townships are surveyed north, south, east, and west from that point.

The north-south line that runs through the initial point is a true meridian and is called the **Principal Meridian**. There are 37 Principal Meridians, each is named, and these names are used to distinguish the various surveys.

The east-west line that runs through the initial point is called a **base line**. This line is perpendicular to the Principal Meridian.

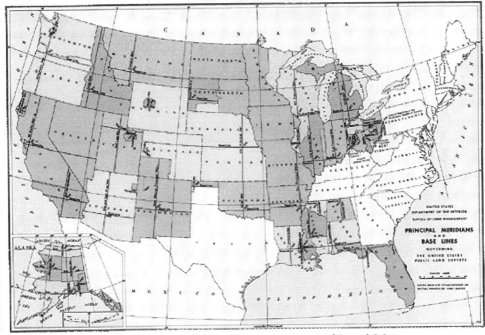

Source: Principal Meridians and Base Lines, Bureau of Land Management

Each township is identified with a township and range designation.

Township designations indicate the location north or south of the baseline, and range designations indicate the location east or west of the Principal Meridian.

For example, a township might be identified as Township 7 North, Range 2 West, which would mean that it was in the 7th tier of townships north of a baseline, and in the 2nd column of townships west of a principal meridian.

A legal land description of a section includes the State, Principal Meridian name, Township and Range designations with directions, and the section number: Nebraska, Sixth Principal Meridian T7N, R2W, sec5.

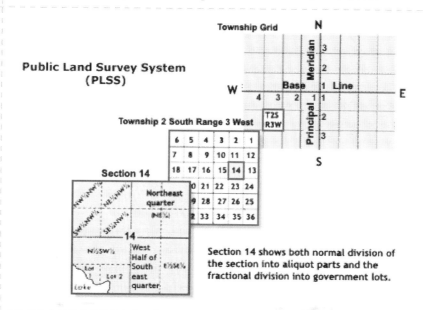

Section 14 shows both normal division of the section into aliquot parts and the fractional division into government lots.

While the original PLSS surveys were supposed to conform to official procedures, some errors were made due either to honest mistakes or to fraudulent surveys. Existing surveys are considered authoritative, and any new surveys must work from existing corners and surveys, in spite of errors in the original surveys and variations from the ideal. This sometimes results in sections that are far from square, or that contain well over or under **640 acres.**

The early surveys in Ohio and Indiana were done when the system currently in use had not yet been fully developed. While these surveys have townships that are 6 miles square, the numbering system used and the types of starting points for the surveys are different from those used elsewhere in the United States. These surveys are also named, although the names are not based on Principal Meridians.

Source: Principal Meridians and Base Lines, Bureau of Land Management

History

Originally proposed by Thomas Jefferson, the PLSS began shortly after the Revolutionary War, when the Federal government became responsible for large areas west of the thirteen original colonies.

The government wished both to distribute land to Revolutionary War soldiers in reward for their service, as well as to sell land as a way of raising money for the nation.

Before this could happen, the land needed to be surveyed. The Land Ordinance of 1785 which provided for the systematic survey and monumentation of public domain lands, and the Northwest Ordinance of 1787 which established a rectangular survey system designed to facilitate the transfer of Federal lands to private citizens, were the beginning of the PLSS.

Under Congressional mandate, cadastral surveys (surveys of the boundaries of land parcels) of public lands were undertaken to create parcels suitable for disposal by the Government. The extension of the rectangular system of surveys over the public domain has been in progress since 1785, and, where it applies, the PLSS forms the basis for most land transfers and ownership today.

The Manual of Instructions for the Survey of the Public Lands Of The United

29

<u>States, 1973</u> documents current official procedures for PLSS surveys.

Certain lands were excluded from the public domain and were not subject to survey and disposal. These lands include the beds of navigable bodies of water, national installations such as military reservations and national parks, and areas such as land grants that had already passed to private ownership prior to subdivision by the Government.

France, Spain, and Mexico all conferred land grants in territory they claimed; many of these grants were confirmed by the U.S Government when the territory in which they were situated was acquired by the United States, and the land was then excluded from the public domain.

Over the past two centuries, almost 1.5 billion acres have been surveyed into townships and sections. The BLM is the Federal Government's official record keeper for over 200 years' worth of cadastral survey records and plats. In addition, BLM is still completing numerous new surveys each year, mostly in Alaska, as well as conducting resurveys to restore obliterated or lost original survey corners.

Commonly Used Terms

Base line—A parallel of latitude, or approximately a parallel of latitude, running through an arbitrary point chosen as the starting point for all sectionalized land within a given area.

Government lot—A subpart of a section which is not described as an aliquot part of the section, but which is designated by number, for example, Lot 3. A lot may be regular or irregular in shape, and its acreage may vary from that of regular aliquot parts. These lots frequently border water areas excluded from the PLSS.

Initial point—The starting point for a survey.

Land Grant—A land grant is an area of land to which title was conferred by a predecessor government and confirmed by the U.S Government after the territory in which it is situated was acquired by the United States. These lands were never part of the original public domain and were not subject to subdivision by the PLSS.

Principal meridian—A meridian line running through an arbitrary point chosen as a starting point for all sectionalized land within a given area.

Public domain—Land owned by the Federal government for the benefit of the citizens. The original public domain included the lands that were turned over to the Federal Government by the Colonial States and the areas acquired later from the native Indians or foreign powers. Sometimes used interchangeably with Public lands.

Public lands—Lands in public ownership, therefore owned by the Federal government. Sometimes used interchangeably with Public domain.

Range—A vertical column of townships in the PLSS.

Section—A one-square-mile block of land, containing 640 acres, or approximately one thirty-sixth of a township. Due to the curvature of the Earth, sections may occasionally be slightly smaller than one square mile.

Township—An approximately 6-mile square area of land, containing 36 sections. Also, a horizontal row of townships in the PLSS.

Subdivision Plat – Lot and Block Numbers

Subdivision Plat will overlay either the Metes and Bounds or the Rectangular Survey System

A sub-divider will break the land into lots, blocks and street addresses. Once completed, the new legal descriptions are recorded.

This map can overlay either main types of measurement.

This map breaks up a large parcel of land into smaller parcels. A sub-divider would break down the individual lots with the Lot and Block numbers system using an engineer or surveyor. The new smaller lots are recorded to give constructive notice to the world.

The map must identify:

1. Individual lots
2. The block in which the lot is located
3. A reference to a platted subdivision or similar
4. A reference to find the cited plat map
5. A description of the map's place of official recording

PLAT MAP

1. Individual lots

2. The block in which the lot is located

3. A reference to a platted subdivision or similar

4. A reference to find the cited plat map

5. A description of the map's place of official recording

MEASURING ELEVATIONS

Datum
A point of reference for measuring elevations.
The United States Geological Survey (USGS) uses mean (average) sea level in New York Harbor.

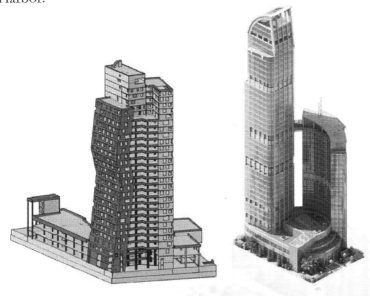

Benchmark
A permanent reference point used primarily to mark elevations.
A monument is a manmade object used as the point of beginning.

Benchmark – The point of certain elevation marked for the purpose of surveying. The standard point of reference.

Datum - The horizontal plane used for elevation measurement.

N 40° 41.350 W 074° 02.673 (NAD 83)
Altitude: 0

Coordinates may not be exact. Altitude is UNKNOWN and location is ADJUSTED. (more info)

Location:

Example of a benchmark

In NEW YORK county, NY View Original Datasheet

Designation:

STATUE OF LIBERTY

CONTOUR MAP

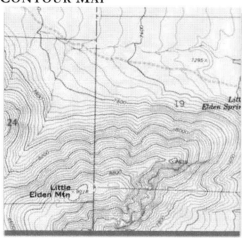

Legal descriptions are used to identify real estate. It is a detailed way of describing a parcel of land in documents such as deeds and mortgages that will be accepted in court of law.

Mineral, Air and Water Rights

When a person owns real estate, they own from the center of the earth up into infinity.

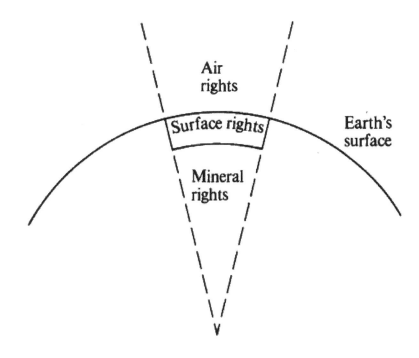

All the minerals under the land surface are included in the definition of real property.

Real Estate extends to air rights which may be called <u>Air Lots.</u>

Real Estate
The land and all things permanently attached to it by either nature or by man (improvements). Can be sold or leased to others.

Surface rights
The land.

Subsurface rights

Mineral rights are property rights to exploit an area for the <u>minerals</u> it harbors. Mineral rights can be separate from property ownership. Subsurface rights may be leased.

To bring oil and gas reserves to market, minerals are conveyed for a specified time to oil companies through a legally binding contract known as a lease.

Air rights

Air rights are the property interest in the "space" above the earth's surface. Generally speaking, owning, or renting, land or a <u>building</u> includes the right to use and develop the space above the land without interference by others.[i]

To promote air commerce, legislators established a legal height for any interests associated with lands; thereby establishing a public right to transit through the higher altitudes.[1]

Water Rights

Riparian
Small river or stream.
The rights of an adjacent landowner to a creek, stream, pond or adjacent small body of water. It gives all owners of land contiguous to the same body of surface water equal reasonable rights to the water whether a landowner uses the water or not.

A landowner cannot deny another landowner downstream from the water by rerouting the water or damming it. If the water right is attached (appurtenant) to the land, it runs with the deed and transfers to the next owner.

Littoral
Large body of water and tidal waters.
Navigable
Tidal Water
Littoral rights give the homeowner shoreline rights.
The land in between the high tide and low tide is set aside for the use and enjoyment of the public.
If the water right is attached (appurtenant) to the land, it runs with the deed and transfers to the next owner.

With **Littoral Water Rights**, strangers are allowed access to the sand in front of an ocean front property at low tide.

Prior Appropriation

With prior appropriation, the first person to take water for a beneficial purpose has the right to continue with the use of taking of the water.

Other landowners may take water as long as it does not infringe on the first user. "Fist in time of use."

Prior Appropriation is used where water is scarce or limited. Government Granted.

Prior Appropriation

Beneficial Purpose

"Fist in time of use."

Prior Appropriation is used where water is scarce or limited.

Government Granted

Prior Appropriation is used in the drier areas of the Country.

Chapter Two

ENCUMBRANCES

Encumbrances and Effects on Property Ownership
Encumbrance means "something burdensome" or something that bothers something.

Encumbrances are something that is bothersome / burdens.

Easements are encumbrances. A mortgage, a property tax bill and a mechanics lien are all encumbrances. A shared driveway, an easement and an encroachment are all encumbrances also.

An encumbrance is a <u>right</u> to, interest in, or legal <u>liability</u> on <u>real property</u> that does not prohibit passing <u>title</u> to the property but that diminishes its value.[1]

Encumbrances can be classified in several ways. They may be financial (ex: <u>liens</u>) or non-financial (ex: <u>easements</u>, private restrictions).

Alternatively, they may be divided into those that affect title or those that affect the use or physical condition of the encumbered property (ex: restrictions, easements, encroachments).[2]

Deed restrictions are encumbrances.

(Example: same mailboxes or You cannot cut down oak trees on your property.)
Deed restrictions are private agreements that affect the use of land. It is also called a limitation on use.

Liens (types and priority)
A lien refers to *non-possessory* security interests.

Liens affect the title. A property tax bill or an unpaid mortgage bill may affect ownership.

Voluntary Liens vs. Involuntary Liens

> **Voluntary Liens**
> A lien voluntarily placed on a property by a property owner.
> A mortgage and trust deed are voluntary liens.

Voluntary Liens

A Mortgage

A Second Mortgage

Involuntary Liens

Tax Liens

Liens can be voluntary or involuntary.

Voluntary Liens

mortgage

chattel mortgage

Involuntary Liens

Tax liens, imposed to secure payment of a tax;

"Weed liens" and "Demolition liens", assessed by the government to rectify a property from being a nuisance and public hazard;

Homeowner Association (HOA) liens for unpaid assessments, fines, late charges, interest, costs, and attorney fees;

Mechanic's liens, which secure payment for work done on property or land;

Judgment liens, imposed to secure payment of a judgment.

Specific Liens vs. General Liens

Specific Liens	General Liens
Specific liens are liens specifically on a single property. **Mortgage liens and Trust Deeds Property taxes** are also liens **Ad Valorem taxes**, meaning according to value. **Special Assessments**: A special assessment is an added tax that is paid for by the people who benefit from an improvement. Taxes take priority. **Mechanics liens**	General liens are liens on everything you own. **A judgment Inheritance taxes Income tax Debts due of a deceased person** A General lien could be a lien on several properties one person owns.

Specific Liens

Mortgage Liens and Trust Deeds

Property Taxes

Ad Valorem Taxes

Special Assessments

Mechanics Liens

Mortgage Liens and Trust Deeds

General Liens

A judgment

Inheritance taxes

Income tax

Debts due of a deceased person

A General lien could be a lien on several properties one person owns.

Statutory Liens vs. Equitable Liens

Statutory Liens
A statutory lien is placed on the property by law.
Real estate property taxes -
ad valorem meaning
"according to value"
Special assessments

Equitable Liens
An equitable lien is placed on the property by written contract to produce fairness.
lis pendens – lawsuit pending – means a lawsuit has been filed
A foreclosure can wipe out a lis pendens.
Mechanics liens

Statutory Liens

Placed on the property by law.

Equitable Liens

Placed on the property by written contract to produce fairness.

Mechanics liens

Taxes take priority.

Taxes take priority.

In most cases taxes are paid first.

After taxes,
liens are paid in the order
they were recorded.

Real estate taxes and special assessments get paid first.

After taxes, liens are paid in the order they were recorded.

When a mechanic's lien is filed for the non-payment of labor or materials used to improve a property, the effective date of the lien is the date the improvement, work or materials were furnished.

Real Estate Tax Liens

Ad valorem tax (ad valorem = according to value) This is your property taxes paid once a year. Taxes are to meet the demand of the government.
Ad valorem are *specific, involuntary, statutory* liens.

Special assessments (improvement taxes)
Always specific and statutory liens.

Mortgage liens and deed of trust liens - voluntary, specific liens used in real estate financing

Mechanic's liens - involuntary, statutory, specific liens.

Judgment lien - involuntary, equitable, general liens

Estate and inheritance tax lien - involuntary, statutory, general liens; they are usually paid during **the probate court proceedings.**

Corporate franchise tax lien - involuntary, statutory, general liens for taxes imposed on corporations as a condition of their conducting business in some states.

Internal Revenue Service (income) tax liens - involuntary, statutory, general liens that result from a person's failure to pay any portion of his or her federal tax liability, such as income and withholding taxes.

Easements

Easement Appurtenant
Right of way in Addition to

ownership of real estate.

Easements "run with the land", meaning that when a real estate owner sells the property, the easement automatically transfers with the property deed.

Easement Appurtenance – An easement is annexed to ownership. It is a right to use another's land. "In addition to. – a right of way that benefits a parcel of land to the detriment of anther parcel of land.

Appurtenant means "in addition to" or "belonging to"

There must be at least two properties for an Easement Appurtenance.

Dominant Tenement
Servient Tenement

Easements "run with the land"

An easement is most like a Right of Way. An easement is recorded and in your deed. An easement can end with the Merging of Titles. Merging of Titles means that one person bought or now owns both properties.

An easement can also end when the Dominant Tenement Easement user releases the easement in favor of the owner of the Servient Tenement.

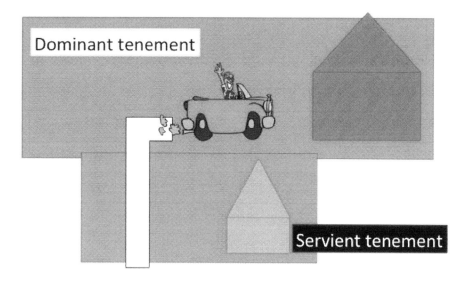

Servient Tenement
The burdened land.
The tenement on which the easement is placed.
The easement on the servient tenement is an encumbrance.

Dominant Tenement
The tenement that benefits from the easement.

Ingress and Egress
In and Exit

In an easement appurtenant, the two tracts of land can be contiguous or noncontiguous.

An easement appurtenant is most like a "right of way".

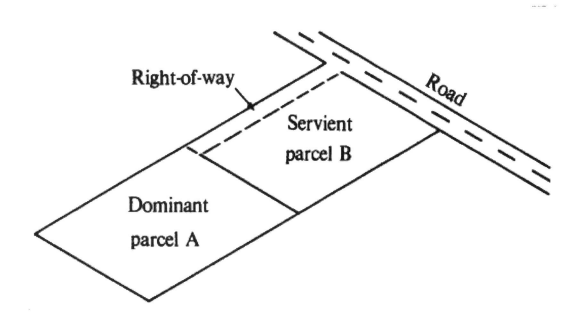

Bob owns his home in a lake front community in addition to a **non-contiguous easement appurtenant** for access to the lake. **Or** Bob owns his home in addition to a "right of way" over his neighbor's property in order to access the lake. (For ingress and egress.)

Noncontiguous:
Things not side by side.

Noncontiguous Easement Appurtenant

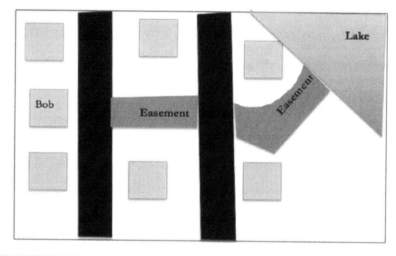

Page 30

Easement in Gross

Frequently for utilities.

Easement in Gross – Utility Company Access. There is no dominant tenement.
All of the homes up against a Gross Easement are Servient Tenements.

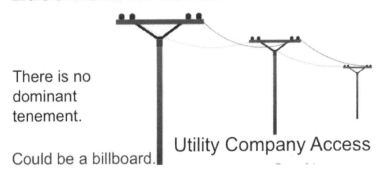

Party Wall Easement

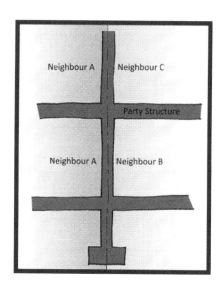

Used for a wall that straddles the property line of adjacent properties with different owners.

Easement by Necessity

A land locked property or a property with no access. Access is needed.

Land locked property. It is because owners must have ingress to and egress from their land.

Easement by Prescription

Easement by Prescription

Continuous
Visible
Open
Notorious

This will be in the form of a time factor question!

Based on the principles of Adverse Possession.

Continuous usage, without the owner's approval. It's usage that is visible, open and notorious. It's based on the principles of **Adverse Possession**. It's when someone has been doing something for a long period of time.

Bob was driving over the northeast corner of Al's property for 10 years. Al knew about it but didn't like it. Al never said anything to Bob. One day, Al decided he wanted to build a home for his daughter on that portion of land that Bob has been driving over. Al asked Bob to stop using his property. Bob took Al to court and was granted permission to continue to drive over Al's property. Al's intention to build his daughter a new home on that section of land had to be abandoned. Bob was granted an Easement by Prescription.

Adverse Possession

Adverse Possession

Open, continuous, notorious and hostile use of another person's property for a statutory period of time.

A way of taking title to another person's property by the open, continuous, notorious and hostile use of another person's property for a statutory period of time.

Easement by Condemnation

Acquired for a public purpose; requires compensation for loss in property value.

Creating an Easement
By express grant in a deed from the owner of the property.
By express reservation by the grantor in a deed of conveyance.
By use.
By implication.

Terminating an Easement
When the purpose for which it was created no longer exists.
By the owner of either the dominant or the servient tenement becoming the owner of both under one legal description. (merger) MERGING OF TITLES
By release of the right of easement to the owner of the servient tenement.

By abandonment of the easement.

By the non-use of a prescriptive easement by its owner.

By adverse possession by the owner of the servient tenement.

By destruction of the servient tenement (for instance, party wall).

By court decision of a quiet title action against someone claiming an easement.

By excessive use (possibly a change in land use).

License

A license is a temporary right to use the land of another.

Bob has granted Tom and his family permission to fish from Bob's pond for the month of May. Bob has granted Tom and his family a license.

A revocable right to use another's land for a specific reason.

  # License

A revocable right to use another's land for a specific reason.

Fishing from pond during the month of August.

Parking in driveway during little league season.

Encroachments

An encroachment is an improvement over onto another's property.

An encroachment is an improvement over onto another's property

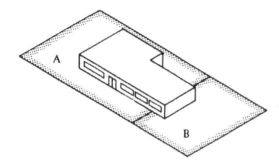

> If Bob's garage extended onto Sally's property it is an encroachment. If many years go by and nothing is done to remove the overextending garage, Bob may be granted a prescriptive easement.

The best way to find an encroachment is to hire a surveyor.

Types of Estate

Freehold - own

Non freehold - lease

Real Property

Real estate plus the interests, benefits, and rights inherent in the ownership of real estate.

Ownership Rights / Sticks:

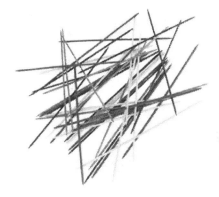

The bundle of legal rights includes the rights of:

Possession—the right to occupy the premises

Control—the right to determine certain interests for others

Enjoyment—possession without harassment or interference

Exclusion—legally refusing to create interests for others

Disposition—determining how the property will be disposed of

Encumbrance—the right to use property as security for loan

1. Severalty
2. Co-Ownership
3. Trust

Ownership in Severalty
One Person

Single Ownership - Ownership in Severalty (Tenancy in Severalty) – One person

Ownership in Severalty is when real property is owned by a single person or entity.

Co Ownerships

Tenancy in Common
Joint Tenancy
Tenancy by the Entirety

Tenancy in Common

Two or more natural or legal owners
Each owner with an undivided fractional interest

Unity of *possession*
Each owner may encumber or convey his or her interest
Each interest is inheritable

Tenancy in Common

Interests do not have to be equal.

A partner can will his/her shares.

Can Partition to separate interests.

Joint Tenancy (with rights of survivorship) JTWROS

Two or more natural owners

Right of survivorship

Creation of joint tenancy requires four unities (PITT)
    A. Possession
All joint tenants holding an undivided right to possession.
    B. Interest
All joint tenants holding equal ownership interests.
    C. Time
All joint tenants acquiring their interest at the same time.
    D. Title
All joint tenants acquiring their interests by the same document.
Termination of joint tenancy occurs when any one unity is terminated.

Joint Tenancy

Equal Interests

The Four Unities

JTWROS

Can partition to separate interests.

More info

The Four Unities in Joint Tenancy

Time

Title

Interest

Possession

Partition in Joint Tenancy

A Court action to partition turns the ownership into Tenancy in Common.

Suit to Partition

A **partition** is a term used in the law of real property to describe an act, by a court order or otherwise, to divide up a concurrent estate into separate portions representing the proportionate interests of the tenants. It is sometimes described as a **forced sale**.

https://en.wikipedia.org/wiki/Partition_(law)

Tenancy by the Entirety

Spouses Only

The Four Unities of Joint Tenancy
PLUS MARRIAGE

Each person is 1/2 person. Together they make up
the one person who owns the property.

Tenancy by the Entirety
Special form of ownership for married couples in certain states.
Husband and wife are considered one legal entity.
Each has undivided interest with inherent right of survivorship.
Both husband and wife must sign any documents to encumber or convey the property.

Termination of Tenancy by Entireties:
Death of either spouse; survivor becomes owner in severalty.
Agreement between both parties (new deed)
Divorce (parties become tenants in common)
Court ordered sale.

Community Property

Married couples only
Husband and wife are equal partners.
All property acquired during the marriage is community property.
Property brought to the marriage or acquired by gift or inheritance is separate property.
Does not have a right of survivorship as joint tenancy does.

"Community property is a marital property regime under which most property acquired during the marriage (except for gifts or inheritances) is owned jointly by both spouses and is divided upon divorce, annulment, or death. Joint ownership is automatically presumed by law in the absence of specific evidence that would point to a contrary conclusion for a particular piece of property.

Generally speaking, the property that each partner brings into the marriage or receives by gift, bequest or devise during marriage is called separate property (not community property
Source: Community property - https://en.wikipedia.org

Ownership In Trust

Title
is held
by a third
Party
for the
benefit
of another.

Ownership by Trusts
Parties to a trust.

Trustor
The person who creates the trust.

Trustee
The party who holds legal title and must carry out the trustor's instructions.

Beneficiary
The person who receives the benefits of the trust.

Living trust
Created while the trustor is alive.

Testamentary trust
Created by the grantor's will.

Land trust
Real estate is the only asset.
Public records do not name beneficiary. (A way of hiding the owner's identity.)

Partition
Termination of co-ownership by suit for partition.
The court may physically divide the property, or order it sold and divide the proceeds among the disputing owners.

General Partnership

All partners are general partners who participate in the partnership and share full liability

Limited Partnership

The general partner provides the management.
The limited partners are only liable to the extent of their investment.

S corporations

Corporations that elect to pass corporate income, losses, deductions, and credits through to their shareholders for federal tax purposes. Shareholders of S corporations report the flow-through of income and losses on their personal tax returns and are assessed tax at their individual income tax rates. This allows S corporations to avoid double taxation on the corporate income. S corporations are responsible for tax on certain built-in gains and passive income at the entity level.

Corporations

A legal entity or A person.
Exist in perpetuity (forever) until formally dissolved
Managed and operated by board of directors.
Provide its shareholders with limited liability.
Corporate profits are usually subject to double taxation unless a S corporation.

Syndicate

A joining together of two or more people or firms.

Limited Liability Companies (LLC)

Members have the limited liability of a corporation, plus the tax advantages of a partnership.
One person can be an LLC.

Joint Venture

Two or more people or firms carry out a single business project.

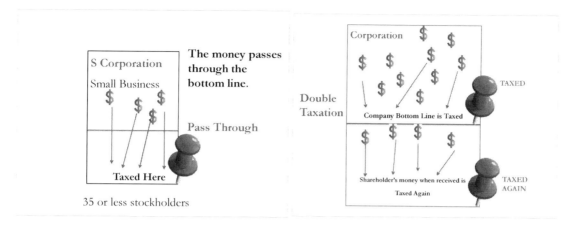

S Corporation

Small Business

The money passes through the bottom line.

Pass Through

Taxed Here

35 or less stockholders

Corporation

Double Taxation

Company Bottom Line is Taxed

TAXED

Shareholder's money when received is Taxed Again

TAXED AGAIN

Types of Estates

Freehold – estate for an indeterminable time.
Non-Freehold – leaseholds

> **Freehold**
> A Freehold estate of real property is when the owner has immediate rights (bundle of rights) to the property for an undefined amount of time.
>
> **A fee Simple Absolute** (highest form of ownership) is a freehold estate that can be inherited.
> A Life Estate is a freehold estate that designates a specific person or persons who will retain possession of the property for as long as they are alive. At the life estate owner's death, the property will pass to the remainder man.

> **Less Than Freehold – Non-Freehold**
> This is an estate of property that allows a user to retain possession for a specific period of time.
> **Leasehold Estates**
>
> Tenancy for Years – A leasehold interest in property with a definite beginning and a definite end.
> Tenancy at Sufferance (holdover tenancy) – A tenant unwilling to vacate. An eviction may be in effect.
> Tenancy at Will – A leasehold estate without a specific amount of time. Either the tenant or landlord can end this lease.
>
> Periodic Tenancy - Tenancy for year-to-year, month-to-month or week-to-week. From period to period.

Freehold Estate

Ownership (bundle of rights)

Ownership for a indeterminable amount of time.

A Life Estate is a freehold estate.

Life Estate

Life tenant is entitled to possession of the property. A life estate holder is not beholden to the future owners.

Reversionary interest

The property returns to the grantor (or the grantor's heirs).

Life Estates

A person will own the property until they die.

Pur Autrie Vie
A life estate based on another's life.

At the death of the life estate holder, the property will convey to a remainder man. He is said to hold the property for the remainder of the property existence.

Carol owned a life estate with the **remainder man** to be Bob. She leased her property to a tenant for nine years. In year three of the lease, she passed away. What is the status of the lease? Voided. The lease is only valid for the duration of Carol's life.

Pur Autrie Vie

A life estate based on the life of another.

Dower

The life estate interest of a wife in the real property of her deceased husband.

Curtesy

The life estate interest of a husband in the real property of his deceased wife.

Community property states do not use dower or curtesy.

Homestead rights

Protects the equity in a residence from a judgment by unsecured creditors.

Fee Simple Absolute

vs.

Fee Simple Defeasible

Fee Simple (fee simple absolute)	Fee Simple Defeasible
Highest interest in ownership. The highest form of ownership in real estate.	Ownership with a condition. If the condition is violated the property will revert back to the original grantor.

A hospital was granted a **fee simple defeasible estate**. They were allowed to keep the property forever as long as they meet the condition of the defeasible deed. It stated that the hospital must remain a no-profit.
If the condition is violated, the deed will revert back to the original grantor.

Fee Simple Absolute

The highest form of ownership.

Bundle of Rights
Ownership Rights
Bundle of Sticks

Fee Simple Defeasible

Highest form of
ownership with
a condition.

**Terms &
Conditions**

**If that condition is violated,
the property reverts back to the original
grantor.**

Less Than Freehold
Non-Freehold

A rental or a leasehold

Estate for Years (tenancy for years)
It does not have to be for a year or years. It can be any amount of time.
There has to be a definite beginning and a definite ending.
No notice is required to terminate.
Does not automatically renew.

Tenancy for Years

A fixed term tenancy.
Has a definite beginning and a
definite end.

Estate from Period to Period (periodic tenancy)
Month to Month. A fixed period of time. Auto renewal.
Notice must be given by either party to terminate.

Holdover Tenancy
Landlord may evict or treat holdover tenant as one who has periodic tenancy.

Estate at Will (tenancy at will)
The consent of the landlord is mandatory.
Informal and usually oral.

Indefinite in length.

Notice must be given to terminate the lease.

Estate at Sufferance (tenancy at sufferance)

An eviction by the landlord or the landlord's representative is eminent. The tenant refuses to vacate.

Federal Fair Housing Act makes it illegal to discriminate on basis of physical disabilities.

Tenants may make reasonable modifications to property but must restore at end of lease term.

Tenancy at Sufferance

The tenant is a trespasser.

Holdover tenancy.

An eviction.

Tenant is making the landlord suffer.

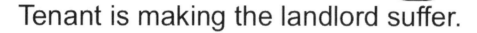

Subleasing

Subleasing is the transfer of **part** of the tenant's interest.

The tenant/sub lessor's interest in a sublease is known as a sandwich lease.

Gross Lease
Landlord pays some of the tenant expenses.
Landlord may be paying gas, electric, trash….

Net Lease
Tenant pays some of landlord expenses.
Tenant may be paying the electric bill in the parking lot, a portion of property taxes….

Gross Lease

Landlord pays
some of the
Tenant's expenses.

Net Lease

Tenant pays some of the landlord expenses.

Taxes

Insurance

N N N
Triple Net Lease

Common Area maintenance

Percentage Lease
Rent based on the percentage of income. (sales)

Percentage Lease

Rent based on a percentage of total sales.

Index Lease
A lease based on an index.
Rent can go up and down based on an economic index.

Index lease is when rent is based off of an economic index.

76

Lease with Obligation to Purchase
A Rent to Own

Ground Lease
Long Term Lease

Ground Lease – Long term lease. The tenant builds on the property.

A Sale-Leaseback is when the owner of real property sells the property and then leases it back.

A Sale Leaseback

The owner of the property sells the property and then rents the property back.

Graduated Lease. Goes up over time

Graduated Lease

A lease that gradually increases over time.

Oil and Gas Lease

Drilling companies most often lease the rights to drill for and produce oil.

Agricultural Lease

Farm Lease

The agriculture sector relies heavily on leases for land and equipment to meet the needs of farmers. With absentee ownership of farmland growing in the United States, farmers and ranchers lease many of the acres they farm and graze today. Either private parties or governmental entities may enter into a leasing arrangement so the complexity and scope of these contracts can vary substantially.

Leasehold Interest
The Tenant's Interest in a Leasehold Estate

Leased Fee Interest
The Landlord's interest in a Leasehold Estate

Leased Fee Interest

Leasehold Interest

The Landlord's interest

Tenant's Interest

Co Owner Properties

Condominiums – Condos
Stock Cooperatives
Time Share Estates

Condominiums – Condos

Real Property

Ownership of an individual home in a collection of homes.

A condo owner owns a percentage of interest in the common areas.

It is possible to hold title as "In Severalty" and "In Common" when owning a condominium. The "In Common" title is the percentage ownership of all the common grounds and appurtenances.

Condos are usually managed by a Home Owners Association.
Homeowner's Dues are associated with ownership for the upkeep of the buildings and common areas.

The real property owner owns the four walls of his unit and the space contained within. Patios may be appurtenant with each owner's interest.

Condominium - Condos

The owner owns the four walls of his unit and the space contained within.

The owner owns a percentage of interest in the common areas.

Patios and parking spaces may be appurtenant with each owner's interest.

Stock Cooperatives

Personal Property

A corporation owns the real estate and the inhabitants own stock in the corporation.
The inhabitants receive a Proprietary Lease.
The amount of stock a person owns determines the size and location of his unit.
The stockholders interview the buyer of the stock to determine the credit worthiness of an applicant.

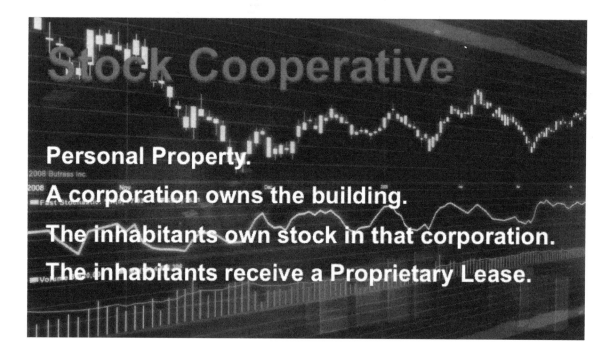

Stock Cooperative

Personal Property.

A corporation owns the building.

The inhabitants own stock in that corporation.

The inhabitants receive a Proprietary Lease.

Time Share Estates

Real Property

Interval Ownership

A timeshare owner owns property along with others owners. Timeshares are most often a vacation home.

The use of the estate is limited to the timeshare interest.

Timeshares are owned as "Tenancy in Common".

Time Share Estate

Real Property

Interval Ownership

Owners are all Tenants in Common.

Usually a vacation home.

Planned Unit Development – PUD

The development of an entire community. Includes, homes, stores, schools, business, parks and so forth.

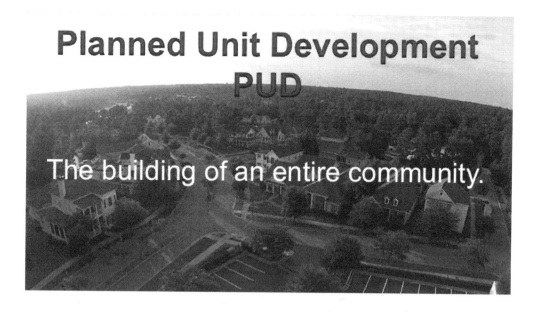

Chapter Four

Land Use Controls and Regulations

Government rights in land

Property Taxes and Special Assessments

Taxes are to meet the public needs of government.

Taxes take priority.

Ad Valorem
According to Value
This is your property tax.

Special Assessments
Only those who benefitted from an improvement pay the special assessment. For example, if a neighborhood needs a new school the city will go and build it. Only the people in that school district will be forced to pay the special assessments.

Only the government can eminent domain. The government can take privately owned property for the good of the public.

Video/Eminent Domain here

Condemnation is compensation to the property owner. Known as "Just Compensation".

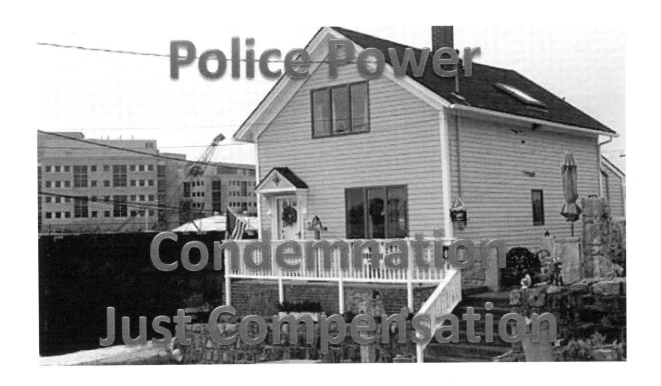

Eminent Domain
The government takes your
property for the use of the public.

The owner is paid <u>Just</u>
<u>Compensation</u>
Through <u>Condemnation.</u>

Reverse Condemnation
The homeowner is forcing the
government to use Eminent
Domain to take his property.

A man at the end of an expanded
airport runway could try <u>Reverse</u>
<u>Condemnation.</u>

Reverse Condemnation
Inverse Condemnation

Only the homeowner can file for reverse condemnation.

Inverse condemnation is a term used in the law to describe a situation in which the government
takes private property but fails to pay the compensation required by the 5th Amendment of the
Constitution, so the property's owner has to sue to obtain the required just compensation.

A claim for damages due to aircraft noise is usually asserted along with a "takings" claim (**action in inverse condemnation**) as alternative theories for a remedy. The takings claim is necessary if the airport's defense is that it has an avigation easement. In some cases courts prefer a takings theory; in fact, in some states the definition of a government taking of property (usually in the state's constitution) includes damage akin to nuisance.

By Howard Beckman

Can a condo complex eminent domain the three houses adjacent to their parking lot in order to expand parking?

Intestate: Three syllables – In test ate

Three Syllables – With out will

Property passes by Descent and Distribution. If no heirs can be found, real estate will escheat to the state because land can-not be ownerless.

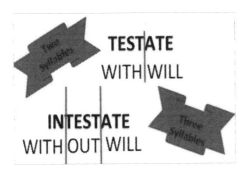

Testate: Two syllables –
Test ate
Two syllables – With will

Testate:
Property passes by Devise. The person who passes and leaves the will is the Devisor. (or is the givor)

The person who is left the property is the Devisee.

In a will, the Divisor specifically states who is going to get what.

Testate – With Will

Devise - The Status
Devisor – The person who dies
Devisee – The person who inherits the gift.

In a will, the Divisor specifically states who is going to get what.

Intestate – With Out Will

Property passes by Descent and Distribution

Escheat

When a person dies intestate (with out will) and no heirs can be found, the government acquires the property. It escheats to the state.
Land cannot be ownerless.

Escheat

When someone passes without a will and no heirs can be found, the property will go to the state.

Land cannot be ownerless.

Government Control on Real Property (PETE)	Police Power
Police Power Eminent Domain Taxation Escheat	Secures the health, safety and general welfare of the public. (Zoning, building codes, EPA)

Cities and local municipalities are allowed to decide their own zoning through State Enabling Acts or Rights.

Public controls based in police power

The police power of the states is the inherent authority to create the regulations necessary to protect the public health, safety and welfare

EXAMPLES

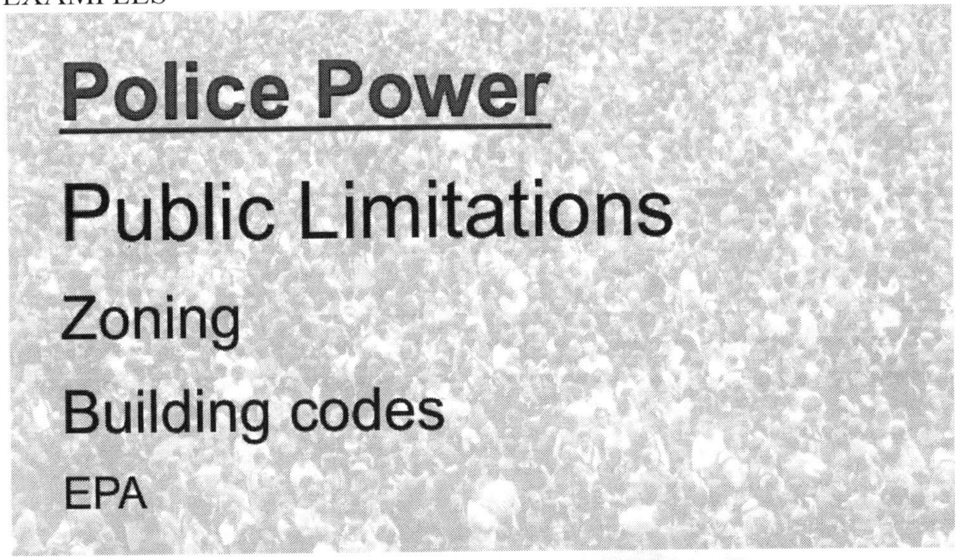

Police Power

Public Limitations

Zoning

Building codes

EPA

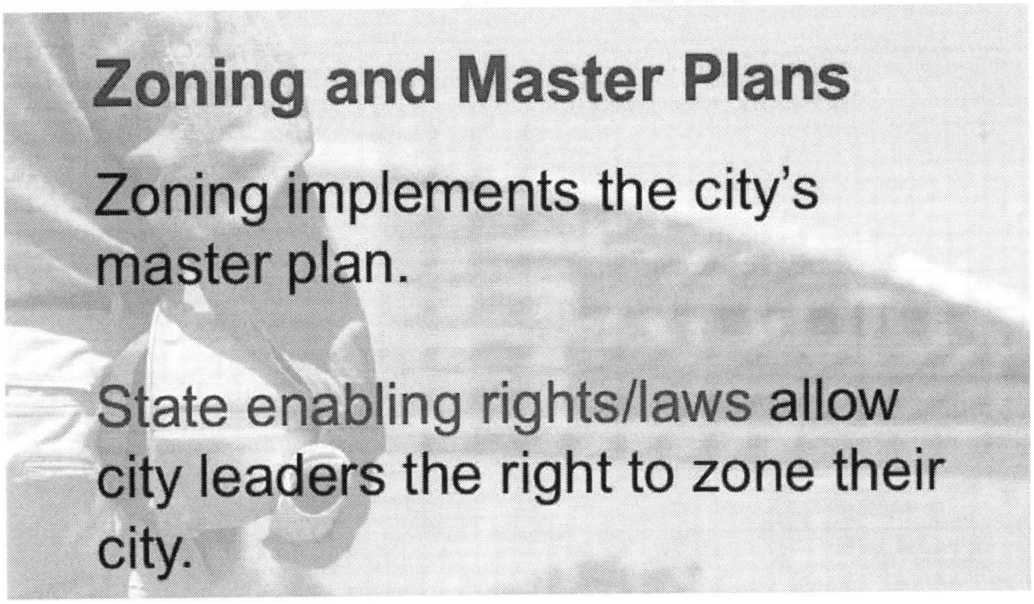

Zoning and Master Plans

Zoning implements the city's master plan.

State enabling rights/laws allow city leaders the right to zone their city.

Zoning implements the city's master plan.

Zoning includes various land use laws falling under the police power rights of state governments and local governments to exercise authority over privately owned real property.

Zoning is the process of dividing land into zones (e.g. residential, industrial) in which certain land uses are permitted or prohibited.

The type of zone determines whether planning permission for a given development is granted.

Zoning may specify a variety of outright and conditional uses of land. It may also indicate the size and dimensions of land area as well as the form and scale of buildings. These guidelines are set in order to guide urban growth and development.

Zoning is the permitted uses of each parcel of land

Lot sizes
Types of structures
Building height
Setbacks
Style and appearance of structures
Density
Protection of natural resources

Local Laws that regulate the use of land.

The division of land uses:

Residential
Commercial
Industrial
Agricultural
Multiple-use, such as
Planned unit developments

Zoning Hearing Boards

Before a zoning permit change is allowed, changes are heard by the zoning board.

Zoning Variance

A deviation from the zoning. For instance, building a fence beyond the neighborhood setback limit.

If a public control and a deed restriction conflict, the more restrictive of the two takes precedence.

Comprehensive Plan or Master Plan

Developed to ensure that social and economic needs are balanced against environmental and aesthetic concerns.

Provides the municipality with the goals and objectives for its future development.

Buffer Zone

A zone separating two areas.

It could be a large park between a mall and a Single Family residential neighborhood.

Buffer Zone

A parcel of land segregating two areas. An example would be a park between a mall and a residential neighborhood.
Parks, playgrounds, may be included to separate residential areas from nonresidential areas.

For use in nature conservation, a buffer zone is often created to enhance the protection of areas under management for their biodiversity importance. The buffer zone of a protected area may be situated around the periphery of the region or may be a connecting zone within it which links two or more protected

Buffer Zone

Aesthetic Zoning

It specifies certain types of architecture.

Bulk Zoning

Zoning a large area of land at one time. It controls density and avoid overcrowding.

Incentive Zoning

It is to ensure that certain types of use are incorporated into developments.

Spot Zoning

A zoning to a particular parcel of land. It could be land rezoned to build a school in a residential neighborhood.

Spot Zoning

A zoning to a particular parcel of land.

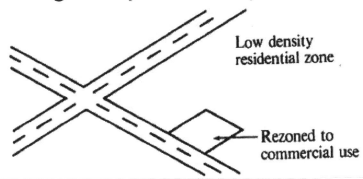

Low density residential zone

Rezoned to commercial use

Downzoning

Rezoning of an area that would be less dense in population. An example would be a neighborhood that downzoned from multi-unit residential zoning to single family residences only. The multi-unit residential properties are grandfathered in, meaning that the new zoning does not apply to them. Usually, if the building burns down or gets destroyed, the new zoning would apply to the new construction.

Downzoning

The permitted density of housing and development is reduced.

Nonconforming Use

A type of zoning variance where a parcel of land may be given an exception from current zoning ordinances due to improvements made by a prior owner or before the current zoning ordinances made the desired use non-conforming under local law.

An example would be a health clinic in the middle of a residential neighborhood.

Conditional Use Permit

A zoning exception which allows the property owner use of his land in a way not otherwise permitted within the particular zoning district. For instance, a medical clinic was granted a zoning variance to build in a neighborhood zoned for residential properties.

Conditional <u>Use</u> Permit

A **conditional use permit** allows the city to consider uses of a specific property which is not allowed as a matter of right within a zoning district.

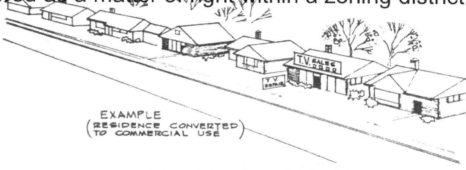

EXAMPLE
(RESIDENCE CONVERTED
TO COMMERCIAL USE)

Conditional <u>Use</u> Permit

To obtain a conditional use permit, the process would Begin through a public hearing process. A **conditional use permit** can provide flexibility within a zoning ordinance.

Variance

A request for a deviation from the Zoning Code. An example would be a homeowner allowed to build a fence closer to a lot line than the zoning allows.

Most zoning systems have a procedure for granting variances (exceptions to the zoning rules), usually because of some perceived hardship due to the particular nature of the property in question. If the variance is not warranted, then it may cause an allegation of spot zoning to arise. Most state zoning-enabling laws prohibit local zoning authorities from engaging in any spot zoning because it would undermine the purpose of a zoning in place.

Setback

The distance which a building or other structure is set back from a street or road, a river or other stream, a shore or flood plain, or any other place which is deemed to need protection. Depending on the jurisdiction, other things like fences, landscaping, septic tanks, and various potential hazards or nuisances might be regulated. Setbacks are generally set in municipal ordinances or zoning. Setbacks along state, provincial, or federal highways may also be set in the laws of the state or province, or the federal government."

Source: Setback (land use) - https://en.wikipedia.org

The minimum distances between buildings and the lot line.

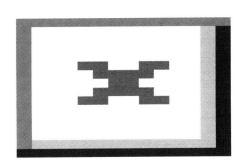

A building code (also building control or building regulations)

A set of rules that specify the standards for constructed objects such as buildings and non-building structures.

Buildings must conform to the code to obtain planning permission, usually from a local council. The main purpose of building codes is to protect public health, safety and general welfare as they relate to the construction and occupancy of buildings and structures. The building code becomes law of a particular jurisdiction when formally enacted by the appropriate governmental or private authority.

Building codes are generally intended to be applied by architects, engineers, interior designers, constructors and regulators but are also used for various purposes by safety inspectors, environmental scientists, real estate developers, subcontractors, manufacturers of building products and materials, insurance companies, facility managers, tenants, and others. Codes regulating the design and construction of structures where adopted into law.

Examples of building codes began in ancient times. In the USA the main codes are the International Commercial or Residential Code [ICC/IRC]"
Source: Building code - https://en.wikipedia.org

Standards for construction

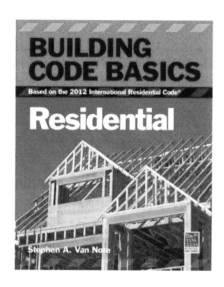

Building Codes

Standards
for
construction

Environmental Impact Statement (EIS)

Under United States environmental law, is a document required by the National Environmental Policy Act (NEPA) for certain actions "significantly affecting the quality of the human environment". An EIS is a tool for decision making. It describes the positive and negative environmental effects of a proposed action, and it usually also lists one or more alternative actions that may be chosen instead of the action described in the EIS.

Several U.S. state governments require that a document similar to an EIS be submitted to the state for certain actions.
Source: Environmental impact statement - https://en.wikipedia.org

For proposed projects.

Environmental Impact Statements/Reports

EISs promote informed decision-making by reporting "detailed information concerning significant environmental impacts.

It describes the positive and negative environmental effects of a proposed project.

The National Flood Insurance Program (NFIP)

A program created by the Congress of the United States in 1968 through the National Flood Insurance Act of 1968 (P.L. 90-448).

The program enables property owners in participating communities to purchase insurance protection, administered by the government, against losses from flooding, and requires flood insurance for all loans or lines of credit that are secured by existing buildings, manufactured homes, or buildings under construction, that are located in a community that participates in the NFIP.

This insurance is designed to provide an insurance alternative to disaster assistance to meet the escalating costs of repairing damage to buildings and their contents caused by floods.
Source: National Flood Insurance Program - https://en.wikipedia.org

Floodplain or Flood Plain

An area of land adjacent to a stream or river that stretches from the banks of its channel to the base of the enclosing valley walls and experiences flooding during periods of high discharge. It includes the floodway, which consists of the stream channel and adjacent areas that actively carry flood flows downstream, and the flood fringe, which are areas inundated by the flood, but which do not experience a strong current.

In other words, a floodplain is an area near a river or a stream which floods when the water level reaches flood stage."

Source: Floodplain - https://en.wikipedia.org

Wetlands

"A wetland is a land area that is saturated with water, either permanently or seasonally, such that it takes on the characteristics of a distinct ecosystem. The primary factor that distinguishes wetlands from other land forms or water bodies is the characteristic vegetation of aquatic plants, adapted to the unique hydric soil.

Wetlands play a number of roles in the environment, principally water purification, flood control, carbon sink and shoreline stability. Wetlands are also considered the most biologically diverse of all ecosystems, serving as home to a wide range of plant and animal life."
Source: Wetland - https://en.wikipedia.org

Wetlands are set aside for conservation.

Shoreline Regulations

Coastal Zone Management Act

A "coastal zone" is defined as the "coastal waters and the adjacent shore lands, as well as includes islands, transitional and intertidal areas, salt marshes, wetlands, and beaches."

The Coastal Zone Management Program (CZMP), also called the National Coastal Zone Management Program, was established under the Coastal Zone Management Act of 1972 and is administered by NOAA's Office for Coastal Management (OCM). This program is designed to set up a basis for protecting, restoring, and establishing a responsibility in preserving and developing the nation's coastal communities and resources, where they are under the highest pressure. The vision of the CZMP is to ensure that "the nation's coast and oceans, including the Great Lakes and island territories, are healthy and thriving for this and future generation". Their mission is "to ensure the conservation and responsible use of our nation's coastal and ocean resources".

The key goals of the National CZM program include: "protecting natural resources, managing development in high hazard areas, giving development priority to coastal-dependent uses, providing public access for recreation, coordinating state and federal actions". Ultimately the outcomes from the CZMP are for "healthy and productive coastal ecosystems, and to have environmentally, economically, and socially vibrant and resilient coastal communities".

Source: File:DelwareSeashoreStateParkCZMP.jpg - https://en.wikipedia.org

Interstate Land Sales Full Disclosure Act

"The Interstate Land Sales Full Disclosure Act of 1968 (ILSFDA or ILSA or "Act") was an act of Congress aimed to facilitate regulation of interstate land sales, to protect consumers from fraud and abuse in the sale or lease of land.

It requires land developers to register subdivisions of (currently 100 or more) non-exempt lots or condominium units.

The responsibility for administering the Act and its regulations is with the Consumer Financial Protection Bureau (CFPB).

A regulated developer is to provide each purchaser with a disclosure document called a Property Report. The Property Report contains relevant information about the subdivision and must be delivered to each purchaser before the signing of the contract or agreement and gives the purchaser at a minimum a 7-day period to cancel the purchase agreement."
Source: Interstate Land Sales Full Disclosure Act of 1968 - https://en.wikipedia.org

Chapter Five

REGULATION OF ENVIRONMENTAL HAZARDS

CERCLA – Comprehensive Environmental Response Compensation and Liability Act

Established a 9 billion dollar fund called **SUPERFUND.**

CERCLA identifies responsible parties and holds them to strict liability for cleanup. Liability can be joint and severable. Cleanup is without excuse. It can also be retroactive.

SARA – Superfund Amendments and Reauthorization Act of 1986

Established stronger cleanup standards. Increased funding for Superfund.

Created the concept of innocent landowner immunity.

Brownfields Revitalization and Environmental Restoration Act – 2001 and 2002

Helps rejuvenate deserted, defunct and derelict toxic industrial waste sites.

Restrictions on Sale or Development of Contaminated Property

IN MORE DETAIL

SUPERFUND: CERCLA OVERVIEW

The Comprehensive Environmental Response, Compensation, and Liability Act (CERCLA), commonly known as Superfund, was enacted by Congress on December 11, 1980. This law created a tax on the chemical and petroleum industries and provided broad Federal authority to respond directly to releases or threatened releases of hazardous substances that may endanger public health or the environment. Over five years, $1.6 billion was collected and the tax went to a trust fund for cleaning up abandoned or uncontrolled hazardous waste sites. CERCLA:

- established prohibitions and requirements concerning closed and abandoned hazardous waste sites;
- provided for liability of persons responsible for releases of hazardous waste at these sites; and
- established a trust fund to provide for cleanup when no responsible party could be identified.

The law authorizes two kinds of response actions:

- Short-term removals, where actions may be taken to address releases or threatened releases requiring prompt response.
- Long-term remedial response actions, that permanently and significantly reduce the dangers associated with releases or threats of releases of hazardous substances that are serious, but not immediately life threatening. These actions can be conducted only at sites listed on EPA's National Priorities List (NPL).

CERCLA also enabled the revision of the National Contingency Plan (NCP). The NCP provided the guidelines and procedures needed to respond to releases and threatened releases of hazardous substances, pollutants, or contaminants. The NCP also established the NPL.

CERCLA was amended by the Superfund Amendments and Reauthorization Act (SARA) on October 17, 1986.

CERCLA

Liability can be joint and severable.

It can also be retroactive.

THE SUPERFUND AMENDMENTS AND REAUTHORIZATION ACT (SARA)

The Superfund Amendments and Reauthorization Act (SARA) amended the Comprehensive Environmental Response, Compensation, and Liability Act (CERCLA) on October 17, 1986. SARA reflected EPA's experience in administering the complex Superfund program during its first six years and made several important changes and additions to the program. SARA:

- stressed the importance of permanent remedies and innovative treatment technologies in cleaning up hazardous waste sites;
- required Superfund actions to consider the standards and requirements found in other State and Federal environmental laws and regulations;
- provided new enforcement authorities and settlement tools;
- increased State involvement in every phase of the Superfund program;
- increased the focus on human health problems posed by hazardous waste sites;
- encouraged greater citizen participation in making decisions on how sites should be cleaned up; and
- increased the size of the trust fund to $8.5 billion.

SARA also required EPA to revise the Hazard Ranking System (HRS) to ensure that it accurately assessed the relative degree of risk to human health and the environment posed by uncontrolled hazardous waste sites that may be placed on the National Priorities List (NPL).

Abatement, mitigation and cleanup requirements

SARA

Superfund Amendments and Reauthorization Act of 1986

Established stronger cleanup standards. Increased funding for Superfund.

Created the concept of **innocent landowner immunity**.

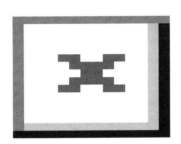

BROWNFIELD OVERVIEW

A brownfield is a property, the expansion, redevelopment, or reuse of which may be complicated by the presence or potential presence of a hazardous substance, pollutant, or contaminant. It is estimated that there are more than 450,000 brownfields in the U.S. Cleaning up and reinvesting in these properties increases local tax bases, facilitates job growth, utilizes existing infrastructure, takes development pressures off of undeveloped, open land, and both improves and protects the environment.

Brownfields Revitalization and Environmental Restoration Act

Helps rejuvenate deserted, defunct and derelict toxic industrial waste sites.

Restrictions on Sale or Development of Contaminated Property

Lead Based Paint

LEAD-BASED PAINT IN HOUSING

Approximately three-quarters of the nation's housing stock built before 1978 (approximately 64 million dwellings) contains some lead-based paint. When properly maintained and managed, this paint poses little risk. However, 1.7 million children have blood- lead levels above safe limits, mostly due to exposure to lead-based paint hazards.

EFFECTS OF LEAD POISONING

Lead poisoning can cause permanent damage to the brain and many other organs and causes reduced intelligence and behavioral problems. Lead can also cause abnormal fetal development in pregnant women.

BACKGROUND

HUD and EPA require the disclosure of known information on lead-based paint and lead-based paint hazards before the sale or lease of most housing built before 1978.

WHAT IS REQUIRED

Before ratification of a contract for housing sale or lease:

Sellers and landlords must disclose known lead-based paint and lead-based paint hazards and provide available reports to buyers or renters.

Sellers and landlords must give buyers and renters the pamphlet, developed by EPA, HUD, and the Consumer Product Safety Commission (CPSC), titled Protect Your Family from Lead in Your Home.

Home buyers will get a 10-day period to conduct a lead-based paint inspection or risk assessment at their own expense. The rule gives the two parties flexibility to negotiate key terms of the evaluation.

Sales contracts and leasing agreements must include certain notification and disclosure language.
!
Sellers, lessors, and real estate agents share responsibility for ensuring compliance.

WHAT IS NOT REQUIRED

This rule does not require any testing or removal of lead-based paint by sellers or landlords.

This rule does not invalidate leasing and sales contracts.

TYPE OF HOUSING COVERED

Most private housing, public housing, Federally owned housing, and housing receiving Federal assistance are affected by this rule.

TYPE OF HOUSING NOT COVERED

Housing built after 1977 (Congress chose not to cover post-1977 housing because the CPSC banned the use of lead-based paint for residential use in 1978).

Zero-bedroom units, such as efficiencies, lofts, and dormitories.

Leases for less than 100 days, such as vacation houses or short-term rentals.

Housing for the elderly (unless children live there).

Housing for the handicapped (unless children live there).

Rental housing that has been inspected by a certified inspector and found to be free of lead-based paint.

Foreclosure sales.

The Buyer has ten days to inspect for lead based paint.

Buyers sign a disclosure acknowledging the possibility of lead based paint.

Sellers do not have to remove it.

Buyers receive the pamphlet; *Protect Your Family from Lead in Your Home.*

Lead can cause mental retardation.

Houses built before **1978** may have potentially high levels of lead based paint.

The buyer has ten days to inspect the property for lead based paint.

The buyer must acknowledge a disclosure of potential lead based paint.

Sellers do not have to remove it.

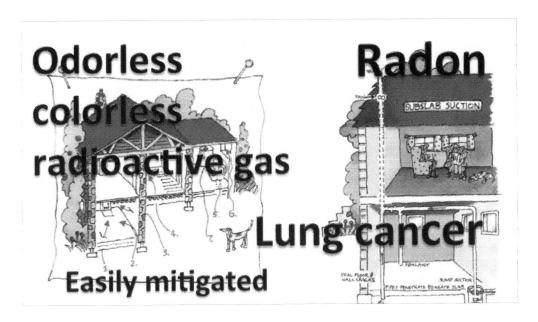

Radon Gas – An odorless, colorless, radioactive gas that causes lung cancer.

Radon is easily mitigated for a cost somewhere around (usually) $500 - $3000.

EXPOSURE TO RADON CAUSES LUNG CANCER IN NON-SMOKERS AND SMOKERS ALIKE

Radon is the number one cause of lung cancer among non-smokers, according to EPA estimates.

EPA 402/K-13/002 | September 2013 (revised) | www.epa.gov/radon

United States
Environmental Protection
Agency

Home Buyer's and Seller's Guide to Radon

Indoor Air Quality (IAQ)

- Consumer's Guide to Radon Reduction: How to Fix Your Home

United States
Environmental Protection
Agency

EPA 402/K-10/005 | 2016 | www.epa.gov/radon

Consumer's Guide
to Radon Reduction
How to Fix Your Home

Indoor Air Quality (IAQ)

Radon Gas

Odorless
Colorless
Radioactive gas
May cause lung cancer.
Enters the house through the basement.
Easily mitigated

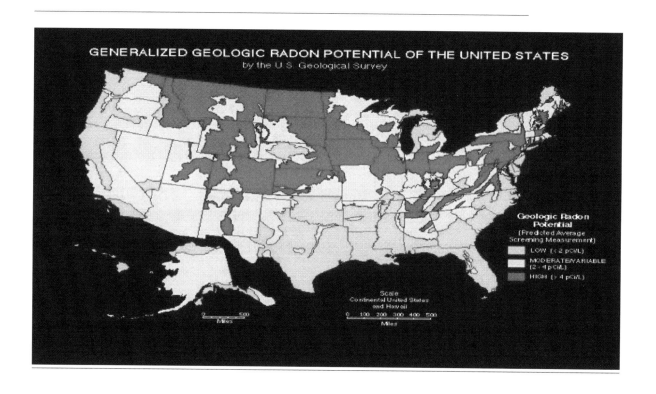

ASBESTOS

Banned in 1978

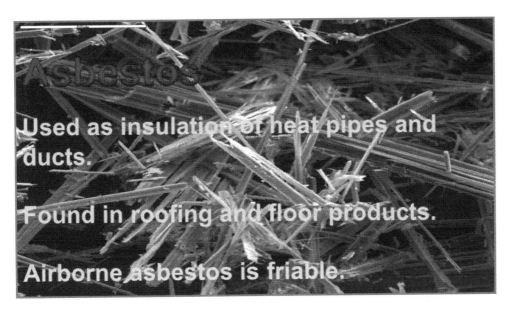

A material used for many years for insulation of heat pipes and ducts. Also, used in roofing and floor products. When asbestos ages it can become airborne.

Asbestos is a mineral fiber that occurs in rock and soil.

Airborne asbestos is called friable. **The best way to handle asbestos is to encapsulate it.** Prolonged inhalation of asbestos fibers can cause serious and fatal illnesses including lung cancer, mesothelioma, and asbestosis (a type of pneumoconiosis).

WHERE CAN I FIND ASBESTOS?

Because of its fiber strength and heat resistance asbestos has been used in a variety of building construction materials for insulation and as a **fire retardant**. Asbestos has also been used in a wide range of manufactured goods, mostly in building materials (roofing shingles, ceiling and floor tiles, paper products, and asbestos cement products), friction products (automobile clutch, brake, and transmission parts), heat-resistant fabrics, packaging, gaskets, and coatings.

Where asbestos may be found:

- Attic and wall insulation produced containing vermiculite
- Vinyl floor tiles and the backing on vinyl sheet flooring and adhesives
- Roofing and siding shingles
- Textured paint and patching compounds used on wall and ceilings
- Walls and floors around wood-burning stoves protected with asbestos paper, millboard, or cement sheets
- Hot water and steam pipes coated with asbestos material or covered with an asbestos blanket or tape
- Oil and coal furnaces and door gaskets with asbestos insulation
- Heat-resistant fabrics
- Automobile clutches and brakes

HOW CAN PEOPLE BE EXPOSED TO ASBESTOS?

Asbestos fibers may be released into the air by the disturbance of asbestos-containing material during product use, demolition work, building or home maintenance, repair, and remodeling. In general, exposure may occur only when the asbestos-containing material is disturbed or damaged in some way to release particles and fibers into the air.

HEALTH EFFECTS FROM EXPOSURE TO ASBESTOS

Exposure to asbestos increases your risk of developing lung disease. That risk is made worse by smoking. In general, the greater the exposure to asbestos, the greater the chance of developing harmful health effects.

Disease symptoms may take many years to develop following exposure.

Asbestos-related conditions can be difficult to identify. Healthcare providers usually identify the possibility of asbestos exposure and related health conditions like lung disease by taking a thorough medical history. This includes looking at the person's medical, work, cultural and environmental history.

After a doctor suspects an asbestos-related health condition, he or she can use a number of tools to help make the actual diagnosis. Some of these tools are physical examination, chest x-ray and pulmonary function tests. Your doctor may also refer you to a specialist who treats diseases caused by asbestos.

Three of the major health effects associated with asbestos exposure are:

- lung cancer
- mesothelioma, a rare form of cancer that is found in the thin lining of the lung, chest and the abdomen and heart
- asbestosis, a serious progressive, long-term, non-cancer disease of the lungs

The use of asbestos in new construction projects has been banned for health and safety reasons.

Prior to the ban, asbestos was widely used in the construction industry in thousands of materials. Some are judged to be more dangerous than others due to the amount of asbestos and the material's friable nature.

Removal of asbestos building components can also remove the **fire protection** they provide; therefore, fire protection substitutes are required for proper fire protection that the asbestos originally provided.

The demolition of buildings containing large amounts of asbestos based materials pose particular problems for builders and property developers – such buildings often have to be deconstructed piece by piece, or the asbestos has to be painstakingly removed before the structure can be razed by mechanical or explosive means.

Used as insulation that was pumped between the walls.

FOAM INSULATION

Urea-formaldehyde insulation

Urea-formaldehyde <u>foam insulation</u> (**UFFI**) dates to the 1930s and made a synthetic insulation. It is a foam, like shaving cream, that is easily injected or pumped into walls.

It is made by using a pump set and hose with a mixing gun to mix the foaming agent, resin and compressed air. The fully expanded foam is pumped into areas in need of insulation. It becomes firm within minutes but cures within a week.

UFFI is generally found in homes built before the 1970s, often in basements, crawl spaces, attics, and unfinished attics.

Visually it looks like oozing liquid that has been hardened. Over time, it tends to vary in shades of butterscotch but new UFFI is a light-yellow color. Early forms of UFFI tended to shrink significantly.

Modern UF insulation with updated catalysts and foaming technology have reduced shrinkage to minimal levels (between 2-4%). The foam dries with a dull matte color with no shine. When cured, it often has a dry and crumbly texture.

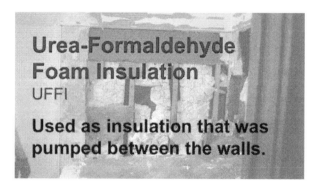

Not used since 1977. Some old PCB products are still functioning.

In general individuals are exposed to PCBs overwhelmingly through food, much less so by breathing contaminated air, and least by skin contact.

Once exposed, some PCBs may change to other chemicals inside the body.
These chemicals or unchanged PCBs can be excreted in feces or may remain in a person's body for years, with half-lives estimated at 10–15 years.

PCBs collect in body fat and milk fat.

PCBs are present in fish and waterfowl of contaminated aquifers.

Infants are exposed to PCBs through breast milk or by intrauterine exposure through trans-placental transfer of PCBs and are at the top of the food chain.

Waste Disposal Sites

Landfills built on the wrong type of soil could pollute ground water.

UNDERGROUND STORAGE TANKS (USTS)

Nearly all USTs regulated by the underground storage tank requirements contain petroleum.

UST owners include marketers who sell gasoline to the public (such as service stations and convenience stores) and non-marketers who use tanks solely for their own needs (such as fleet service operators and local governments).

The greatest potential hazard from a leaking UST is that the petroleum or other hazardous substance **can seep into the soil and contaminate groundwater**, the source of drinking water for nearly half of all Americans. A leaking UST can present other health and environmental risks, including the potential for fire and explosion.

Underground Storage Tanks
Leaking Underground Storage Tanks
LUST
Leaking tanks must be removed along with all the polluted material.

LEAKING UNDERGROUND STORAGE TANKS – LUST

Legislation aimed at protecting ground water. Leaking underground storage tanks can pollute ground water. Leaking tanks must be removed along with all the polluted material.

Suspected of causing cancer.

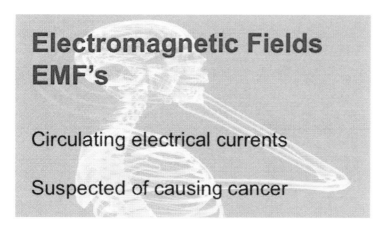

Electromagnetic fields (EMF) are a combination of electric and magnetic fields of energy that surround any electrical device that is plugged in and turned on.

- Scientific experiments have not clearly shown whether or not exposure to EMF increases cancer risk. Scientists continue to conduct research on the issue.
- The strength of electromagnetic fields fades with distance from the source. Limiting the amount of time spent around a source and increasing the distance from a source reduces exposure

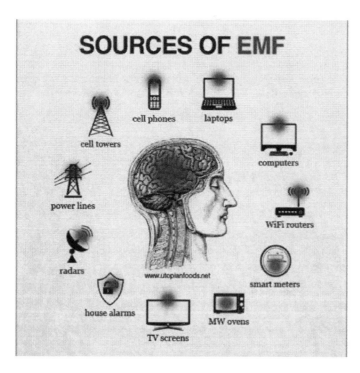

EMFs are found near power lines and other electronic devices such as smart meters. Electric and magnetic fields become weaker as you move further away from them. The fields from power lines and electrical devices have a much lower frequency than other types of EMF, such as microwaves or radio waves. EMF from power lines is considered to be extremely low frequency. Scientific studies have not clearly shown whether exposure to EMF increases cancer risk. Scientists continue to conduct research on the issue.

CARBON MONOXIDE
Colorless, odorless gas byproduct of burning fuels due to incomplete combustion Improper ventilation of equipment, malfunction.

Detectors are available, mandatory in some areas

May cause allergic reactions. Mold can be found around wet areas.

Mold

May cause allergic reactions.
Mold can be found around wet areas.

Black Mold

Stachybotrys Chartarum

Black Mold - Stachybotrys Chartarum

Molds are part of the natural environment, and can be found everywhere, indoors and outdoors. Mold is not usually a problem, unless it begins growing indoors.

Allergic reactions to mold are common. They can be immediate or delayed. Molds can also cause asthma attacks in people with asthma who are allergic to mold. In addition, mold exposure can irritate the eyes, skin, nose, throat, and lungs of both mold-allergic and non-allergic people. Symptoms other than the allergic and irritant types are not commonly reported as a result of

AN INSIDIOUS MOLD
CBS NEWS

Melinda Ballard and Ron Allison thought theirs was a dream house: a 22-room mansion on 72 acres outside of Austin, Texas.

Ballard, a former New York City public relations executive, thought it offered the perfect way to escape from the big city. "It was my baby," she said. "And it was truly a dream house for me."

It's not a dream anymore. Ballard and Allison abandoned their home; they were forced to move out when their house was invaded by a mold that they say made everyone in their family sick. Erin Moriarty reports.

The couple's son Reese was the first to become ill at age 4. "(He was) coughing up blood," Ballard said. "His equilibrium was completely shot; very bad stomach problems; diarrhea; vomiting - it just spanned the whole globe in terms of symptoms."

Soon Ballard became sick; she says she had trouble staying on her feet. Then Allison, an investment banker, began having trouble breathing. He started coughing up blood, Ballard said.

Experts say the family was being poisoned by a black toxic mold, called Stachybotrys. The mold, which has been found in all 50 states, in homes, businesses and schools, had invaded their house. Some strains of Stachybotrys cause allergies, asthma and skin rashes. Others produce mycotoxins, released into the air. These toxins can seriously damage the lungs and central nervous system.

In April 1999, Dr. David Straus, one of the nation's leading mold experts, ordered the Ballards to evacuate their house. They had to leave at a moment's notice. They left dishes in the dishwasher and food in the refrigerator.

Dr. Straus believed they became sick from breathing in mycotoxins. The mold most commonly grows as a result of water damage, according to Dr. Straus.

This mold began with a leak in the downstairs bathroom, Ballard said.

"It needs water and it needs some type of organic food source," said Dr. Straus, who is at Texas Tech University. "They like cellulose," he added. "Most of the material we use to build houses - like Sheetrock, ceiling tile, wood - fungi can grow on."

The mold infiltrated under the flooring, 2,500 square feet of a wooden floor, according to Ballard.

And the mold contaminated all of the family's possessions, including photographs, Dr. Straus said. It got into the air-conditioning unit and spread toxins throughout the house. Removing every trace of the mycotoxins may be impossible, said experts hired by the Ballards.

"This is like what happens in a huge flood; you lose everything," Ballard said.

The toxins affected her husband, she added. He became very forgetful: When he'd go to the grocery store, he'd leave the groceries there, she said.

Allison says his memory loss affected his work.

His co-worker Harold Babbitt noticed the change. "I would walk into his office, and he would just be staring, like someone who had a stroke," Babbitt said. "There were deals that should have been completed that weren't completed."

Allison finally resigned.

Since Ballard left the house, her symptoms disappeared.

But Reese developed asthma and had trouble in school. Allison went to New York with Reese to see a doctor specializing in treatment of mold exposure illnesses: Dr. Eckhardt Johanning, of Albany, who has studied more than 600 patients exposed to toxic mold.

Dr. Johanning found that both Reese and his father had low levels of antibodies, which suggested exposure to a toxin.

Ballard said that Dr. Johanning said Reese should never again be exposed to the mold.

"I'm not saying this is necessarily a permanent condition," Dr. Johanning said. "The brain can repair itself a lot. But it may take some time to do. Stachybotrys produces very potent chemicals that can cause brain fogginess, tremors, problems with the memory."

Allison, Ballard and their son are not the only family to have trouble with the mold. In Southern California, Julie and Richard Licon found Stachybotrys in the walls and floors of their condominium.

"All the wood was pretty much black from the mold," said Richard Licon.

The couple's homeowner's association agreed to move the Licons and their six children to a hotel while the house was cleaned of mold.

Seven months later, the Licons moved back. But they became convinced the mold was still there. During the seven months in the hotel, the children were not sick, Julie Licon said. When they moved back into their condominium, however, the kids got sick, she noted.

Their son Jordan, then 2, had seizures form mold exposure. These seizures resumed when they moved back, the Licons said. Their other children also experienced a variety of symptoms, from nosebleeds to headaches and dizziness.

They retested their house and found massive amounts of Stachybotrys in the air. A spore had grown inside the air-conditioning unit.

So, the Licons moved out again. "The only thing we can take, literally, is the clothes on our back," Richard Licon said.

In some cases, Stachybotrys may even kill.

Chapter Six

WATER RIGHTS

Federal Flood Insurance Program

The National Flood Insurance Program (NFIP) is a program created by Congress.

This insurance is designed to provide an insurance alternative to disaster assistance to meet the escalating costs of repairing damage to buildings and their contents caused by floods.

Administered by the Federal Emergency Management Agency (FEMA)
Program subsidizes flood damage insurance.
Required on all properties located in flood-prone area ("flood plains") if property is financed with federally related mortgage loans.
Maps of flood-prone areas prepared by Army Corps of Engineers

Land areas that are at high risk for flooding are called special flood hazard areas or floodplains. These areas are indicated on flood insurance rate maps.

In high-risk areas, there is at least a 1 in 4 chance of flooding during a 30-year mortgage.

Alluvium

The increase in the area of land without any act being taken by the owner. The typical cause is sediment (alluvium) deposited by a river. This changes the size of a piece of land (a process called accession) and thus its value over time."

Accretion

The opposite of erosion.
The process of coastal sediment returning to the visible portion of a beach or foreshore following a submersion event. A sustainable beach or foreshore often goes through a cycle of submersion during rough weather then accretion during calmer periods. If a coastline is not in a healthy sustainable state, then erosion can be more serious and accretion does not fully restore the original volume of the visible beach or foreshore leading to permanent beach loss."

Avulsion

A sudden loss or addition to land, which results from the action of water. It differs from accretion, which describes a gradual loss or addition to land resulting from the action of water.

Erosion

The action of surface processes (such as water flow or wind) that remove soil, rock, or dissolved material from one location on the Earth's crust, then transport it away to another location. A gradual wearing a way of land.

Water rights

The right of a user to use water from a water source, e.g., a river, stream, pond or source of groundwater. In areas with plentiful water and few users, such systems are generally not complicated or contentious. In other areas, especially arid areas where irrigation is practiced, such systems are often the source of conflict, both legal and physical. Some systems treat surface water and ground water in the same manner, while others use different principles for each."
Source: Water right - https://en.wikipedia.org

Riparian

Rights to an adjacent non-navigable river or stream. (A creek.)
Access to and use of the water. (rivers and streams.)
Runs with the land. (Meaning it stays with the deed when the property is sold.)

> **Riparian**
>
> Small river or stream.
>
> The rights of an adjacent landowner to a creek, stream, pond or adjacent small body of water.
>
> It gives all owners of land contiguous to the same body of surface water equal reasonable rights to the water whether a landowner uses the water or not.
> A landowner cannot deny another landowner downstream from the water by re-routing the water or damming it.
>
> If the water right is attached (appurtenant) to the land, it runs with the deed and transfers to the next owner.

Littoral

The littoral zone is the part of a sea, lake or river that is close to the shore.

In coastal environments the littoral zone extends from the high water mark, which is rarely inundated, to shoreline areas that are permanently submerged.

Rights to an adjacent navigable body of water.

Littoral Water Rights "run with the land". (It stays with the deed when the property is sold.)

Littoral

Large body of water and tidal waters.

Navigable

Littoral rights give the homeowner shoreline rights.

The land in between the high tide and low tide are set aside for the use and enjoyment of the public.

If the water right is attached (**appurtenant**) to the land, it runs with the deed and transfers to the next owner.

Littoral: When owning ocean front property, strangers are allowed access in front of your property on the sand at low tide. The owner owns up to the high tide mark.

The Mississippi River is littoral.

Prior Appropriation

Prior appropriation water rights is the legal doctrine that the first person to take a quantity of water from a water source for "beneficial use"—agricultural, industrial or household —has the right to continue to use that quantity of water for that purpose. Subsequent users can take the remaining water for their own beneficial use provided that they do not impinge on the rights of previous users.

In the western states, water supplies are very limited and must be allocated sparingly based on the productivity of its use. The right is also allotted to those who are "first in time of use."

The legal details vary from state to state; however, the general principle is that water rights are unconnected to land ownership, and can be sold or mortgaged like other property. These rights can be lost over time if non-use of the water source is demonstrated or if the water has not been used for a certain number of years.

Beneficial use is commonly defined as agricultural, industrial or household use.

Each water right has a yearly quantity and an appropriation date. Each year, the user with the earliest appropriation date (known as the "senior appropriator") may use up to their full allocation (provided the water source can supply it). Then the user with the next earliest appropriation date may use their full allocation and so on. In times of drought, users with junior appropriation dates might not receive their full allocation or even any water at all.

When a water right is sold, it retains its original appropriation date. Only the amount of water historically consumed can be transferred if a water right is sold.

If a water right is not used for a beneficial purpose for a period of time it may lapse under the doctrine of abandonment.

The right to use water is controlled by the state. Usually found in the drier areas or deserts.

(The First in Use and Beneficial Purpose.)

Prior Appropriation is found in the drier areas of the country and the desserts.

Prior Appropriation

With **prior appropriation,** the first person to take water for a beneficial purpose has the right to continue the use.

Other landowners may take water as long as it does not infringed on the first user. "Fist in time of use."
Prior Appropriation is used where water is scarce or limited.

Government Granted.

If farmers believe that the new farmer up stream will be taking too much water out of a stream leaving no water for the downstream farmers, they can be granted Prior Appropriation. (First in Use will limit or stop the upstream farmer from taking water.)

Prior Appropriation is used in the drier areas of the Country.

Chapter Seven

PRIVATE CONTROLS

Private Land-Use Controls

Private Land Use Controls

Deed Restriction – Private Limitations

A limitation of use upon an individual's real estate.

Obstructing a view of a neighbor
How *and* where to build a fence
Removing trees
Color homes, pet restrictions, vehicle parking............

The people who live in the neighborhood enforce the restrictive covenants.

Why there are Deed Restrictions

To control and maintain the desirable quality and character of a property or Subdivision'

A subdivision is the result of dividing land into pieces that are easier to sell or otherwise develop, usually via a plat.

The former single piece as a whole is then known in the United States as a subdivision.

If it is used for housing it is typically known as a housing subdivision or housing development, although some developers tend to call these areas communities."
Source: Subdivision (land) - https://en.wikipedia.org

Deed Restrictions and Homeowners Associations

A Deed Restriction (Deed Conditions or Restrictions)

Limitation on use

Violating a deed restriction could cause imprisonment and / or a fine.

A copy of the CC&Rs is transferred at the close or before.

Restrictive Covenants

A promise to engage in or refrain from a specified action

Restrictive Covenants set standards for all the parcels in a subdivision including
1. The type of building allowed on the property
2. The use to which the land may be put
3. The type of construction
4. Height, setbacks, square footage

Covenants, Conditions and Restrictions (CC&Rs)

Rules and regulations placed upon the homeowner.

These are the Homeowners Association (HOA) Rules and Regulations

Regulations are enforced by the HOA. (homeowners of the neighborhood)

If restrictions conflict with the zoning ordinances, the more restrictive of the two will take precedence.

Covenants, Conditions and Restrictions (CC&Rs)

Restrictive covenants are included in a subdivision plat or separate recorded document are to set standards for all the parcels in a subdivision including:

The type of building allowed on the property.
The use to which the land may be put.
The type of construction.
Height, setbacks, square footage.
Legal Issues regarding private restrictions.
Violating a deed restriction could cause imprisonment and / or a fine.
Regulations are enforced by the HOA. (Homeowners of the neighborhood)

Chapter Eight

VALUATION AND MARKET ANALYSIS

Value - Appraisal

An appraisal is an opinion of a professional appraiser.

Value – Appraisal

An appraisal is an opinion from a professional appraiser.

The Appraisal Foundation (TAF) is the primary standards body; its Appraisal Standards Board (ASB) promulgates and updates best practices as codified in the Uniform Standards of Professional Appraisal Practice (USPAP), while its Appraisal Qualifications Board (AQB) promulgates minimum standards for appraiser certification and licensing.

Uniform Standards of Professional Appraisal Practice – **USPAP** – The quality control standards for real estate appraisers.

The Uniform Standards of Professional Appraisal Practice (USPAP) has always required appraisers to identify the scope of work needed to produce credible results.[2]

An appraisal is a professional appraiser's opinion of value.

---

[2] https://en.wikipedia.org/wiki/Uniform_Standards_of_Professional_Appraisal_Practice

Uniform Standards of Professional Appraisal Practice
USPAP

The quality control standards for real estate appraisers.

Financial Institutions Reform, Recovery, and Enforcement Act of 1989 (FIRREA)

This is a United States federal law enacted in the wake of the savings and loan crisis of the 1980s.

It gives both Freddie Mac and Fannie May additional responsibility to support mortgages for low and moderate income families.

FIRREA

The Financial Institutions Reform, Recovery, and Enforcement Act of 1989 (FIRREA), is a United States federal law enacted in the wake of the savings and loan crisis of the 1980s.

FIRREA gives both Freddie Mac and Fannie Mae additional responsibility to support mortgages for low- and moderate-income families .

The Financial Institutions Reform, Recovery, and Enforcement Act of 1989 (FIRREA) demanded all the states to develop systems for licensing and certifying real estate appraisers.

"An appraiser is one who sets a value upon property, real or personal."
Source: Appraiser - https://en.wikipedia.org

Appraiser Trainee:

Someone who is qualified to appraise those properties, which the supervising certified appraiser is qualified to appraise.

LICENSED REAL PROPERTY APPRAISER:

Someone who is qualified to appraise non-complex one to four units having a transaction value less than $1,000,000 and complex one to four residential units having a transaction value less than $250,000. This classification does not include the appraisal of subdivisions.

CERTIFIED RESIDENTIAL REAL PROPERTY APPRAISER:

Someone who is qualified to appraise one to four residential units without regard to value or complexity. This classification does not include the appraisal of subdivisions. To be a state certified residential appraiser qualified to do appraisals for federally related transactions, a state must have requirements that meet or exceed this minimum standard.

CERTIFIED GENERAL REAL PROPERTY APPRAISER:

Someone who is qualified to appraise all types of real property. To be a state certified general appraiser qualified to do appraisals for federally related transactions, a state must have requirements that meet or exceed this minimum standard.

Appraisals are for a certain type of value (e.g., foreclosure value, fair market value, distressed sale value, investment value).

The most commonly used definition of value is Market Value.

> Market Value / Open Market Value
>
> The most probable selling price in an open market with an arm's length transaction.
> The future worth.

Market value

The price at which an asset would trade in a competitive setting.

Market value is usually interchangeable with *open market value* or *fair value*

Market Value / Open Market Value

The most probable selling price.

The future worth.

MARKET VALUE – the estimated amount for which an asset or liability should exchange on the open market between a willing buyer and a willing seller in an arm's length transaction, after proper marketing and where the parties had each acted knowledgeably, prudently and without compulsion.

Market Price

The actual selling price.

HIGHEST AND BEST USE

144

"It is the concept in real estate appraisal that shows how the highest value for a property is arrived at. In any case where the market value of real property is sought, that value must be based on its highest and best use. Highest and best use is always that use that would produce the highest value for a property, regardless of its actual current use."
Source: Highest and best use - https://en.wikipedia.org

The highest and best use of a property is its most profitable legally and physically permitted use, that is, the use that will at present provide the highest income. The highest and best use evolves from an analysis of the community, neighborhood, site, and improvements.

Highest and Best Use

Simply ask,
"what is the best purpose for this property that would give it the most value"?

Supply and Demand

> A developer was building a neighborhood of homes where the demand for the housing was constant. Which home would most likely sell for the most?
>
> The last one.
>
> The least? The first one.

Property values will rise as demand increases and/or supply decreases.

Value in Use

The net present value (NPV) of a cash flow or other benefits that an asset generates for a specific owner under a specific use."
Source: Value-in-use - https://en.wikipedia.org

The value of a cash flow that an asset generates for a specific owner under a specific use.

Value-in-use is the value to one particular user, and may be above or below the market value of a property.

Investment value

Differences between the *investment value* of an asset and its *market value* provide the motivation for buyers or sellers to enter the marketplace

> The value of an asset to the owner or a prospective owner for individual investment or operational objectives.

Insurable value

The value of real property covered by an insurance policy.

Generally, it does not include the site value.

"Liquidation value

The likely price of an asset when it is allowed insufficient time to sell on the open market, thereby reducing its exposure to potential buyers. Liquidation value is typically lower than fair market value."
Source: Liquidation value - https://en.wikipedia.org

While Uniform Standards of Professional Appraisal Practice (USPAP) does not define Market Value, it provides general guidance for how Market Value should be defined:

A type of value, stated as an opinion, that presumes the transfer of a property (i.e., a right of ownership or a bundle of such rights), as of a certain date, under specific conditions set forth in the definition of the term identified by the appraiser as applicable in an appraisal.

MASS APPRAISAL AND AUTOMATED VALUATION MODELS

"Automated valuation model (AVM) is the name given to a service that can provide real estate property valuations using mathematical modelling combined with a database.

Most AVMs calculate a property's value at a specific point in time by analyzing values of comparable properties. Some also take into account previous surveyor valuations, historical house price movements and user inputs (e.g. number of bedrooms, property improvements, etc.).

Appraisers, investment professionals and lending institutions use AVM technology in their

---

An AVM typically includes:

An indicative market value for many residential properties nationwide.

The tax assessor's indication of value, if available.

Information on a subject property and recent sales history.

Comparable sales analysis of like properties.

---

analysis of residential property.

An AVM is a residential valuation report that can be obtained in a matter of seconds. It is a technology-driven report.

The product of an automated valuation technology comes from analysis of public record data and computer decision logic combined to provide a calculated estimate of a probable selling price of a residential property. An AVM generally uses a combination of two types of evaluation, a hedonic model and a repeat sales index. The results of each are weighted, analyzed and then reported as a final estimate of value based on a requested date.

Source: Automated valuation model - https://en.wikipedia.org

While AVMs can be quite accurate, particularly when used in a very homogeneous area, there is also evidence that AVMs are not accurate in other instances such as when they are used in rural areas, or when the appraised property does not conform well to the neighborhood.

THREE APPROACHES TO VALUE

There are three traditional groups of methodologies for determining value. These are usually referred to as the "three approaches to value" which are generally independent of each other:

> The sales comparison approach (comparing a property's characteristics with those of comparable properties that have recently sold in similar transactions).
>
> The cost approach (the buyer will not pay more for a property than it would cost to build an equivalent).
>
> The income approach (similar to the methods used for financial valuation, securities analysis or bond pricing).

An appraiser can choose from three approaches to determine value.

One or two of these approaches will usually be most applicable, with the other approach or approaches usually being less useful.

The appraiser has to think about the way that most buyers usually buy a given type of property. What appraisal method do most buyers use for the type of property being valued? This generally guides the appraiser's thinking on the best valuation method, in conjunction with the available data.

For instance, appraisals of properties that are typically purchased by investors (e.g., office buildings) may give greater weight to the Income Approach.

Buyers interested in purchasing single family residential property would rather compare price, in this case the Sales Comparison Approach (market analysis approach) would be more applicable. The third and final approach to value is the Cost Approach to value.

THE SALES COMPARISON APPROACH

The sales comparison approach is based primarily on the principle of substitution. This approach assumes a prudent (or rational) individual will pay no more for a property than it would cost to purchase a comparable substitute property.

The approach recognizes that a typical buyer will compare asking prices and seek to purchase the property that meets his or her wants and needs for the lowest cost. In developing the sales comparison approach, the appraiser attempts to interpret and measure the actions of parties involved in the marketplace, including buyers, sellers, and investors.

Data collection methods and valuation process

Data is collected on recent sales of properties similar to the subject being valued, called "comparable". Only SOLD properties may be used in an appraisal and determination of a property's value, as they represent amounts actually paid or agreed upon for properties.

Sources of comparable data include real estate publications, public records, buyers, sellers, real estate brokers and/or agents, appraisers, and so on. Important details of each comparable sale are described in the appraisal report. Since comparable sales are not identical to the subject property, adjustments may be made for date of sale, location, style, amenities, square footage, site size, etc.

The main idea is to simulate the price that would have been paid if each comparable sale were identical to the subject property.

If the comparable is superior to the subject in a factor or aspect, then a downward adjustment is needed.

Likewise, if the comparable is inferior to the subject in an aspect, then an upward adjustment for that aspect is needed.

The adjustment is somewhat subjective and relies on the appraiser's training and experience.

Steps in the sales comparison approach

1. Research the market to obtain information pertaining to sales, and pending sales that are similar to the subject property
2. Investigate the market data to determine whether they are factually correct and accurate
3. Determine relevant units of comparison (e.g., sales price per square foot), and develop a comparative analysis for each
4. Compare the subject and comparable sales according to the elements of comparison and adjust as appropriate
5. Reconcile the multiple value indications that result from the adjustment (upward or downward) of the comparable sales into a single value indication

Selecting and Adjusting the Comparable

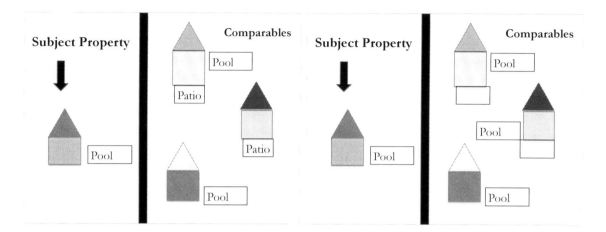

When finding comparable properties always use the closest properties to the subject property.

Always adjust the comparable properties.
Make the comparable properties look like the subject property.

The date of sale of the comparable properties is important.

You do not want to use properties sold a year ago or two years ago. Use the most recent sales.

The Subject house had a $5000 patio, which the comparable home does not. What would be the adjustment made?

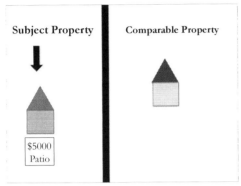

Add $5000 to the comparable property.

The comparable home had a $5000 patio, which the Subject house does not. What would be the adjustment made?

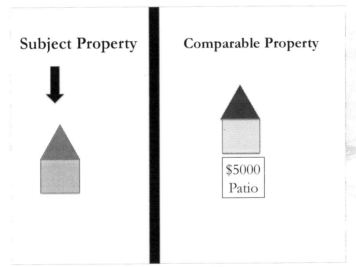

Subtract $5000 from the comparable property.

Even though a builder built an identical home using the same floor plan, materials and subcontractors two towns over, you must use the home that sold next door and last week for the comparable even though it has less square footage.

The **cost approach** was once called the summation approach.

Replacement Cost or Summation Approach

Based on the principle of substitution.
Special purpose buildings.
Library, City Hall, Church, Hospital.....

The theory is that the value of a property can be estimated by adding the land value and the improvements.

The value of the improvements is often referred to by the abbreviation RCNLD (for "reproduction/replacement cost new less depreciation").

Reproduction refers to reproducing an exact replica.

Replacement cost refers to the cost of building a house or other improvement which has the same utility, but using modern design, workmanship and materials.

In practice, appraisers almost always use replacement cost.

An exception to the general rule of using the replacement cost, is for some insurance value appraisals. In those cases, reproduction of the exact asset after a destructive event like a fire is the goal.

The cost approach is considered most reliable when used on newer structures, but the method tends to become less reliable for older properties.

The **Cost Approach** to value is most useful in determining insurable value, and cost to construct a new structure or building.

Special Purpose Properties

The cost approach is often the only reliable approach when dealing with special purpose properties (e.g., public assembly, marinas).

If you get a question on using the Cost Approach on a residential home, they are talking about an historic home.

An example could be Elvis Presley's Graceland.

Replacement Cost or Summation Approach

Historic Homes

Graceland, Beauvoir, Rowan Oak.......

THE COST APPROACH

Basic steps in the cost approach are:

1. Estimate the value of the land as if vacant
2. Estimate the replacement cost new of the improvements
3. Estimate the loss in value from all forms of depreciation
4. Deduct the total amount of depreciation from the replacement cost new
5. Estimate the same amount for any other improvements
6. Add the land value estimate to the depreciated cost value to arrive at the total property value

Step One, land valuation, may involve any of the methods already mentioned(allocation, abstraction, etc.)

Step Two, estimating the replacement cost new of the improvements, requires that a distinction be made between replacement cost and reproduction cost.

Replacement cost is defined as: the cost and overhead that would be incurred in constructing an improvement having the same utility as the original, without necessarily reproducing exactly the same characteristics of the property, but using today's materials, labor, and building techniques. In other words, replacement cost represents the cost to create an equally desirable substitute property

Reproduction cost is defined as: the cost, including material, labor, and overhead, that would be incurred in constructing an improvement having exactly the same characteristics as the original improvement.

Reproduction cost is sometimes difficult to measure because the same building materials or methods are not available. Reproduction cost for an older building with 12-foot ceilings, working fireplaces in every room (as opposed to modern central heating systems), and elaborate trim would be computed on the basis of creating an identical structure today. The reproduction costs of these types of physical characteristics in older structures often tends to create an element of depreciation(value loss) identified as functional obsolescence. This is illustrated using the principle of substitution, which states that in a competitive market, a buyer will typically not pay more for a particular property than the amount to acquire a similar property with comparable utility (a satisfactory substitution). Thus, reproduction cost may often require adjustments for construction techniques, building materials and various forms of depreciation to be indicative of current market value.

There are several methods used to arrive at a cost value: the quantity survey method, the unit-in-place method, and the square foot method.

The quantity survey method requires that the appraiser create a detailed inventory of every item of material, equipment, labor, overhead, and fees involved in the construction of a property. This method is not routinely used by appraisers because it is extremely time consuming.

The unit-in-place method is less detailed than the quantity survey method, but still reasonably accurate and complete. This method combines direct and indirect costs into a single cost for a building component (the unit-in-place) which is then multiplied by the area of the portion of the building being valued to arrive at a total cost for that component. This is the method used in the Construction Cost Manual prescribed by the Arizona Department of Revenue, for many building components. These allow the appraiser to make adjustments for individual components for various types of structures.

The square foot method combines all the costs for a particular type and quality of structure into one value as a cost per square foot (or cubic foot). This method produces a value based on the floor area of the structure. The cubic foot method is used when the wall height varies within a building class, such as warehouses or factories. Generally the square foot or cubic foot methods are not considered sufficiently accurate compared to the first two methods for estimating cost.

Income Approaches

GRM – Gross Rent Multiplier

GIM – Gross Income Multiplier

The income capitalization approach (often referred to simply as the "income approach") is used to value commercial and investment properties. Because it is intended to directly reflect or model the expectations and behaviors of typical market participants, this approach is generally considered the most applicable valuation technique for income-producing properties, where sufficient market data exists.

In a commercial income-producing property this approach capitalizes an income stream into a value indication. This can be done using revenue multipliers or capitalization rates applied to a Net Operating Income (NOI).

Capitalization rate (or "Cap Rate") is a real estate valuation measure used to compare different real estate investments. Although there are many variations, a cap rate is often calculated as the ratio between the net operating income produced by an asset and the original capital cost (the price paid to buy the asset) or alternatively its current market value.

Income Approach

Capitalization rate

It determines the value of income producing properties.

The RETURN on investment.

Capitalization rates are an indirect measure of how fast an investment will pay for itself.

GRM – GROSS RENT MULTIPLIER

Capitalization Rate – An investor's rate of return on an investment.

Residential Property

Gross Yearly Income

The ratio of the price of an investment to its yearly rental income before expenses
It calculates the number of months the property would take to pay for itself in gross received rents.

Gross Rent Multiplier is the ratio of the price of a real estate investment to its annual rental income **before** accounting for expenses such as property taxes, insurance, utilities, etc. To sum up Gross Rent Multiplier, it is the number of years the property would take to pay for itself in gross received rent. For the investor looking to purchase, a higher GRM (perhaps over 12) is a poorer opportunity, whereas a lower one (perhaps under 8) is better.

GIM – GROSS INCOME MULTIPLIER

Commercial Real Estate and Commercial Residential

Net yearly Income **after** expenses

Finds the rate of annual return.

> **A less than arm's length** transaction is usually done between people who are related. An example would be a mother selling her house to her daughter for 50% of it's true market value.

> An **arm's length** transaction is a standard, regular, common transaction where the buyer and seller do not know each other.

Appraisers do not use less than arm's length transactions as comparable properties when appraising.

An arm's length transaction
Less than arms length

Appraisers do not use less than arm's length transactions as comparable properties when appraising.

COMPETITIVE MARKET ANALYSIS/ CMA /COMPARATIVE MARKET ANALYSIS

A tool for real estate professionals. It is NOT an appraisal. It does NOT indicate value. A CMA can help a seller determine a listing range.

A CMA is an estimate of a home's value done by a real estate broker to establish a listing or offer price. This service is usually offered free of charge and without obligation. A CMA should only be used as a reference for deciding at what price you should list or buy a home.

A real estate appraisal is done by a licensed real estate appraiser and is most often used by lenders when issuing mortgages for refinancing or buying/selling a home.

Competitive/Comparative Market Analysis (CMA)

A tool a real estate agent uses to help a seller find a listing range.

A CMA does not determine value.

Only an appraisal can determine value.

NEIGHBORHOOD FEATURES - Ideally, the comparable properties should be adjacent to the subject property. The comparable properties should be in the same neighborhood; but if they are located in another neighborhood, it should be a neighborhood very similar to the one in which the subject property is located, based
upon the appraiser's analysis of neighborhood characteristics.

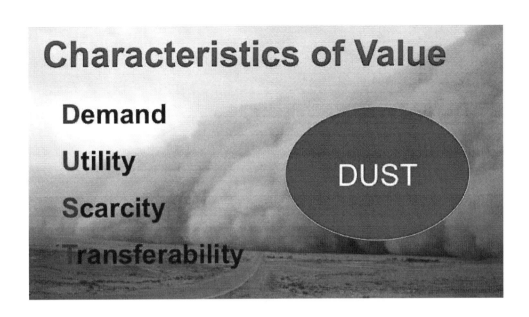

CHARACTERISTICS OF VALUE

(DUST)
Demand
Utility
Scarcity
Transferability

URAR – Uniform Residential Appraisal Report

The form appraisers use.

MARKET CYCLES AND OTHER FACTORS AFFECTING PROPERTY VALUE

Market cycles, economic conditions, social factors (example: aging population), physical conditions (example: run down properties) and Government (legal and zoning) factors affect value.

Price Per Square Foot
Both appraisals and CMAs use price per square foot.

Highest and Best Use
The reasonably probable and legal use of property, which results in the highest value.

Conformity
Conformity is desirable in maintaining overall value.

Conformity

The concept that a property will maintain or increase in value due to nearby properties being similar.

Depreciation
Wasting Assets. Land does not depreciate. Only the improvements (buildings) depreciate.

Depreciation

Wasting Assets

Land does not depreciate.

Straight-line Method of Depreciation is the simplest and most often used method.

Anticipation
The expectation that there will be a property value increase because of a future event.

A woman decided not to sell her property because she found out about a large shopping center that will be built nearby. She believes that the value of her property will increase due to the new development. She plans to sell when the construction is complete and the stores are open. She is basing her decision on **anticipation**.

Anticipation

The belief that a property's value will increase due to some future event.

Increasing Returns

Relates to adding improvements to a piece of real estate that will add value at more than what was spent on the improvement. Does a pool add value?

Decreasing Returns

Diminishing Returns - Relates to adding improvements to a piece of real estate where the improvement will add less or no value compared to what was spent on the improvement.

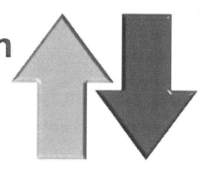

Increasing Returns
add value with improvements

Decreasing Return
Diminishing Returns
no extra value

Supply and Demand

Prices will generally drop as supply increases relative to demand
Prices will generally rise as demand increases relative to supply

Factors Affecting Supply:

Labor force
Construction costs
Government controls at all levels
Government fiscal and monetary policies

Factors Affecting Demand:

Population
Demographics—the make-up of the population including mobility, financial stability, and size and nature of family unit
Employment and wage levels—where and how money is spent; perceived job security

Amenities

A neighborhood benefit off the property. (Examples: Parks, bike trails, hiking trails or a neighborhood pool.)

Regression – The largest home in a neighborhood of smaller homes suffers from regression.

Progression – The smallest home in a neighborhood full of larger homes will benefit from progression.

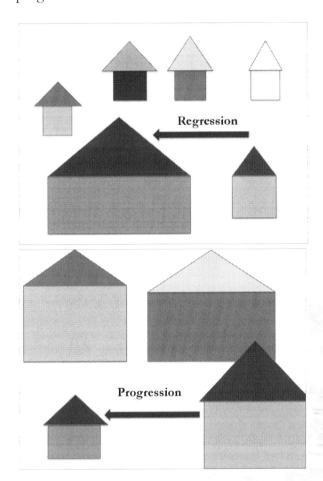

Bob overbuilt for his neighborhood. He suffers from Regression. He has the largest home in a neighborhood of smaller homes. He now wants to add an Olympic swimming pool, Jacuzzi and tennis court.

If Bob adds those improvements, he most likely will be suffering from **Diminishing Returns as well as Regression**. He will not get his investment back when he sells the property. In other words, the improvements cost more than the rise in value to his property.

Physical and Functional Obsolescence

Inside the building. May or may not be curable.

A home with 5 bedrooms and one bathroom. A home with 4 bedrooms on the second floor and one bathroom on the first floor. A poor floor plan. A one-car garage.

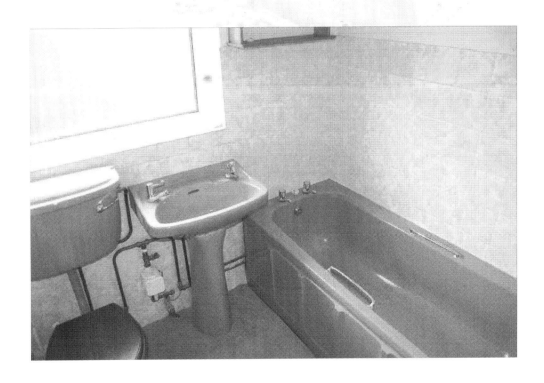

Functional obsolescence is a loss in value to the improvements due to certain existing physical characteristics, and can be divided into four types:

1. poor design or style; inefficient floor plan; excessive ceiling height
2. lack of modern facilities
3. out-of-date equipment
4. (over improvement), or inadequacy (under improvement)

Economic/External obsolescence is caused by conditions outside the property such as economic changes, legal restrictions, development of new processes, etc. It may be divided into five types:

1. proximity to negative environmental influences
2. zoning restrictions
3. adverse influences of supply and demand
4. changes in neighborhood social or economic factors
5. changes in locational demands

External (economic) Obsolescence

Outside factors. Not curable.

A deteriorating neighborhood. A smelly business. An airport runway with planes shaking your house. A tainted water well. A dumpsite. Train tracks.

Physical deterioration, as the name implies, is a loss in value due to normal aging and deterioration. It can be subdivided into four types:

1. wear and tear from normal use
2. negligent care or lack of maintenance
3. damage from dry rot, pests, etc.
4. wear and tear from the elements (wind, rain, etc.)

Neighborhood Stages

Growth, Stability, Decline and Revitalization

GROWTH

STABILITY

169

DECLINE

REVITALIZATION

Amenities
off the property

Features
on the property

Amenities: A community pool; a neighborhood park; a bike trail

Features: A pool in the back yard; a three-car garage

Chapter Nine

FINANCING
PART A

Mortgagor = borrower   Mortgagee = lender

"A mortgage loan, also referred to as a mortgage, is used either by purchasers of real property to raise funds to buy real estate; or alternatively by existing property owners to raise funds for any purpose, while putting a lien on the property being mortgaged.

The loan is "secured" on the borrower's property. This means that a legal mechanism is put in place which allows the lender to take possession and sell the secured property ("foreclosure" or "repossession") to pay off the loan in the event that the borrower defaults on the loan or otherwise fails to abide by its terms.

Mortgage can also be described as "a borrower giving consideration in the form of a collateral for a benefit (loan).""
Source: Mortgage loan - https://en.wikipedia.org

Mortgage Loan Instruments - Two documents must be signed

The promissory note (financing document), the written promise to repay the debt.

The mortgage (security document), the document that creates the lien or transfers an interest to the creditor.

Lenders and creditors must inform rejected credit applicants, in writing within 30 days, why credit was denied or terminated.

Types of security interests in realty

Three types of security over real property are commonly used in the United States: the title mortgage, lien mortgage, and deed of trust. In the United States, these security instruments proceed off of debt instruments drawn up in the form of promissory notes and which are known variously as mortgage notes, lender's notes, or real estate lien notes.

The mortgage

A mortgage is a security interest in realty created by a written instrument (traditionally a deed) that either conveys legal title or hypothecates title by way of a non-possessory lien to a lender for the performance under the terms of a mortgage note. In slightly less than half of states, a mortgage creates a lien on the title to the mortgaged property. Foreclosure of that lien almost always requires a judicial proceeding declaring the debt to be due and in default and ordering a sale of the property to pay the debt. Many mortgages contain a power of sale clause, also known as no judicial foreclosure clause, making them equivalent to a deed of trust.

The deed of trust

Main article: deed of trust (real estate)

The deed of trust is a conveyance of title made by the borrower to a trustee (not the lender) for the purposes of securing a debt.

In lien-theory states, it is reinterpreted as merely imposing a lien on the title and not a title transfer, regardless of its terms. It differs from a mortgage in that, in many states, it can be foreclosed by a non-judicial sale held by the trustee through a power of sale. It is also possible to foreclose them through a judicial proceeding.[

Deeds of trust to secure repayments of debts should not be confused with trust instruments that are sometimes called deeds of trust but that are used to create trusts for other purposes, such as estate planning. Though there are superficial similarities in the form, many states hold deeds of trust to secure repayment of debts do not create true trust arrangements.[

Mortgage	Deeds of Trust
A property owner (mortgagor) agrees to pay a lien secured by real estate. The mortgagee will place a lien on the property in favor of the mortgagee.	Three party instruments used instead of a mortgage.
	The trustee holds the deed on behalf of the lender.
When the mortgage is paid, the buyer receives a Satisfaction of Mortgage document.	The seller holds legal title to the property. The buyer holds equitable title.
	The deed of trust is the lien.
	When paid in full, the buyer receives a re-conveyance deed.
	Deed of trust Similar to, but not identical to, a mortgage Creates a three-party agreement Generally provides simpler and faster foreclosure than a mortgage

The Mortgage Note

The mortgage note is a legal document that provides evidence of your indebtedness and your formal promise to repay the mortgage loan, according to the terms you've agreed to. These terms include the amount you owe, the interest rate of the mortgage loan, the dates when the payments are to be made, the length of time for repayment and the place where the payments are to be sent.

The note also explains the consequences of failing to make your monthly mortgage payments.

The mortgage or deed of trust is the security instrument that you give to the lender that protects the lender's interest in your property. When you sign the mortgage or the deed of trust (depending on the state where you live), you are giving the lender the right to take the property by foreclosure if you fail to pay your mortgage according to the terms you've agreed to. Financing a house is very similar to financing an automobile; in both cases the property is the security for the loan.

The mortgage or deed of trust states most of the information contained in the note. It also establishes your responsibility to keep the house in good repair, insure it, pay your real property taxes and make your payments on time.

The Deed

A deed is a document that transfers ownership of the property to you. It contains the names of the previous and new owners and a legal description of the property and is signed by the person transferring the property. The deed gives you title to the property, but the title is conveyed to a neutral third party (called a trustee) until you pay the mortgage loan in full.

Lien Theory vs. Title Theory States

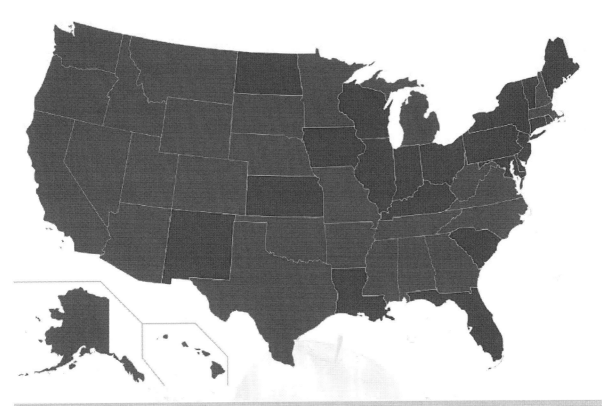

In lien-theory states, mortgages and deeds of trust have been redesigned so that they now impose a non-possessory lien on the title to the mortgaged property, while the mortgagor still holds both <u>legal and equitable title</u>.

In title-theory states, a mortgage continues to be a conveyance of legal title to secure a debt, while the mortgagor still <u>retains equitable title</u>.

Hypothecation

"The debtor retains ownership of the collateral, but the creditor has the right to seize ownership if the debtor defaults."
Source: Hypothecation - https://en.wikipedia.org

Pledging property as collateral without giving up its possession

Hypothecation

It's having a loan on something without having to give up possession of it.

A car loan. A mortgage.

The Promissory Note

"A promissory note, sometimes referred to as a note payable, is a legal instrument (more particularly, a financial instrument, and more specifically a debt instrument), in which one party (the maker or issuer) promises in writing to pay a determinate sum of money to the other (the payee), either at a fixed or determinable future time or on demand of the payee, under specific terms. If the promissory note is unconditional and readily saleable, it is called a negotiable instrument."

Source: Promissory note - https://en.wikipedia.org

Will contain the amount of the debt, the time and method of payment, and the rate of interest.

If used with a mortgage, will be payable to the lender.

If used with a deed of trust, can be payable "to bearer".

Can refer to or repeat several of the clauses contained in the mortgage or the deed of trust.

Is a negotiable instrument; holder of note—payee; may transfer rights to the future payments.

Interest

A charge for the use of money.

Legal Title

The actual owner has legal title until the owner passes the deed to another.

Equitable Title

The buyer holds equitable title.

Usury

"The practice of making unethical or immoral monetary loans that unfairly enrich the lender.

A loan may be considered usurious because of excessive or abusive interest rates or other factors.

Someone who practices usury can be called a usurer, but a more common term in contemporary English is loan shark.

The term may be used in a moral sense—condemning, taking advantage of others' misfortunes—or in a legal sense where interest rates may be regulated by law.
Source: Usury - https://en.wikipedia.org

Charging interest in excess of maximum rate that may be legally charged
Maximum rate generally set by state law.

Usury laws protect the public.

Loan origination fees

The expense that is paid to the lender for generating the loan.

Discount points

Used to increase the yield (true rate of interest) required by an investor who would purchase a loan.

One discount point equals 1 percent of the loan amount

Discount points are used to buy down the interest rates, temporarily or permanently.

> **Points**, sometimes also called "**discount points**", are a form of pre-paid interest. One point equals one percent of the loan amount. By charging a borrower points, a lender effectively increases the yield on the loan above the amount of the stated interest rate. Borrowers can offer to pay a lender points as a method to reduce the interest rate on the loan, thus obtaining a lower monthly payment in exchange for this up-front payment.

Prepayment

Borrower may pay off loan in full at any time before the end of the term of the loan, or make additional payments to principal during the term.

Penalties may be assessed by the lender to compensate for unearned interest when a loan is paid in full prior to the scheduled end of the loan term.

Prepayment penalties are prohibited on mortgage loans insured or guaranteed by the federal government or sold to Fannie Mae or Freddie Mac.

Assignment of the mortgage

The note can be sold to a third-party investor.
The securing mortgage or deed of trust will be assigned with the note to its purchaser.

A Satisfaction of mortgage is issued to the mortgager when the loan is paid in full.

Tax and insurance reserves / Impound Account

Required for some mortgages by the lender; called reserve fund, impound, or trust or escrow account.

RESPA limits the amount that can be held as reserves.

Loan to Value is equity. The difference between the value of property and the loan amount.

Private mortgage insurance, or PMI, is typically required with most conventional (non-government backed) mortgage programs when the down payment or equity position is less than 20% of the property value.

Borrower paid private mortgage insurance, or BPMI, is the most common type of PMI in today's mortgage lending marketplace. BPMI allows borrowers to obtain a mortgage without having to provide 20% down payment, by covering the lender for the added risk of a high loan-to-value (LTV) mortgage.

Lender paid private mortgage insurance, or LPMI, is similar to BPMI except that it is paid by the lender and built into the interest rate of the mortgage.

Loan Processor— The loan processor's job is to prepare your mortgage loan information and application for presentation to the underwriter. The loan processor will ask you for many documents, including documents about your income, your employment, your monthly bills and how much you have in the bank. In addition, the loan processor must make sure that all proper documentation is included, that all numbers are calculated correctly and double checked and that everything is stacked in the proper order. A well-processed loan file can decrease the amount of time it takes for a decision about your mortgage loan application.

Mortgage Underwriter— The mortgage underwriter is the professional authorized to assess if you are eligible for the mortgage loan you are applying for. The mortgage underwriter will approve or reject your mortgage loan application based on your credit history, employment history, assets, debts and other factors.

Mortgage Lender and Servicer— The mortgage lender is the financial institution that provides funds for your mortgage. A mortgage servicer is the financial institution or entity that is responsible for collecting your ongoing mortgage payments. If you have difficulty paying your mortgage on time after you become a homeowner, be sure to contact your mortgage servicer who can provide you with a variety of options to help you stay in or sell your home. Your mortgage servicer may be the same as your lender, or may be a different company depending on who your lender is or how they manage your mortgage going forward. It is not uncommon for your lender to transfer the servicing of your mortgage to a different company after you close on your home.

Pre-Approval
Once the application is complete, your loan officer will review it with you and ask you and any co-borrowers to sign it. Your loan officer will then send it through their organization to obtain approvals. If it's approved, you will receive a pre-approval letter, which is the lender's conditional commitment to lend you a specific amount of money for the purchase of your home.
With that pre-approval, you will know just how much house you can afford to buy. While this is helpful information, you need to decide for yourself if you can live comfortably with the amount of your suggested mortgage and the associated monthly mortgage payment.

The Loan Estimate
Within three business days of submitting the application, your loan officer must provide you with a Loan Estimate. The Loan Estimate provides you with an estimate of your mortgage loan terms and settlement charges (also called closing charges, or costs to complete your mortgage transaction) if you are approved for a mortgage loan.

The Loan Estimate is a three-page form with summary information of your loan terms, monthly payment and money needed at closing on the first page, details of your closing costs on the second page and additional information about your loan on the third page.

You can use your Loan Estimate to compare rates and settlement charges from other lenders. As the legal mortgage terminology used in the Loan Estimate may seem confusing, the following definitions should help you understand some of the most important information on this form.

Loan Terms — This section defines the basic terms of your mortgage loan, including the initial loan amount, interest rate and initial monthly payment. This section also includes important information indicating if your interest rate can rise and if your loan has a prepayment penalty.

Escrow Account Information— Most lenders require you to pay in advance for some items that will be due after closing. These prepaid items generally include homeowner's insurance premiums and property taxes. The first page of the Loan Estimate indicates whether or not an escrow account is required and estimates the amount of your monthly escrow payment.

Closing Cost Details— Your closing costs include Loan Costs and Other Costs. Loan costs are divided into three categories:

Origination charges are fees charged by your lender for preparing and submitting your completed loan application and underwriting your loan. The Origination Charges can include an application fee, an underwriting fee and an origination charge or points. One point equals one percent (1%) of your mortgage amount.

Other Costs include:

(1) Taxes and government fees such as recording fees and taxes and transfer taxes;

(2) Prepaid such as homeowner's insurance premiums for the first year of your loan term, prepaid interest and property taxes; and

(3) Initial escrow payments at closing, which generally include two (2) months of homeowner's insurance premiums and property taxes.

Government recording charges — the fee required to register the property under your name and record the mortgage or deed of trust.

The APR is not the interest rate for which you applied. This percentage rate takes into account the various loan charges, including loan discounts, origination fees, prepaid interest and other credit costs. <u>The APR is important because it gives the true cost of borrowing since all of the finance charges associated with the mortgage loan are considered.</u>

The Closing Disclosure
Your loan officer should provide you with a copy of the Closing Disclosure at least 3 business days before you sign the mortgage loan documents at your closing. This document discloses the actual dollar amounts you will pay for the various fees and services associated with the closing of your mortgage loan. Your closing costs can typically range from 3 percent to 7 percent of the mortgage loan amount, so it's important that you are aware of these costs and ask questions about them.

The Closing Disclosure contains the final terms of your loan, as well as the final loan charges that you will pay at closing. In addition to the disclosures contained in the Loan Estimate, the Closing Disclosure provides information regarding certain features of your loan, the amount financed, the finance charge and the total of payments.

Adjustable-Rate Mortgage (ARM): Also known as a variable-rate loan, an ARM usually offers a lower initial rate than a fixed-rate loan, but your payment can go up at set times and by set amounts. The interest rate can change at a specified time, known as an adjustment period, based on a published financial index that tracks changes in the current financial market. ARMs also have caps and floors, or a maximum and minimum that the interest rate can change at each adjustment period, as well as over the life of the loan.

Amortization: Paying off a loan over a period of time and at the interest rate specified in the loan documents. The amortization of a loan includes the payment of interest and a part of the amount borrowed in each mortgage payment. For instance, on a 30-year fixed-rate mortgage, the amortization period is 30 years.

Annual Percentage Rate (APR): How much a loan costs over the loan term expressed as a rate. The APR includes the interest rate, points, broker fees and certain other credit charges a borrower is required to pay. This is not the interest rate that is used in setting your monthly payment.

Collateral: Property which is used as security for a debt. In the case of a mortgage, the collateral is the house and land.

Credit Bureau: A company that gathers information on consumers who use credit. Lenders will ask for your permission before getting a copy of your credit report from these companies.

Credit Report: A document used by the lender to examine your use of credit. It provides information on money that you've borrowed from credit institutions, the amount of available credit you have in your name and your payment history. Lenders obtain credit reports from credit bureaus.

Credit Score: A computer-generated number that summarizes your credit profile and predicts the likelihood that you'll repay future debts.

Debt: Money owed by one person or institution to another person or institution.

Default: Failure to fulfill a legal obligation, like paying your mortgage. A default includes failure to pay on a financial obligation, but may also be a failure to perform some action or service that is non-monetary. For example, a mortgage requires the borrower to maintain the property.

Down Payment: A portion of the price of a home, paid upfront and not part of your mortgage.

Earnest Money: Funds from you to the seller, held on deposit, to show that you're committed to buying the home. The deposit will not be refunded to you after the seller accepts your offer. It will go toward your total closing costs and any remaining amount will then go toward your down payment, unless one of the sales contract contingencies is not fulfilled.

Escrow: A deposit by a borrower to the lender of funds to pay property taxes, insurance premiums and similar expenses when they become due.

Equity: The value of your home above the total mortgage amount you owe for your home. If you owe $100,000 on your house but it is worth $130,000, you have $30,000 of equity. Your equity can fluctuate over time, based not only on your outstanding loan balance, but home price values in your local market area.

Fixed-Rate Mortgage: A mortgage with an interest rate that does not change during the entire term of the loan.

Foreclosure: A legal action that ends all ownership rights to a home when the homeowner fails to make a series of mortgage payments or is otherwise in default under the terms of the mortgage.

Liabilities: Your debts and other financial obligations.

Lien: A claim or charge on property for payment of a debt. A mortgage is a lien, meaning the lender has the right to take the title to your property if you don't make the mortgage payments.

Loan: Money you borrow from a bank or other lender with a written promise to pay it back later. Banks and other lenders charge you fees and interest to borrow money.

Loan Estimate: A document that provides you with an estimate of the costs associated with your mortgage loan, as well as some other features of your loan. Your loan officer must provide you with a Loan Estimate within three business days of submitting the loan application.

Loan Origination Fees: Fees paid to your mortgage lender for processing the mortgage loan application. These fees are usually in the form of points. One point equals one percent of the mortgage amount. For instance on a $100,000 mortgage, one point is $1,000.

Mortgage Broker: A home finance professional who specializes in bringing together borrowers and lenders to facilitate real estate mortgages.

Mortgage Insurance: Insurance that protects mortgage lenders against loss in the event of default by the borrower. If you make a down payment of less than twenty percent, your lender will generally require mortgage insurance.

Mortgage Lender: The lender providing funds for a mortgage. Lenders also manage the credit and financial information review, the property review and the mortgage loan application process through closing.

Mortgage Rate: The interest rate you pay to borrow the money to buy your house.

Mortgage Servicer: The financial institution or entity that is responsible for collecting your mortgage loan payments.

Principal: The amount of money borrowed from the lender to buy your house or the amount of the mortgage loan that has not yet been repaid to the lender. This does not include the interest you will pay to borrow that money. The principal balance (sometimes called the outstanding or unpaid principal balance) is the amount owed on the loan minus the amount you repaid.

Underwriting: The process that your lender uses to assess your eligibility to receive a mortgage loan. Underwriting involves the evaluation of your ability to repay the mortgage loan.

Title: Written evidence of the right to ownership in a property.

Title Insurance: Insurance providing protection against loss arising from problems connected to the title to your property.

Uniform Residential Loan Application: A standard mortgage loan application form on which you provide the lender with information required to assess your ability to repay the loan amount and to help the lender decide whether to lend you money.

Lender Requirements, Equity, Qualifying Buyers, Loan Application Procedures

When you apply for a mortgage, your loan officer will forward your application and the supporting documentation to an underwriter. It's the underwriter's responsibility to review your loan scenario and the supporting documentation to ensure that it meets the loan program guidelines, to determine whether or not you qualify for the loan.

The underwriter looks at your application to see if it meets these basic criteria:
Your ability to repay the loan. This requirement basically asks, "Is your income enough to cover the new mortgage payment and all your other monthly expenses?" To figure this out, lenders use your debt-to-income ratio (DTI). Most lenders want your debt-to-income ratio to be 36% or less, but the ratio that works best for you is the one that you can comfortably afford.

Your likelihood to repay the loan. Your payment history and credit score are indicators to lenders of your likelihood to make payments in the future.

The home value. The underwriter carefully looks at the home value (based on a professional appraisal ordered by your lender) of the property you are purchasing to verify that it meets or exceeds the purchase price. This will also help them ensure the loan-to-value (LTV) ratio fits within the loan program guidelines. (For more complete information, read The home appraisal process.) To qualify for a conventional loan, most lenders require you to have a loan-to-value ratio of no more than 80-95%. The higher your home's value and the less you owe on it, the lower your LTV ratio.

For a purchase, the source of funds for your down payment. The underwriter will verify your down payment funds. If you have a down payment of less than 20%, you will typically be required to pay private mortgage insurance (PMI), which increases your monthly mortgage payment. The underwriter will review your documentation to estimate whether you have enough money to cover closing costs. You may also be required to have set aside two or more monthly mortgage payments as reserves, depending on the loan program and/or loan amount. Lenders typically require reserves to cover your mortgage payment in case of emergencies or unforeseen events.
Bank of America

"THE REAL ESTATE SETTLEMENT PROCEDURES ACT (RESPA) was a law passed by the United States Congress.

The main objective was to protect homeowners by assisting them in becoming better educated while shopping for real estate services, and eliminating kickbacks and referral fees that add unnecessary costs to settlement services.

RESPA requires lenders and others involved in mortgage lending to provide borrowers with pertinent and timely disclosures regarding the nature and costs of a real estate settlement process.

RESPA was also designed to prohibit potentially abusive practices such as **kickbacks** and referral fees, the practice of dual tracking, and imposes limitations on the use of escrow accounts."

Source: Real Estate Settlement Procedures Act - https://en.wikipedia.org

Buying subject to or assuming a seller's mortgage or deed of trust

Subject to:	Assumption:
The purchaser is not personally liable for the debt.	The purchaser is personally liable for the debt.
The purchaser gets a new loan.	In the event of a foreclosure, the purchaser may be held liable for any deficiency.
In the event of a foreclosure, the purchaser is not personally liable for a deficiency.	Unless specifically released by the lender, the original borrower may also be liable for the debt or any deficiency

Priority of Mortgages and Deeds of Trust

Priority is established by the date and time of recordation.
Generally, the loan for the purchase is the first lien.
Subsequently recorded liens are second mortgages (junior liens).
Lien priorities can be changed with *subordination* **agreements.**

Subordination is the process by which a creditor is placed in a lower priority for the collection of its debt from its debtor's assets than the priority the creditor previously had.

The priority of right to collect the debt is important when a debtor owes more than one creditor but has assets of insufficient value to pay them all in full at the time of a default.

Except in bankruptcy proceedings, the creditor with the first priority for collection will generally have the first claim on the debtor's assets for its debt and the creditors whose rights are subordinate will thus have fewer assets to satisfy their claims.

Subordination can take place by operation of law or by agreement among the creditors.

Subordination Agreement

An agreement between banks.
The first lien holder agrees to take a
second position in favor of another lien
holder.

Foreclosure

"Foreclosure is a legal process in which a lender attempts to recover the balance of a loan from a borrower, who has stopped making payments to the lender, by forcing the sale of the asset used as the collateral for the loan.

Formally, a mortgage lender (mortgagee), or other lienholder, obtains a termination of a mortgage borrower (mortgagor)'s equitable right of redemption, either by court order or by operation of law (after following a specific statutory procedure)."

Source: Foreclosure - https://en.wikipedia.org

Judicial Foreclosure	**Non-judicial Foreclosure**	**Strict Foreclosure**
Legal event whereas the lender receives a court order. The sale of the property is approved by the court. Property is usually sold to the highest bidder.	Standard in a Deed of Trust. Allows the Trustee to sell the property to the highest bidder for the lender. Seller financing often has a Deed of Trust because it's easier to foreclose on the property.	A decree orders the debt to be paid within a set time limit. If the payment is not met, the mortgagor's right of equitable redemption is forever lost. The lien holder takes possession when the court awards title to him.

A legal foreclosure kills the relationship with the second lien holder's secured property. It becomes an unsecured loan that will follow the mortgagor.

Short Sale – The lien holder negotiates to avoid foreclosure. The lien holder accepts less than the loan amount.

Deed in Lieu of Foreclosure

A "friendly foreclosure".
The borrower forfeits any equity in the property and deeds it to the lender.
Any junior liens remain and become the lender's liability.

"A deed in lieu of foreclosure is a deed instrument in which a mortgagor (i.e. the borrower) conveys all interest in a real property to the mortgagee (i.e. the lender) to satisfy a loan that is in default and avoid foreclosure proceedings.

The deed in lieu of foreclosure offers several advantages to both the borrower and the lender. The principal advantage to the borrower is that it immediately releases him/her from most or all of the personal indebtedness associated with the defaulted loan. The borrower also avoids the public notoriety of a foreclosure proceeding and may receive more generous terms than he/she would in a formal foreclosure. Another benefit to the borrower is that it hurts his/her credit less than a foreclosure does.

Advantages to a lender include a reduction in the time and cost of a repossession, lower risk of borrower revenge (metal theft and vandalism of the property before sheriff eviction), and additional advantages if the borrower subsequently files for bankruptcy.

If there are any junior liens a deed in lieu is a less attractive option for the lender. The lender will likely not want to assume the liability of the junior liens from the property owner, and accordingly, the lender will prefer to foreclose in order to clean the title."
Source: Deed in lieu of foreclosure - https://en.wikipedia.org

Deficiency Judgment

Issued to cover the difference between the amount received at the foreclosure sale and the principal balance owed.

Becomes a judgment against the debtor.

"A **deficiency judgment** is an unsecured money judgment against a borrower whose mortgage foreclosure sale did not produce sufficient funds to pay the underlying promissory note, or loan, in full. The availability of a deficiency judgment depends on whether the lender has a recourse or nonrecourse loan, which is largely a matter of state law. In some jurisdictions, the original loan(s) obtained to purchase property is/are non-recourse, but subsequent refinancing of a first mortgage and/or acquisition of a 2nd (3rd, etc.) are recourse loans."
Source: Deficiency judgment - https://en.wikipedia.org

Equitable Redemption Occurs prior to the sales. The borrower pays the stated amount and the mortgage is reinstated.	been foreclosed upon and sold to reclaim the money to repay the amount of the debt.

Redemption

The final repayment or the end of the scheduled term or a lump sum redemption, typically when the borrower decides to sell the property. A closed mortgage account is said to be "redeemed".

REO – Real Estate Owned. Bank ownership. The property has been foreclosed and is now owned by the bank.

Federal Deposit Insurance Corporation (FDIC)

Insurance of bank deposits up to $250,000.

"The Federal Deposit Insurance Corporation (FDIC) is a United States government corporation providing deposit insurance to depositors in US banks.

The FDIC was created during the Great Depression to restore trust in the American banking system; more than one-third of banks failed in the years before the FDIC's creation, and bank runs were common.

Since the passage of the Dodd–Frank Wall Street Reform and Consumer Protection Act in 2011, the FDIC insures deposits in member banks up to US **$250,000** per ownership category."
Source: Federal Deposit Insurance Corporation - https://en.wikipedia.org

> **Insurance companies investing in mortgages**
> Prefer income-producing commercial and industrial properties.

Mortgage Brokers

Act as **intermediaries b**etween borrowers and lenders.
Locate borrowers, process their loan applications, and submit them to lenders.
Do not service the loan once it has been made.
Mortgage brokers have much more product to sell than mortgage bankers.

"A mortgage broker acts as an intermediary who brokers mortgage loans on behalf of individuals or businesses.

Traditionally, banks and other lending institutions have sold their own products. As markets for mortgages have become more competitive, however, the role of the mortgage broker has become more popular.

Mortgage brokers exist to find a bank or a direct lender that will be willing to make specific loan an individual is seeking. Many mortgage brokers are regulated to assure compliance with banking and finance laws in the jurisdiction of the consumer. The extent of the regulation depends on the jurisdiction."
Source: Mortgage broker - https://en.wikipedia.org

Mortgage Bankers

They work for a bank. They originate mortgages by selling the bank's products. They have less product to sell than mortgage bankers.

Mortgage bankers are companies or individuals that originate mortgage loans, sell them to other investors, service the monthly payments, and may act as agents to dispense funds for taxes and insurance.

Mortgage brokers present homebuyers with loans from a variety of loan sources. Their income comes from the lender making the loan, just like with any other bank. Because they can tap a variety of lenders, they can shop on behalf of the borrower and achieve the best available terms.

Mortgage Brokers

Self-Employed

Originates loans for lenders.

Has more product than a mortgage banker.

Mortgage Brokers
Act as intermediaries between borrowers and lenders.
Locate borrowers, process their loan applications, and submit them to lenders.
Do not service the loan once it has been made.

Mortgage Bankers

Employee - Work for the bank.

Loans the bank's money.

Limited to his bank's products.

Who has more product? Mortgage Brokers or Mortgage Bankers?

MORTGAGE BANKERS ASSOCIATION
M E M B E R

Mortgage Brokers

Self-Employed

Originates loans for lenders.

Has more product than a mortgage banker.

Mortgage Bankers

Employee - Works for the bank.

Loans the bank's money.

Limited to his bank's products.

> **VA Loans** are guaranteed.
> Will lend up to appraisal.
>
>
> **FHA Loans** are insured.
> Down payment as low as 3.5%

FHA-Insured Loans

"An FHA insured loan is a US Federal Housing Administration mortgage insurance backed mortgage loan which is provided by an FHA-approved lender. FHA insured loans are a type of federal assistance and have historically allowed lower income Americans to borrow money for the purchase of a home that they would not otherwise be able to afford.

There is also a monthly mortgage insurance premium (MIP) which varies based on the amortization term and loan-to-value- ratio.

The basic FHA mortgage insurance program is Mortgage Insurance for One-to-Four-Family Homes.
Over time, private mortgage insurance (PMI) companies came into play, and now FHA primarily serves people who cannot afford a conventional down payment or otherwise do not qualify for PMI."
Source: FHA insured loan - https://en.wikipedia.org

FHA allows first time homebuyers to put down as little as 3.5% and receive up to 6% towards closing costs.

FHA —part of the Department of Housing and Urban Development (HUD).

FHA insures real estate loans made by approved lending institutions.

FHA sets standards for the type and construction of buildings and neighborhoods and qualifications for borrowers.

The property must be appraised by an FHA-approved appraiser.

FHA sets maximum loan amounts.

FHA loan limits are geographically based. Different parts of the country have different amounts. You can look up your county here.

Your Door to
FHA
HOMEOWNERSHIP

Buying your first home?
FHA might be just what you need. Your down payment can be as low as 3.5% of the purchase price. Available on 1-4 unit properties.

FHA insured loans require mortgage insurance to protect lenders against losses that result from defaults on home mortgages.

FHA Loan Limits
FHA lending limits vary based on a variety of housing types and the state and county in which the property is located.

FHA Loan Limits
The FHA loan limit maximum amount of $729,750 will only be applicable to extremely high-cost metropolitan areas. Loan limits vary from area to area. You will have to know the loan limit of $729,750.

FHA.com
another American dream comes true

VA-guaranteed loans

The Department of Veterans Affairs (DVA)

"A VA loan is a mortgage loan in the United States **guaranteed** by the United States Department of Veterans Affairs (VA). The loan may be issued by qualified lenders."

"The VA loan was designed to offer long-term financing to eligible American veterans or their surviving spouses (provided they do not remarry). The basic intention of the VA direct home loan program is to supply home financing to eligible veterans in areas where private financing is not generally available and to help veterans purchase properties with no down payment. Eligible areas are designated by the VA as housing credit shortage areas and are generally rural areas and small cities and towns not near metropolitan or commuting areas of large cities.

The VA loan allows veterans 103.3 percent financing without private mortgage insurance or a 20 percent second mortgage and up to $6,000 for energy efficient improvements.

A VA funding fee of 0 to 3.3% of the loan amount is paid to the VA; this fee may also be financed. In a purchase, veterans may borrow up to 103.3% of the sales price or reasonable value of the home, whichever is less.

Since there is no monthly PMI, more of the mortgage payment goes directly towards qualifying for the loan amount, allowing for larger loans with the same payment.

In a refinance, where a new VA loan is created, veterans may borrow up to 100% of reasonable value, where allowed by state laws.

"VA loans allow veterans to qualify for loan amounts larger than traditional Fannie Mae / conforming loans. VA will insure a mortgage where the monthly payment of the loan is up to 41% of the gross monthly income vs. 28% for a conforming loan assuming the veteran has no monthly bills.

The maximum VA loan guarantee varies by county. As of 1 January 2017, the maximum VA loan amount with no down payment is usually $424,100, although this amount may rise to as much as $721,050 in certain specified "high-cost counties".

Source: VA loan

The VA will issue a **certificate of reasonable value** (the VA approved appraisal). To indicate the property's maximum value for guarantee purposes.

If property appraises for less than the sales price, veteran can make a down payment in cash to make up the difference between the appraisal and sale price.

Discount points - can be paid by the veteran, seller, or another person

Prepayment privileges - can prepay without any penalty

VA Loan Assumption rules

VA must approve the buyer and assumption agreement.

Original borrower remains liable for the loan, unless VA approves a **release of liability**.

Non-veterans may assume the loan.

VA Home Loans are provided by private lenders, such as banks and mortgage companies. VA guarantees a portion of the loan, enabling the lender to provide you with more favorable terms

---

The basic entitlement available to each eligible Veteran is $36,000. Lenders will generally loan up to 4 times a Veteran's available entitlement without a down payment, provided the Veteran is income and credit qualified and the property appraises for the asking price. http://www.benefits.va.gov

---

VA Loans

The basic entitlement available to each eligible Veteran is $36,000.

Lenders will generally loan up to 4 times a Veteran's available entitlement.

Remaining Entitlement

Veterans who had a VA loan before may still have "remaining entitlement" to use for another VA loan. Most lenders require that a combination of the guaranty entitlement and any cash down payment must equal at least 25 percent of the reasonable value or sales price of the property, whichever is less. Thus, for example, $23,500 remaining entitlement would probably meet a lender's minimum guaranty requirement for a no-down payment loan to buy a property valued at and selling for $94,000. You could also combine a down payment with the remaining entitlement for a larger loan amount.

Qualifications for a VA Loan

A Veteran

A qualified non-veteran

An un-remarried surviving spouse

National Guard Members and

Reservists with six years of service.

VA

Guaranteed

Loan can be up to the appraised value.

Loan is from a qualified lender.

Assumable by non-veterans

As well as veterans.

No prepayment penalty.

FHA

Insured

As low as a 3.5% down payment.

Loan is from a qualified lender.

Assumable

No prepayment penalty.

FHA is insured. **DVA** is guaranteed. They insure or guarantee the bank

Farm Service Agency Loan (FSA)

"The Consolidated Farm and Rural Development Act authorizes the **Farm Service Agency** (formerly FmHA) to make direct and guaranteed farm ownership loans to eligible family farmers.

One of the functions of the FO loan program is to assist farmers, especially beginning farmers, in the purchase and enlargement of farms. An eligible borrower must be unable to obtain sufficient credit from a commercial lender, but must assure reasonable prospects of success in the farm operation. Loans are made for up to 40 years.

The interest rate is determined by USDA, and cannot exceed the cost of funds to the Government plus 1 percentage point.

However, direct loans to limited resource borrowers can be made at significantly below the federal cost of funds.

The interest rate on guaranteed loans is negotiated between the borrower and the lender.

USDA guarantees the timely repayment of 90% of principal and interest on guaranteed loans, and in some cases can subsidize the interest rate on these loans.

The amount USDA can directly lend or guarantee each year is determined in the annual congressional appropriations process."

Source: Farm ownership loans

Provides loans to help purchase or improve properties in rural areas, primarily farms and single-family residences.

Loans to low/moderate income families at low interest rates.

Committed to the future of rural communities.

"USDA Office of Rural Development (RD) is an agency with the United States Department of Agriculture which runs programs intended to improve the economy and quality of life in rural America.

Source: USDA Rural Development

USDA Rural Development offer loans, grants and loan guarantees to support essential services such as housing, economic development, health care, first responder services and equipment, and water, electric and communications infrastructure.

They promote economic development by supporting loans to businesses through banks, credit unions and community-managed lending pools. We offer technical assistance and information to help agricultural producers and cooperatives get started and improve the effectiveness of their operations.

They provide technical assistance to help communities undertake community empowerment programs. We help rural residents buy or rent safe, affordable housing and make health and safety repairs to their homes.

USDA Rural Development has a $216 billion portfolio of loans. We will administer $38 billion in loans, loan guarantees and grants through our programs in the current fiscal year.

Conventional Mortgage

Not insured by the government.

May be sold on the secondary mortgage market.

Conventional Mortgage

A conventional mortgage is any type of homebuyer's loan that is not offered or secured by a government entity, like the Federal Housing Administration (FHA), the U.S. Department of Veterans Affairs (VA) or the USDA Rural Housing Service, but rather available through or guaranteed a private lender (banks, credit unions, mortgage companies) or the two government-sponsored enterprises, the Federal National Mortgage Association (Fannie Mae) and the Federal Home Loan Mortgage Corporation (Freddie Mac).

Read more: Conventional Mortgage http://www.investopedia.com/terms/c/conventionalmortgage.asp#ixzz4fZCewY2s

Package loans

One loan covering both real and personal property

Blanket loans

Are one loan secured by multiple parcels of property as collateral
Are usually used in the financing of subdivision developments

Partial Release Clause

A clause usually found in a sub-divider or developer loan.

Partial Release Clause

Used by sub-dividers and developers with a blanket loan. Sub dividers will get one large loan on a large parcel. The loan is called a Blanket Mortgage. As the plots become ready for resale, the developer is allowed to pay a certain amount of money to the lien holder. A certain portion of the lots will be released from the lien. Allows for a partial payment to release a parcel or parcels of land.

Seller/Owner Financing
Purchase Money Mortgage

Usually used when the buyer cannot secure bank financing.

Purchase-money mortgages
Seller/Owner Financing / A Purchase Money Mortgage

Seller financing is a loan provided by the seller of a property or business to the purchaser. When used in the context of residential real estate, it is also called "owner financing." Usually, the purchaser will make some sort of down payment to the seller, and then make installment payments (usually on a monthly basis) over a specified time, at an agreed-upon interest rate, until the loan is fully repaid. In layman's terms, this is when the seller in a transaction offers the buyer a loan rather than the buyer obtaining one from a bank. To a seller, this is an investment in which the return is guaranteed only by the buyer's credit-worthiness or ability and motivation to pay the mortgage. For a buyer it is often beneficial, because he/she may not be able to obtain a loan from a bank. In general, the loan is secured by the property being sold. In the event that the buyer defaults, the property is repossessed or foreclosed on exactly as it would be by a bank.

There are no universal requirements mandated for seller financing. In order to protect both the buyer's and seller's interests, a legally binding purchase agreement should be drawn up with the assistance of an attorney and then signed by both parties.

This is when the Seller provides the buyer with the loan. It is usually done when the buyer cannot secure bank financing.

Often refers to an extension of credit by the seller to the buyer that enables the buyer to purchase the property; the seller "takes back" a note for some or all of the purchase price

Wraparound Loans

Allow the new lender to assume responsibility for the payment of the existing loan (the underlying obligation), and give the borrower a new increased loan at a higher interest rate May be prevented by an acceleration and alienation or due-on-sale clause in the original mortgage.

A wraparound mortgage, more commonly known as a "wrap", is a form of secondary financing for the purchase of real property. The seller extends to the buyer a junior mortgage which wraps around and exists in addition to any superior mortgages already secured by the property. Under a wrap, a seller accepts a secured promissory note from the buyer for the amount due on the underlying mortgage plus an amount up to the remaining purchase money balance.

The new purchaser makes monthly payments to the seller, who is then responsible for making the payments to the underlying mortgagee(s). Should the new purchaser default on those payments, the seller then has the right of foreclosure to recapture the subject property. Because wraps are a form of seller financing, they have the effect of lowering the barriers to ownership of real property; they also can expedite the process of purchasing a home.

An example of a Wraparound Mortgage:

> The seller, who has the original mortgage sells his home with the existing first mortgage in place and a second mortgage which he "carries back" from the buyer. The mortgage he takes from the buyer is for the amount of the first mortgage plus a negotiated amount less than or up to the sales price, minus any down payment and closing costs. The monthly payments are made by the buyer to the seller, who then continues to pay the first mortgage with the proceeds. When the buyer either sells or refinances the property, all mortgages are paid off in full, with the seller entitled to the difference in the payoff of the wrap and any underlying loan payoffs.
>
> Typically, the seller also charges a spread. For example, a seller may have a mortgage at 6% and sell the property at a rate of 8% on a wraparound mortgage. He then would be making a 2% spread on the payments each month (roughly). The difference in principal amounts and amortization schedules will affect the actual spread made).

CONSTRUCTION LOANS

Construction Loans are often extended for developers who are seeking to build something but sell it immediately after building it. In this case, a special appraisal is ordered to attempt to predict the future sales value of the project.
Periodic payments often called "draws"
Made to the general contractor at predetermined progress points
Paid off and replaced by a permanent or "take out" loan

Source: Construction Loan- https://en.wikipedia.org

Sales and Leasebacks

"Leaseback, short for 'sale-and-leaseback,' is a financial transaction, where one sells an asset and leases it back for the long-term; therefore, one continues to be able to use the asset but no longer owns it. The transaction is generally done for fixed assets, notably real estate, as well as for durable and capital goods such as airplanes and trains."
Source: Leaseback - https://en.wikipedia.org

Buydown

Some of the buyer's future interest paid in advance to the lender by the seller or some other individual.

Used frequently by home builders as an incentive to buyers

Home Equity Line of Credit HELOC

Equity Loans
It's much like a credit card.
A line of credit.
A loan based on the equity in a property.

Home equity loans

"A home equity loan is a type of loan in which the borrower uses the equity of his or her home as collateral. The loan amount is determined by the value of the property, and the value of the property is determined by an appraiser from the lending institution. Home equity loans are often used to finance major expenses such as home repairs, medical bills, or college education. A home equity loan creates a lien against the borrower's house and reduces actual home equity.

Most home equity loans require good to excellent credit history, reasonable loan-to-value and combined loan-to-value ratios. Home equity loans come in two types: closed end (traditionally just called a home-equity loan) and open end (a.k.a. a home-equity line of credit). Both are usually referred to as second mortgages, because they are secured against the value of the property, just like a traditional mortgage. Home equity loans and lines of credit are usually, but not always, for a shorter term than first mortgages. Home equity loan can be used as a person's main mortgage in place of a traditional mortgage. However, one cannot purchase a home using a home equity loan, one can only use a home equity loan to refinance.

In the United States, in most cases it is possible to deduct home equity loan interest on one's personal income taxes."
Source: Home equity loan - https://en.wikipedia.org

Usually junior to the loan obtained to purchase the property.
Can be an equity line of credit or a fixed amount.

A **non-conforming loan** is a loan that fails to meet bank criteria for funding.

Interest Only Loan

In the United States, a five- or ten-year interest-only period is typical. After this time, the principal balance is amortized for the remaining term. In other words, if a borrower had a thirty-year mortgage loan and the first ten years were interest only, at the end of the first ten years, the principal balance would be amortized for the remaining period of twenty years. The practical result is that the early payments (in the interest-only period) are substantially lower than the later payments. This gives the borrower more flexibility because the borrower is not forced to make payments towards principal. Indeed, it also enables a borrower who expects to increase his salary substantially over the course of the loan to borrow more than the borrower would have otherwise been able to afford, or investors to generate cash flow when they might not otherwise be able to.

During the interest-only years of the mortgage, the loan balance will not decrease unless the borrower makes additional payments towards principal. Under a conventional amortizing mortgage, the portion of a payment that applies to principal is significantly smaller than the portion that applies to interest in the early years (the same period of time that would be interest-only).

Interest-only loans represent a somewhat higher risk for lenders, and therefore are subject to a slightly higher interest rate. Combined with little or no down payment, the adjustable rate (ARM) variety of interest only mortgages are sometimes indicative of a buyer taking on too much risk—especially when that buyer is unlikely to qualify under more conservative loan structures. Because a homeowner does not build any equity in an interest-only loan he may be adversely affected by prevailing market conditions at the time the borrower is either ready to sell the house or refinance. The borrower may find themselves unable to afford the higher regularly amortized payments at the end of the interest only period, unable to refinance due to lack of equity, and unable to sell if demand for housing has weakened.

Due to the speculative aspects of relying on home appreciation which may or may not happen, many financial experts such as Suze Orman advise against interest-only loans for which a borrower would not otherwise qualify.

Interest only with a balloon payment being the final payment.

A term loan is a monetary loan that is repaid in regular payments over a set period of time. Term loans usually last between one and ten years, but may last as long as 30 years in some cases.

What is a 'Term Loan'

A term loan is a loan from a bank for a specific amount that has a specified repayment schedule and a fixed or floating interest rate. For example, many banks have term-loan programs that can offer small businesses the cash they need to operate from month to month. Often, a small business uses the cash from a term loan to purchase fixed assets such as equipment for its production process.

Read more: Term Loan http://www.investopedia.com/terms/t/termloan.asp#ixzz4fZP7w4eT
Follow us: Investopedia on Facebook

PARTIALLY AMORTIZED

Partial Payment
Balloon Payment

Partially Amortized (balloon) Loans

Payment of some principle and interest. Has a balloon payment for the final payment.

Amortized – Fully Amortized

Direct Reduction Loan

Fixed payment

Interest payment decreases over time.

Principal payment increases over time.

Amortized Loan (direct reduction loan)

Fixed payment. The amount of principle paid increases and the amount of interest paid decreases over time. The monthly payment stays the same.

It reverses over time.

The amount applied to the interest decreases with each payment.
The amount applied to the principal increases with each payment.

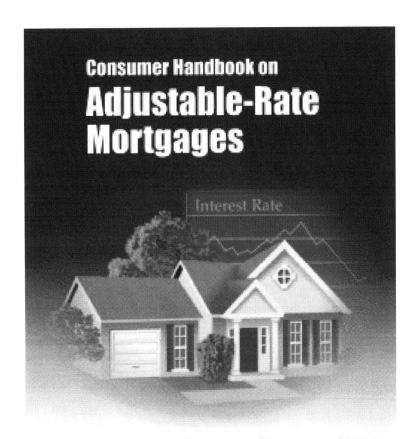

Adjustable Rate Mortgage (ARM) loans – Interest rate is based on an index.

Adjustable rate mortgage (ARM) loans

An adjustable-rate mortgage (ARM), is a mortgage loan with the interest rate on the note periodically adjusted based on an index.

ARMs generally permit borrowers to lower their initial payments if they are willing to assume the risk of interest rate changes.

Loan caps provide payment protection against payment shock, and allow a measure of interest rate certainty to those who gamble with initial fixed rates on ARM loans.

Lifetime Cap: Most First Mortgage loans have a 5% or 6% Life Cap above the Start Rate (this ultimately varies by the lender and credit grade).

A variable-rate mortgage, adjustable-rate mortgage(ARM), or tracker mortgage is a mortgage loan with the interest rate on the note periodically adjusted based on an index which reflects the cost to the lender of borrowing on the credit markets.

Growing-equity Mortgages (GEMs)

Known as a rapid-payoff mortgage

A fixed rate mortgage on which the monthly payments increase over time according to a set schedule. The interest rate on the loan does not change, and there is never any negative amortization. In other words, the first payment is a fully amortizing payment. As the payments increase, the additional amount above and beyond what would be a fully amortizing payment is applied directly to the remaining balance of the mortgage, shortening the life of the mortgage and increasing interest savings.

Read more: Growing-Equity
Mortgage http://www.investopedia.com/terms/g/growing_equity_mortgage.asp#ixzz4fZS9AUDQ
Follow us: Investopedia on Facebook

Negative Amortization Mortgage

The quickest way to go underwater.

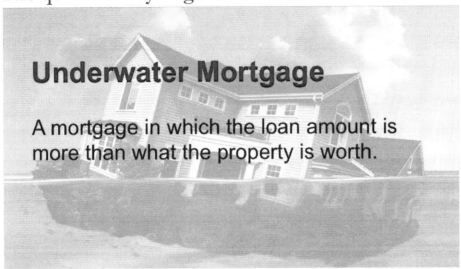

Occurs in loans in which the periodic payment does not cover the amount of interest due for that loan period. The unpaid accrued interest is then capitalized monthly into the outstanding principal balance. The result of this is that the loan balance (or principal) increases by the amount of the unpaid interest on a monthly basis.

All NegAM home loans eventually require full repayment of principal and interest according to the original term of the mortgage and note signed by the borrower. Most loans only allow NegAM to happen for no more than 5 years.

There are typically 4 payment options (listed from highest to lowest):

- 15-year payment

Amortized over a period of 15 years at the Fully Indexed Rate

- 30-year payment

Amortized over a period of 30 years at the Fully Indexed Rate

- Interest only payment
- Minimum payment

Based on the minimal start rate determined by the lender. When paying the minimum payment, the difference between the interest only payment and the minimum payment is deferred to the balance of the loan increasing what is owed on the mortgage.

In a very hot real estate market a buyer may use a negative-amortizing mortgage to purchase a property with the plan to sell the property at a higher price before the end of the loan period. Therefore, an informed investor could purchase several properties with minimal monthly obligations and make a great profit over a five-year plan in a rising real-estate market.

If property values decrease, it is likely that the borrower will owe more on the property than it is worth, known colloquially in the mortgage industry as "being underwater." In this situation, if the property owner cannot make the new monthly payment, he or she may be faced with foreclosure or having to refinance with a very high loan-to-value ratio, requiring additional monthly obligations, such as mortgage insurance, and higher rates and payments due to the adversity of a high loan-to-value ratio.*

---

* Wikipedia

Reverse Mortgages

Home Equity Conversion Mortgages for Seniors (HECM)
Homeowner must be 62 years or older. Turning the equity in a primary residence into cash free income.

What is a reverse mortgage?

A reverse mortgage is a special type of home loan that lets you convert a portion of the equity in your home into cash. The equity that you built up over years of making mortgage payments can be paid to you. However, unlike a traditional home equity loan or second mortgage, HECM borrowers do not have to repay the HECM loan until the borrowers no longer use the home as their principal residence or fail to meet the obligations of the mortgage. You can also use a HECM to purchase a primary residence if you are able to use cash on hand to pay the difference between the HECM proceeds and the sales price plus closing costs for the property you are purchasing.

Subprime Loans

A loan a bank will use when the borrower has a less than good credit rating. Higher fees and interest charged by the bank are used to offset the risk.

Subprime Loans

Less than good credit rating

Higher fees and interest charged to offset the risk.

Graduated payment mortgage loan

Have increasing costs over time and are geared to young borrowers who expect wage increases over time.

Balloon payment mortgages

Balloon Payment

A large and final payment agreed upon for a predetermined date.

Have only partial amortization, meaning that amount of monthly payments due are calculated (amortized) over a certain term, but the outstanding principal balance is due at some point short of that term, and at the end of the term a balloon payment is due. **A large and final payment set at a pre-determined date.**

Bi Weekly Mortgage

"Lenders will only accept monthly payments, they will not accept partial payments or biweekly payments; except extra money to be applied to the monthly payment that is included in the monthly payment. There is NO mortgage loan payment plan in the United States which the borrower makes payments toward the principal and interest every two weeks instead of once monthly. Regulation allows the mortgage loan companies to not accept partial payments. That was our government's answer to the Mortgage Loan Companies demands of compensating for losing the right to charge prepayment penalties. The government compromised. All other loans can be paid every two weeks. The monthly payment would pay the interest and pay to the principal, the second payment made two weeks later (in any amount you wish) will go directly to the principal of that loan and will save the consumer a large amount of money paid to interest only. This Biweekly Savings Plan or Biweekly Equity building plan in NOT paying a half a mortgage payment every two weeks. (I'll have to finish this later)"

"Buy Down (Paying Points)

A mortgage financing technique where the buyer attempts to obtain a lower interest rate for at least the first few years of the mortgage. The seller of the property usually provides payments to the mortgage lending institution, which, in turn, lowers the buyer's monthly interest rate and therefore monthly payment. This is typically done for a period of about one to five years. In a seller's market the seller might raise the purchase price to compensate for the costs of the buy down but in most markets, it would not be to their advantage to use a buy down as an enticement if they are going to offset the benefit by raising the price. In most cases, the buy down does not even involve the seller. It is an arrangement between the lender and the buyer.

You may also use the buy down option on a refinance.
Source: Buy down - <u>*https://en.wikipedia.org*</u>

Flexible mortgage

refers to a residential mortgage loan that offers flexibility in the requirements to make monthly repayments.

COMMERCIAL MORTGAGE

A mortgage loan secured by commercial property, such as an office building, shopping center, industrial warehouse, or apartment complex. The proceeds from a commercial mortgage are typically used to acquire, refinance, or redevelop commercial property.

Commercial mortgages are structured to meet the needs of the borrower and the lender. Key terms include the loan amount (sometimes referred to as "loan proceeds"), interest rate, term (sometimes referred to as the "maturity"), amortization schedule, and prepayment flexibility. Commercial mortgages are generally subject to extensive underwriting and due diligence prior to closing. The lender's underwriting process may include a financial review of the property and the property owner (or "sponsor"), as well as commissioning and review of various third-party reports, such as an appraisal.

Participation Mortgage or Participating Mortgage

A mortgage loan, or sometimes a group of them, in which two or more persons have fractional equitable interests. In this arrangement the lender, or mortgagee, is entitled to share in the rental or resale proceeds from a property owned by the borrower, or mortgagor. The mortgage is evidenced by the bank or other fiduciary that has legal title to the mortgage and sells the fractional shares to investors or makes the investment for the certificate holders. A participation mortgage may or may not require principal and interest payments and may or may not contain a balloon payment.

For instance, John has a loan for a strip mall including six separate units. All are rented/leased and in addition to the principal and interest he pays to the lender, he is required to pay a certain percentage of the incoming funds. The lender is then participating in the income stream provided by the particular property.

Bridge Loan

A type of short-term loan, typically taken out for a period of 2 weeks to 3 years pending the arrangement of larger or longer-term financing. It is usually called a bridging loan in the United Kingdom, also known as a "caveat loan," and also known in some applications as a swing loan. In South African usage, the term bridging finance is more common, but is used in a more restricted sense than is common elsewhere.

A bridge loan is interim financing for an individual or business until permanent financing or the next stage of financing is obtained. Money from the new financing is generally used to "take out" (i.e. to pay back) the bridge loan, as well as other capitalization needs.

Bridge loans are typically more expensive than conventional financing, to compensate for the additional risk. Bridge loans typically have a higher interest rate, points (points are essentially fees, 1 point equals 1% of loan amount), and other costs that are amortized over a shorter period, and various fees and other "sweeteners" (such as equity participation by the lender in some loans). The lender also may require cross-collateralization and a lower loan-to-value ratio. On the other hand, they are typically arranged quickly with relatively little documentation.
Source: Bridge loan - https://en.wikipedia.org

Hard Money Loan

A specific type of asset-based loan financing through which a borrower receives funds secured by real property. Hard money loans are typically issued by private investors or companies.

Interest rates are typically higher than conventional commercial or residential property loans, starting at 7.7%, because of the higher risk and shorter duration of the loan.

Most hard money loans are used for projects lasting from a few months to a few years. Hard money is similar to a bridge loan, which usually has similar criteria for lending as well as cost to the borrowers. The primary difference is that a bridge loan often refers to a commercial property or investment property that may be in transition and does not yet qualify for traditional financing, whereas hard money often refers to not only an asset-based loan with a high interest rate, but possibly a distressed financial situation, such as arrears on the existing mortgage, or where bankruptcy and foreclosure proceedings are occurring.
Source: Hard money loan - https://en.wikipedia.org

Land Contract/Contract for Deed

"Other terms for a **land contract** include:
terms contract

contract for deed

agreement for deed

land installment contract

installment sale agreement"
Source: Land contract - https://en.wikipedia.org

Contract for Deed or Land Contract
Land Contract for Deed
Land Installment

The seller finances the buyer.

The seller holds the legal title. The buyer holds equitable title.

The buyer has possession of the property but does not own the property.

Community Reinvestment Act of 1977 (CRA)

The Community Reinvestment Act is a United States federal law designed to encourage commercial banks and savings associations to help meet the needs of borrowers in all segments of their communities, including low- and moderate-income neighborhoods.

Congress passed the Act in 1977 to reduce discriminatory credit practices against low-income neighborhoods, a practice known as **redlining**.

Financial institutions are expected to meet deposit and credit needs of community, participate in development and rehabilitation projects and loan programs.

Broker Commissions

Fees paid to the broker for services.

Mortgage Insurance (PMI) – Private Mortgage Insurance

Insurance to offset losses in the case where a mortgagor is not able to repay the loan and the lender is not able to recover its costs after foreclosure and sale of the mortgaged property.

Protects the lender against loss on the top 20% or 25% of the loan. PMI may be dropped when the equity of the property reaches 80% or 85%.

Lender Requirements

Minimum requirement of the borrower set by the lender.

Other Finance Methods

Home Affordable Refinance Program (HARP) – Established for homeowners who have little or no equity. They must be current on their payments. Ends September 30, 2017.

Assumption – The buyer becomes responsible to pay the existing current mortgage.
The purchaser is personally liable for the debt
In the event of a foreclosure, the purchaser may be held liable for any deficiency
Unless specifically released by the lender, the original borrower may also be liable for the debt or any deficiency.

Subject to – The Seller remains responsible to pay the existing current mortgage. The buyer gets a new loan.

The purchaser is not personally liable for the debt.

In the event of a foreclosure, the purchaser is not personally liable for a deficiency.

Due-on-Sale – When the property is sold, the bank will allow for either an assumption or a "subject to".

Due-on-Sale Clause

When the property sells, the loan money becomes due.

Prepayment – A clause in the mortgage that allows the mortgagor to pay or not pay his mortgage early.

Release – Giving up your interest in a property.

Prepayment
Paying off the mortgage earlier than the due date.

Release
Giving up your interest in a property.

Acceleration Clause

In case of a **Default.** All money becomes due.

Alienation Clause

Selling without lender approval. All money becomes due.

ALIENATION – When a mortgagor <u>sells</u> the property without the lender's approval, an alienation clause calls the money due. Voluntary and involuntary. Voluntary would be a sale. Involuntary could be a foreclosure.

ACCELERATION – In case of a <u>Default.</u> All money becomes due.

The FED regulates the money market.

The US Treasury is the nation's fiscal manager.

The US Treasury is the nation's fiscal manager

Primary Mortgage Market

The bank where the purchaser will apply for a loan. The bank where the mortgage is originated.

A formal appraisal has to be done.

Regulated by the FED. (Federal Reserve System)

Examples: Savings and loans, commercial banks, life insurance companies and mutual savings banks.

Primary Mortgage Market

The bank where the mortgage is originated.

Savings and loans, commercial banks, life insurance companies and mutual savings banks.

Regulated by the FED. (Federal Reserve System)

Sources of Loan Money

There are different ways of real estate financing:

- SAVINGS AND LOAN ASSOCIATIONS
- COMMERCIAL BANKS

- SAVINGS BANKS
- MORTGAGE BANKERS AND BROKERS

Mortgage bankers are companies or individuals that originate mortgage loans, sell them to other investors, service the monthly payments, and may act as agents to dispense funds for taxes and insurance.

Mortgage brokers present homebuyers with loans from a variety of loan sources. Their income comes from the lender making the loan, just like with any other bank. Because they can tap a variety of lenders, they can shop on behalf of the borrower and achieve the best available terms.

- CREDIT UNIONS
- FEDERALLY SUPPORTED AGENCIES
- REAL ESTATE INVESTMENT TRUSTS
- OTHER SOURCES
- Individual investors

In addition, homebuyers or builders can save their money using FSBO (For Sale by Owner) in order not to pay extra fees.

Secondary Mortgage Market

Loans being bought and sold after the origination.

Bank buying and selling loans from each other.

Freddie Mac, Fannie Mae and Ginnie Mae provide a secondary market for residential FHA-insured loans, VA-guaranteed loans and conventional mortgages.

Secondary Mortgage Market

A formal appraisal has to be done just like on the Primary Mortgage Market.

The secondary mortgage market is the market for the sale of securities or bonds collateralized by the value of mortgage loans. A mortgage lender, commercial banks, or specialized firm will group together many loans (from the "primary mortgage market") and sell grouped loans known as collateralized mortgage obligations (CMOs) or mortgage-backed securities (MBS) to investors such as pension funds, insurance companies and hedge funds. Mortgage-backed securities were often combined into collateralized debt obligations (CDOs), which may include other types of debt obligations such as corporate loans.

The secondary mortgage market was intended to provide a new source of capital for the market when the traditional source in one market—such as a Savings and loan association (S&L) or "thrift" in the United States—was unable to. It also was hoped to be more efficient than the old localized market for funds which might have a shortage or surplus depending on the location. In theory, the risk of default on individual loans was greatly reduced by this aggregation process, such that even high-risk individual loans could be treated as part of an AAA-risk (safest possible) investment.

"A mortgage-backed security (MBS) is a type of asset-backed security that is secured by a mortgage or collection of mortgages. The mortgages are sold to a group of individuals (a government agency or investment bank) that securitizes, or packages, the loans together into a security that investors can buy.

Fannie Mae or Freddie Mac, or they can be "private-label", issued by structures set up by investment banks.

Source: Mortgage-backed security - https://en.wikipedia.org

Major Warehousing Agencies

Federal National Mortgage Association (FNMA)

Government National Mortgage Association (GNMA)

Federal Home Loan Mortgage Corporation FHLMC (Freddie Mac)

Lets break them down.

MAJOR WAREHOUSING AGENCIES

Federal National Mortgage Association (FNMA)	Government National Mortgage Association (GNMA)	Federal Home Loan Mortgage Corporation – FHLMC (Freddie Mac)
Publically Traded.	Federal Agency.	Government Sponsored
Government. Sponsored	Expands affordable housing. Guarantees mortgage backed securities offered by mortgage lenders.	Created for conventional mortgage on the secondary market. Sells mortgage backed securities. Increases supply of money for mortgages. (Brother of FNMA)
Raises money by selling government guaranteed bonds. Purpose is to expand the secondary mortgage mkt. Secures mortgages and sells them under mortgage backed securities. Allows lenders to reinvest.	Authorized to purchase FHA, VA and Rural Development Loans.	Can buy FHA and VA loans, pool them and sell bonds in the open market.
Works with GNMA in the tandem plan.	Works with FNMA in the tandem plan.	

TANDEM PLAN

FNMA and GNMA work together with the tandem plan.
A United States subsidized mortgage purchase program where the loans enable builders and developers to create non-profit public housing.

Funds in times of high interest rates.

Under the Tandem Plan, the Government National Mortgage Association (GNMA / Ginnie Mae) buys mortgages at discounted market price and then sells them through the Federal National Mortgage Association (FNMA / Fannie Mae) and the Federal Home Loan Mortgage Corp. (FHLMC / Freddie Mac).

Federal National Mortgage Association (FNMA) Fannie Mae

Publically traded

Gov. sponsored enterprise.

Raises money by selling government guaranteed bonds.

Works with GNMA in the tandem plan.

The purpose is to expand the secondary mortgage market.

Secures mortgages into mortgage backed securities.

Allows lenders to reinvest their assets.

Government National Mortgage Association (GNMA) Ginnie Mae

Federal Agency

Expands affordable housing finance

Authorized to purchase FHA, VA and Rural Development Loans.

Works with FNMA in the tandem plan.

Guarantees mortgage-backed securities offered by mortgage lenders.

Federal Home Loan Mortgage Corporation FHLMC (Freddie Mac)

Government Sponsored Enterprise (Brother to Fannie)

Created for conventional mortgage on the secondary market.

Sells Mortgage backed securities.

Increases supply of money for mortgages.

Financing/Credit Laws
Your Equal Credit Opportunity Rights

People use credit to pay for education or a house, a remodeling job or a car, or to finance a loan to keep their business operating.

The Federal Trade Commission (FTC), the nation's consumer protection agency, enforces the Equal Credit Opportunity Act (ECOA), which prohibits credit discrimination on the basis of

race

color

religion

national origin

sex

marital status

age

because you get public assistance.

Creditors may ask you for most of this information in certain situations, but they may not use it when deciding whether to give you credit or when setting the terms of your credit. Not everyone who applies for credit gets it or gets the same terms: Factors like income, expenses, debts, and credit history are among the considerations lenders use to determine your creditworthiness.

The law provides protections when you deal with any organizations or people who regularly extend credit, including banks, small loan and finance companies, retail and department stores, credit card companies, and credit unions. Everyone who participates in the decision to grant credit or in setting the terms of that credit, including real estate brokers who arrange financing, must comply with the ECOA.[3]

---

[3] https://www.consumer.ftc.gov/articles/0347-your-equal-credit-opportunity-rights

Regulation Z / Truth in Lending / TILA

Loans

Advertising

APR

Trigger Terms

Three Day Right of Rescission

Purpose of the TILA and Regulation Z

The TILA is intended to ensure that credit terms are disclosed in a meaningful way so consumers can compare credit terms more readily and knowledgeably.

Before its enactment, consumers were faced with a bewildering array of credit terms and rates.

It was difficult to compare loans because they were seldom presented in the same format.

Now, all creditors must use the same credit terminology and expressions of rates. In addition to providing a uniform system for disclosures, the act:

Protects consumers against inaccurate and unfair credit billing and credit card practices;

Provides consumers with rescission rights;

Provides for rate caps on certain dwelling-secured loans;

Imposes limitations on home equity lines of credit and certain closed-end home mortgages; and

Delineates and prohibits unfair or deceptive mortgage lending practices.

The TILA and Regulation Z do not, however, tell financial institutions how much interest they may charge or whether they must grant a consumer a loan.

Exempt Transactions

Credit extended primarily for a business, commercial, or agricultural purpose;

Credit extended to other than a natural person (including credit to government agencies or Instrumentalities.

The APR

is a measure of the cost of credit, expressed as a nominal yearly rate.
It relates the amount and timing of value received by the consumer to the amount and timing of payments made.

The disclosure of the APR is central to the uniform credit cost disclosure envisioned by the TILA.

Advertising

Triggering Terms - The following are triggering terms that require additional disclosures:

The amount or percentage of any down payment;

The number of payments or period of repayment;

The amount of any payment; and

The amount of any finance charge.

An advertisement stating a triggering term must also state the following terms as applicable:

The amount or percentage of any down payment;

The terms of repayment, which reflect the repayment obligations over the full term of the loan, including any balloon payment; and

The "annual percentage rate," using that term, and, if the rate may be increased after consummation, that fact.

Regulation Z allows for a **three day right of rescission** if a loan is secured by a person's primary residence.

RESPA / Real Estate Settlement Procedures Act

The main objective was to protect homeowners by assisting them in becoming better educated while shopping for real estate services, and eliminating kickbacks and referral fees which add unnecessary costs to settlement services. RESPA requires lenders and others involved in mortgage lending to provide borrowers with pertinent and timely disclosures regarding the nature and costs of a real estate settlement process. RESPA was also designed to prohibit potentially abusive practices such as kickbacks and referral fees, the practice of dual tracking, and imposes limitations on the use of escrow accounts.[4]

*Integrated Disclosure Rule (TRID) ***

For more than 30 years, Federal law has required lenders to provide two different disclosure forms to consumers applying for a mortgage.

The law also generally has required two different forms at or shortly before closing on the loan.

Two different Federal agencies developed these forms separately, under two Federal statutes: the **Truth in Lending Act (TILA) and the Real Estate Settlement Procedures Act (RESPA)**. The information on these forms is overlapping and the language is inconsistent.

Consumers often find the forms confusing, and lenders and settlement agents find the forms burdensome to provide and explain.

The Dodd-Frank Wall Street Reform and Consumer Protection Act (Dodd-Frank Act) directs the Consumer Financial Protection Bureau (Bureau) to integrate the mortgage loan disclosures under **TILA and RESPA**.

First, the **Good Faith Estimate (GFE)** and the initial **Truth-in-Lending disclosure** (initial TIL) have been combined into a new form, the **Loan Estimate**.

Similar to those forms, the new **Loan Estimate form** is designed to provide disclosures that will be helpful to consumers in understanding the key features, costs, and risks of the mortgage loan for which they are applying, and must be provided to consumers no later than the third business day after they submit a loan application.

Second, the **HUD-1** and final **Truth-in-Lending** disclosure have been combined into another new form, the **Closing Disclosure**, which is designed to provide disclosures that will be helpful to consumers in understanding all of the costs of the transaction.

---

[4] https://www.federalreserve.gov/boarddocs/supmanual/cch/respa.pdf

Fraud and Lending Practices

The FBI is committed to aggressively pursuing those who endanger the stability of our banking system and the safety of assets and personal information the public has entrusted to its care.

Fraud in Lending Practices

Investigated by the FBI
up to 30 years in prison
1 million dollars.

Predatory Lending Practices

Poor people targeted most.

In financial institution fraud (FIF) investigations, the Bureau continues to concentrate its efforts on organized criminal groups that prey on banks and engage in patterns of activity that lead to large aggregate losses.

Fraud for housing: This type of fraud is typically represented by illegal actions taken by a borrower motivated to acquire or maintain ownership of a house. The borrower may, for example, misrepresent income and asset information on a loan application or entice an appraiser to manipulate a property's appraised value.

Common Mortgage Fraud Schemes

- **Foreclosure rescue schemes:** The perpetrators identify homeowners who are in foreclosure or at risk of defaulting on their mortgage loan and then mislead them into believing they can save their homes by transferring the deed or putting the property in the name of an investor. The perpetrators profit by selling the property to an investor or straw borrower, creating equity using a fraudulent appraisal, and stealing the seller proceeds or fees paid by the homeowners. The homeowners are sometimes told they can pay rent for at least a year and repurchase the property once their credit has been reestablished. However, the perpetrators fail to make the mortgage payments and usually the property goes into foreclosure.
- **Loan modification schemes:** Similar to foreclosure rescue scams, these schemes involve perpetrators purporting to assist homeowners who are delinquent in their mortgage payments and are on the verge of losing their home by offering to renegotiate the terms of the homeowners' loan with the lender. The scammers, however, demand large fees up front and often negotiate unfavorable terms for the clients, or do not negotiate at all. Usually, the homeowners ultimately lose their homes.

- **Illegal property flipping:** Property is purchased, falsely appraised at a higher value, and then quickly sold. What makes property flipping illegal is the fraudulent appraisal information or false information provided during the transactions. The schemes typically involve one or more of the following: fraudulent appraisals; falsified loan documentation; inflated buyer income; or kickbacks to buyers, investors, property/loan brokers, appraisers, and title company employees.

- **Builder bailout/condo conversion:** Builders facing rising inventory and declining demand for newly constructed homes employ bailout schemes to offset losses. Builders find buyers who obtain loans for the properties but who then allow the properties to go into foreclosure. In a condo conversion scheme, apartment complexes purchased by developers during a housing boom are converted into condos, and in a declining real estate market, developers often have excess inventory of units. So, developers recruit straw buyers with cash-back incentives and inflate the value of the condos to obtain a larger sales price at closing. In addition to failing to disclose the cash-back incentives to the lender, the straw buyers' income and asset information are often inflated in order for them to qualify for properties that they otherwise would be ineligible or unqualified to purchase.

- **Equity skimming:** An investor may use a straw buyer, false income documents, and false credit reports to obtain a mortgage loan in the straw buyer's name. Subsequent to closing, the straw buyer signs the property over to the investor in a quit claim deed, which relinquishes all rights to the property and provides no guaranty to title. The investor does not make any mortgage payments and rents the property until foreclosure takes place several months later.

- **Silent second:** The buyer of a property borrows the down payment from the seller through the issuance of a non-disclosed second mortgage. The primary lender believes the borrower has invested his own money in the down payment, when in fact, it is borrowed. The second mortgage may not be recorded to further conceal its status from the primary lender.

- **Home equity conversion mortgage (HECM):** A HECM is a reverse mortgage loan product insured by the Federal Housing Administration to borrowers who are 62 years or older, own their own property (or have a small mortgage balance), occupy the property as their primary residence, and participate in HECM counseling. It provides homeowners access to equity in their homes, usually in a lump sum payment. Perpetrators taking advantage of the HECM program recruit seniors through local churches, investment seminars, and television, radio, billboard, and mailer advertisements. The scammers then obtain a HECM in the name of the recruited homeowner to convert equity in the homes into cash. The scammers keep the cash and pay a fee to the senior citizen or take the full amount unbeknownst to the senior citizen. No loan payment or repayment is required until the borrower no longer uses the house as a primary residence. In the scheme, the appraisals on the home are vastly inflated and the lender does not detect the fraud until the homeowner dies and the true value of the property is discovered.

- **Commercial real estate loans:** Owners of distressed commercial real estate (or those acting on their behalf) obtain financing by manipulating the property's appraised value. Bogus leases may be created to exaggerate the building's profitability, thus inflating the value as determined using the 'income method' for property valuation. Fraudulent appraisals trick lenders into extending loans to the owner. As cash flows are lower than stated, the borrower struggles to maintain the property and repairs are neglected. By the time the commercial loans are in default, the lender is often left with dilapidated or difficult-to-rent commercial property. Many of the methods of committing mortgage fraud that are found in residential real estate are also present in commercial loan fraud.

- **Air loans:** This is a nonexistent property loan where there is usually no collateral. Air loans involve brokers who invent borrowers and properties, establish accounts for payments, and maintain custodial accounts for escrows. They may establish an office with a bank of telephones, each one used as the fake employer, appraiser, credit agency, etc., to fraudulently deceive creditors who attempt to verify information on loan applications.[5]

Penalty for Fraud is up to one million dollars and up to ten years in jail.

Predatory lending practices (risks to clients)

The practice of a lender deceptively convincing borrowers to agree to unfair and abusive loan terms, or systematically violating those terms in ways that make it difficult for the borrower to defend against[6]

Usury lending laws

Regulations governing the amount of interest that can be charged on a loan. These laws protect the consumer.

Usury Lending Laws

Taking advantage of a situation and charging a higher interest.

Lending laws protect the consumer.

---

[5] https://www.fbi.gov/investigate/white-collar-crime/mortgage-fraud
[6] https://www.consumerfinance.gov/

A rejected credit applicant must be informed within 30 days of the reasons for the rejection.

Down Payment Assistant Programs

The U.S. Department of Housing and Urban Development (HUD) provides grants to state and local organizations through the HOME Investment Partnerships Program and the Community Development Block Grant Program. The Neighborhood Stabilization Program, for example, is among the many homebuyer assistance programs that HUD helps fund. To find the programs in your state, go to HUD's on-line listing or the handy new tool from Down Payment Resource.

State and local housing finance agencies (HFAs) administer many of these programs, and we work with many of them. Freddie Mac even offers an enhanced 3-percent-down mortgage product, HFA Advantage^{SM}, for use through these agencies. The National Council of State Housing Agencies (NCSHA) offers a state-by-state listing of HFAs. The National Association of Local Housing Finance Agencies (NALHFA) provides local-level program information.

The three main types of down payment assistance are grants, second mortgage loans, and tax credits.

Depending on the program, assistance may be limited to first-time homebuyers and/or low- and moderate-income homebuyers. And homebuyer education counseling may be required. (It would be helpful in any case.)

Chapter Ten

GENERAL PRINCIPLES OF AGENCY

> Delegated authority
> and consent to act
> create agency.

Agency Relationships are the fundamental basics in real estate. It is the duties owed clients and customers from Agents.

Principle is the Client – The principal /client delegates authority to the agent. The agent consents to act.

Delegated authority and consent to act create agency.

Types of Agents and Agencies

Types of Agents

Special Agent

General Agent

Universal Agent

Transactional Agent

Designated Agent

Let's break it down.

Special Agent
An agent hired to do one specific act.

Special Agent

One Specific Act
A Listing Broker
A Selling Broker

Examples would be a listing or a buyer's agent.

General Agent
An agent that has general duties. (Example would be a property manager.) A property manager's primary responsibility is to get the highest net return for the owner.

General Agent

General Duties
A Property Manager

A property manager's primary responsibility is to get the highest net return for the owner.

The General Manager is the Property Manager.

A Listing Agreement makes a Seller's Agent a **Special Agent**. A Seller's Agent has been hired to do one specific act. As opposed to a Property Manager who is a **General Agent** and hired to do general duties.

Universal Agent
A person who holds a power of attorney.

Transactional Agent
A non-agent. Does not represent either party. Facilitates the transaction. Collects all documents and makes sure everything is fine.

Transactional Agent

The closing attorney.
The escrow agent.

Basically a non agent.

Designated Agent
Used in a dual agency situation. An agent that gets designated to work with a client or customer.

Designated Agent

An agent designated to represent one party.

Usually used in a dual agency.

Sub Agency / Sub Agent

Lasting until the early 1990s, the broker provided a conventional full-service, commission-based brokerage relationship under a signed listing agreement only with a seller, thus creating an agency relationship with fiduciary obligations under common law. The seller was then a client of the broker.

However, no such agency relationship existed with the buyer, and the broker's agents helped the buyer (who was typically known as his or her "customer"). In this situation, during the entire period in which the buyer looked at properties, entered into a real estate contract, and finally closed on one, that broker/agent functioned solely as the sub-agent of the seller's broker.

Client

The contract between the Seller and the **Seller's Agent** is the **Listing Agreement**.

The Listing Agreement can be considered an employment contract.

Fiduciary Relationships

A fiduciary relationship is one of trust and confidence; it involves one party acting for the benefit of another.

Fiduciary Duties due the Client /Principal
Confidentiality
Obedience
Loyalty
Disclosure
Accountability
Care

(C O L D . A C)

Fiduciary Duties

Confidentiality
Obedience
Loyalty
Disclosure
Accountability
Care

Customer

The Customer is due Fair and Honest Dealings.

The Buyer's Agent is called the **Selling Agent.**
A Customer is not represented.

The Seller's Agent has earned a commission when he brings a ready, willing and able buyer that meets the terms of the listing agreement.

If a Seller's Agent brings a ready, willing and able buyer who meets the terms of the listing agreement, the Seller must pay a commission even if the Seller changes his mind and doesn't want to sell.

The earnest money deposit of the buyer is returned to the buyer and the Seller's Agent should look to the seller for compensation.

The Seller's Agent has met his obligations in the Listing Agreement.

Creation and Disclosure of Agency and Agency Agreements

You must disclose to the party that you don't represent, that you represent someone else.

Single Agency – Working "for" or "with" one party in the transaction.

Dual Agency – Working with the buyer and the seller in one transaction.
Dual Agency is when an Agent represents both Buyer and Seller with the written expressed acceptance of both the Buyer and Seller.

Responsibilities of the Agent/Principal

The Broker and the Agents/Salespersons have an employment contract in which defines what is expected of each party.

If the Broker in the deal dies, all deals and listings die. The Agents/salespersons would need to move to another responsible Broker and execute all new contracts and disclosures because one of the parties in the transaction have changed.

If an Agent/salespersons die, it has no effect on any listings or transactions.

A Broker cannot pay another responsible Broker's Agent unless the deal on which the Broker is paying was generated while the Sub Agent was under the direct supervision of that responsible Broker.

An Agent/Salesperson cannot accept any payment or bonus unless it is from the responsible Broker to which their license is held. If a client or customer gives an Agent/salesperson a bonus, the Agent/Salesperson must turn that bonus over to her responsible Broker.

A responsible Broker is responsible for the real estate activities of his agents/Salespersons.

The Listing Agreement

An Employment Agreement

A Unilateral Agreement

Seller

A listing agreement is between the Seller and the Seller's Agent.

Seller's Agent

Fiduciary Duties

Confidentiality
Obedience
Loyalty
Disclosure
Accountability
Care

General Requirements for Valid Listing – Listings must be in writing, state the exact rate or amount of commission, listing price or range, a description of the property, brokers name and be acknowledged by the seller.

Everything in real estate has to be in writing to be enforceable in court. A judge will not hear a complaint based on verbal agreements.

The broker owns all the listings. If a listing agent moves to another broker, the listing stays with the old broker unless there is a contract that states otherwise.

Procuring Cause / Procured the Buyer
The person responsible for the transaction moving forward.

Procuring Cause
Procured the Buyer

The person responsible for
putting the transaction into motion.

The procuring cause gets paid.

Now lets talk about these listing types.

Listing Agreements are employment contracts between the sellers of real estate and real estate brokers. The listing agreement creates an agency and fiduciary relationship. The seller being the principal / client and the broker is his agent. The broker represents the seller. Listings are unilateral contracts.

Listing Agreements

Exclusive Right Listing
Exclusive Listing
Open Listing

Net Listing

Exclusive Right Listing

An exclusive listing agreement whereas the agent will get paid no matter who procures the buyer. You always get paid even if the Seller sells it herself. (Thus, if it doesn't say RIGHT, then it's wrong for you.) The listing Agent will get paid no matter who brings the buyer.

Exclusive __Right__ Listing

The agent gets paid no matter who procures the buyer.

$

Exclusive Listing

The owner wants to hire one agent and have their property listed on the MLS but they also want to reserve the right to sell it themselves without paying a commission. The listing agent would need to prove they were the **Procuring Cause** to get paid. (Procured the Buyer) An agent may not be paid at all if the seller procures the buyer.

Exclusive Listing

The Seller reserves the right to sell it. If the Seller sells it, the agent has not earned a commission.

?

Open Listing

The seller hires many agents. The agent that gets paid is the one that can prove they were the procuring cause.

Open Listing

The Seller hires any number of agents. Commission is paid to the agent who procures the buyer.

#

Net Listing

A net listing can be any of the listings above. A net listing is when the seller would like to get a definite amount of money from the sale and the agent gets to keep anything else in the transaction. They are considered unethical.

Exclusive Right Listing
Exclusive Listing
Open Listing

Net Listing

A net listing can be combined with any listing.

Listings are **Unilateral Contracts.** (A promise of one person to do something if another person completes an act.).

In a listing, the broker will need to bring a ready, willing and able buyer to meet the terms of the listing agreement to earn his commission. A seller is not obligated to accept less than asking price. If the seller does accept less than asking price, the seller's agent has also earned a commission by bringing a ready, willing and able buyer.

In every listing agreement, there is a **"Protection Clause"**. The protection clause protects the agent from unscrupulous sellers who are trying to save on commission. In the protection clause, it will say something to the effect of: "If the seller sells this listed property after _____ days/months of the expiration of the listing to a person that the listing real estate agent introduced to the seller, the listing agent has earned his/her commission.

Unilateral Contracts
Only one person is forced into doing something.
An open listing. An Option.

Bilateral Contracts
A promise for a promise. A Purchase Agreement.

Bilateral Contracts – A promise for a promise
The Purchase Agreement is a bilateral contract.

Disclose Agent Owned Properties. Always disclose when you are selling your own home.

Disclose when you are buying.

Disclose when you are in a transaction with a relative.

Scenario One

Bob the broker has an agent / salesperson named Sally. Sally just got a listing agreement with a seller. This weekend she plans on having an "open house".

While Sally was at the open house, her broker, Bob got a phone call from a prospective buyer. Broker Bob was asked by the buyer if he could meet him at the open house. While at the open house, the buyer asked Broker Bob to write an offer for him. Who does Broker Bob represent?

Answer: Broker Bob represents the Seller. This situation would put Broker Bob in a dual agency.

Scenario Two

Salesperson Tom just got his license. He was able to get his first listing right away. Tom was so excited about his listing, he decided to have an open house. While at the open house, Tom's college roommate showed up. The college roommate asked Tom to write an offer for $150,000. After the offer was written, the roommate told Tom that if the seller doesn't take his offer, he can go as high as $190,000.

What does agent Tom have to do?

Answer: he has to tell the seller that his roommate will go as high as $190,000. He owed fiduciary duties to his client which include "full disclosure".

Offers

Earnest Money Deposit – When a buyer makes a written off to the seller, he will supply an earnest money deposit to show his true intentions to move forward with the deal. (Money talks)

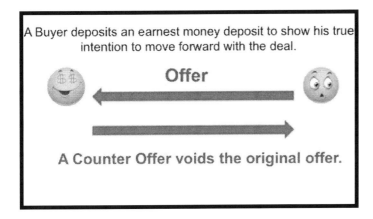

Counteroffer cancels (voids) original offer – A counter offer voids the original offer.

A potential buyer can withdraw the offer before
the seller accepts it and get his/her earnest money deposit
back.

A Seller can withdraw a counter offer before the buyer
accepts it and then accept a better offer.

Priority of multiple counteroffers – All offers get presented as soon as possible. An agent cannot hold back offers. An agent needs to advise his client not to respond to multiple counter offers all at the same time. He needs to be responsible for one at a time.

The OFFER and the PURCHASE Agreements are the same document.

The Purchase Agreement is between the Seller and Buyer. It defines the legal rights of the Seller and Buyer. Defines the legal rights of the Seller and Buyer.

A Buyer can withdraw his offer at any time BEFORE the Seller accepts it and he will get his earnest money deposit back.

A SELLER can withdraw a counter offer before the buyer accepts it and decide to accept another offer

When offer becomes binding (notification) an offer is complete when it is delivered and accepted by the Seller and Buyer (Offer, acceptance and delivery.)

After making an offer, a buyer may withdraw that offer and get his earnest money deposit back if withdrawn before the seller accepts it. A seller can withdraw a counter offer before the buyer accepts it and accept a better offer.

Single Agency – working for or with one party in a transaction

Dual Agency – working for or with both parties in a transaction

PURCHASE AGREEMENTS

The Purchase Agreement is a bilateral contract.

Seller

The contract between the Seller and the **Seller's Agent** is the **Listing Agreement**.
The Listing Agreement can be considered an employment contract. A Listing Agreement is also a unilateral agreement.

The Seller's Agent has earned a commission when he brings a ready, willing and able buyer that meets the terms of the listing agreement.

Steps to an accepted offer.
 1. There must be a listing agreement between a seller and an agent.

2. A buyer makes an offer and puts down an earnest money deposit. (earnest money deposits are not mandated)

3. If the seller makes a counter offer, the counter offer voids the original offer.

4. Once there is a "Meeting of the Minds", another blank OFFER/Purchase Agreement is filled in with the correct information that both parties agreed to.

The buyer holds equitable title before the close.

The seller holds legal title before the close.

Both titles can be inherited.

Time is of the Essence

Punctual performance.

Everything has to be on time.

If a party holds up the contract, they may cause a breach of contract.

SCENARIO ONE:

If the buyer defaults during escrow or after the accepted offer, there will be money set aside called "liquidated damages" that will be paid to the seller. The buyer would be in breach of the contract and the seller can receive the liquidate damages amount.

SCENARIO TWO:

If while in escrow the seller decides to NOT move forward with the transaction, the buyer's earnest money deposit gets returned to the buyer. The listing agent has met his contract with the seller by bringing a **ready, willing and able buyer**, therefore, he has earned his commission. The listing agent should look toward the seller for compensation.

If a Buyer feels that the Seller has defrauded him and hid several problems about the property, a lawsuit from the buyer against the Seller's Agent would not be heard in court. The Purchase Agreement is between the Seller and Buyer not the Seller's Agent and Buyer.

SINGLE AGENCY is working with either the buyer or seller.

DUAL AGENCY is working with both sides.

Single Agency

Dual Agency

Dual agency has to be accepted by both seller and buyer in writing.

TERMINATION OF AGENCY

Even if a Buyer and Seller agree to back out of a Purchase Agreement, the Listing Agent is still due a full commission.

The agent fulfilled his duties under the Listing Agreement.

The Listing Agreement states that when the Seller's Agent brings a ready, willing and able buyer to meet the terms of the listing agreement, the agent has earned his commission.

An agency will end when the agency has been fully executed.

A legal event involving a principle or the death of a principle will end a contract. Legal event examples are bankruptcy or insanity.

Death of Principal will end a contract.

Listings can end by expiration.

A legal event involving a principle or the death of a principle can end a contract.

If the broker goes insane, the deal dies.

Bankruptcy can end a deal.

If the the Broker dies, all contracts end.

A Sub Agent's death has no bearing on contracts.

Termination of agency
Expiration
Completion/performance
Termination by force of law
Destruction of property/death of principal
Mutual agreement

Death of the Buyer or Seller will end a
contract.

The property has to be delivered to the buyer in the same
condition at the close as it was when there was a
meeting of the minds.

THE BROKER OWNS ALL CONTRACTS

AGREEMENTS WITH BUYERS

> There are three types of buyer agreements that mirror the three types of listings.
>
> Exclusive Right Buyer Agency Agreement
>
> Exclusive Buyer Agency Agreement
>
> Open Buyer Agency Agreement

Listing agreements between seller and brokers have been, and continue to be, the most common employment agreements in real estate.

Commercial brokers have long used buyer listing agreements, sometimes called agreements to find real property.

The Buyer's Agent is called the **Selling Agent.**

Buyer Agency Agreement – An employment contract, whereas the broker represents the buyer—the buyer becomes the principal / client. There are 3 types of buyer agreements that mirror the 3 types of listing agreements.

Exclusive Right Buyer Agency
(Exclusive right to represent)
The buyer must pay the broker (unless otherwise stated) if he buys property during the term of the agreement, even if the buyer finds the property himself.

Exclusive Agency Buyer
One broker is the exclusive agent of the buyer, but the buyer does not have to pay a commission to the broker if the buyer finds the property himself.

Non-Exclusive
The buyer hires any number of agents and the buyer may also find the property on his own. Only the agent responsible for finding the property purchased is entitled to payment.

> Present all Offers.
>
> An offer becomes binding when it has been delivered and accepted.
>
> A deed transfers title when the Buyer accepts it.

Accounting for Money

The Broker does not deposit the earnest money until there is a mutually accepted offer or agreement. The Buyer and Seller must have a "Meeting of the Minds".

Brokers are responsible at all times for earnest money deposits. Brokers should deposit earnest money deposits into a non-interest bearing account (Demand Account).

Brokers should use standard accounting practices.

All money collected by a salesperson must be given to his broker.

If a Broker cannot determine where an earnest money deposit should go, he must turn it over to the courts to decide.

The form the broker will use is called an Interpleader.

Trust / Escrow Account
Business Account

TRUST / ESCROW ACCOUNT

Trust / Escrow Account

Client and Customer funds

Not assets of the Broker.

Non interest demand account

Client and Customer Funds
Trust / Escrow money are not assets of the broker.
No moneys from this account may be used for the broker's business or personal expenses.
Money from this account may not be transferred to the broker's account. It is called commingling.

BUSINESS ACCOUNT

Business Account

Broker Funds

Commissions come in and out.

Bills get paid from here.

Rent, electric, gas, rent, expenses

Business money
Broker's assets
Commissions come in and out of this account.
This account pays things like rent, electric, gas and other business related expenses.

Money can be taken out of the Business Account and put into the Trust / Escrow account.

Client or customer funds do not pay the fees associated with their accounts. It's a broker expense.

The broker needs to use his own funds to open a trust account.

Brokers must keep accurate records.

No Commingling

A broker may use money from his business account to open a trust account or to pay any fees associated with it.

A broker will spend more advertising money on the **Exclusive Right Listing**.

Do you know why?

Chapter Twelve

PROPERTY CONDITION AND DISCLOSURE

Purchase Agreements have an inspection period when the buyer will hire a professional to inspect the property. During this time, the buyer may decide not to purchase the property. The Buyer will seek the opinion of professionals as to the condition of a property during the inspection period. An inspection by a professional is not a warranty.

State law requires that the transferor (seller) of any of the following categories of real property will prepare and deliver to the transferee (buyer) a written **"Property Condition Disclosure Statement"**:

PSYCHOLOGICALLY IMPACTED OR STIGMATIZED PROPERTIES

Dr. Lawrence Hasbrouck

Properties that have been the scenes of murders, suicides, or are alleged to be haunted, are stigmatized. In fact, buyers have sued their real estate salespersons because the salespersons didn't disclose the property's history. With this in mind, licensees should determine whether sellers have any knowledge about their properties' histories that should be disclosed. When in doubt, licensees should make full disclosure.

The statutes do not define clearly what is a required material disclosure for stigmatized properties. A licensee should tell the seller any facts he or she thinks need to be disclosed and get the seller's approval. This may prevent the seller from claiming the licensee violated confidentiality or a fiduciary duty. If the seller refuses to give permission to disclose a suicide, for example, the broker must decide whether listing the property is worth the risk

---

Stambovsky v. Ackley, commonly known as the **Ghostbusters ruling**, is a case in the New York Supreme Court, Appellate Division, that held that a house, which the owner had previously advertised to the public as haunted by ghosts, legally was haunted for the purpose of an action for rescission brought by a subsequent purchaser of the house. Because of its unique holding, the case has been frequently printed in textbooks on contracts and property law and widely taught in U.S. law school classes, and is often cited by other courts.

FACTS AND PRIOR HISTORY

During the course of her ownership of the property at issue, which was located in Nyack, New York, Helen Ackley and members of her family had reported the existence of numerous poltergeists in the house. Ackley had reported the existence of ghosts in the house to both Reader's Digest and a local newspaper on three occasions between 1977 and 1989, when the house was included on a five-home walking tour of the city. She recounted to the press several instances in which the poltergeists interacted directly with members of her family. She claimed that grandchildren received "gifts" of baby rings, all of which suddenly disappeared later. She also claimed that one ghost would wake her daughter, Cynthia each morning by shaking her bed She claimed that when spring break arrived Cynthia proclaimed loudly that she did not have to wake up early and she would like to sleep in; her bed did not shake the next morning. Neither Ackley nor her real estate broker, Ellis Realty, revealed the haunting to Jeffrey Stambovsky before he entered a contract to purchase the house in 1989 or 1990. Stambovsky made a $32,500 down payment on the agreed price of $650,000 for the house. Stambovsky was from New York City and was not aware of the folklore of Nyack, including the widely known haunting story.

When Stambovsky learned of the haunting story, he filed an action requesting rescission of the contract of sale and for damages for fraudulent misrepresentation by Ackley and Ellis Realty. Stambovsky did not attend the closing which caused him to forfeit the down payment (although he was then not obligated to buy the house). A New York Supreme Court (trial court) dismissed the action, and Stambovsky appealed.

THE CASE
MAJORITY OPINION
Near the beginning of the majority opinion (three out of five justices) appears its most well-known conclusion: "having reported [the ghosts'] presence in both a national publication… and the local press… defendant is estopped to deny their existence and, as a matter of law, the house is haunted." The court noted that regardless of whether the house was truly haunted or not, the fact that the house had been widely reported as being haunted greatly affected its value.

Notwithstanding these conclusions, the court affirmed the dismissal of the fraudulent misrepresentation action and stated that the realtor was under no duty to disclose the haunting to potential buyers. Thus, no damages were available to Stambovsky because New York, at the time, adhered to property law doctrine of caveat emptor.

The appellate court reversed the trial court's decision regarding the rescission action, however, as it went on to note that "haunting" was not a condition that a buyer or potential buyer of real property can and should be able to ascertain upon reasonable inspection of the property.

According to the court, though the doctrine of caveat emptor would normally operate to bar a rescission action, causing seller to have no duty to disclose information about the property to be sold (but also preventing the seller from affirmatively misrepresenting the condition of the property), the doctrine, in a merged law and equity system, can be modified to do justice to the parties. In this case, "the most meticulous inspection and the search would not reveal the presence of poltergeists at the premises or unearth the property's ghoulish reputation in the community," thus equity would allow Stambovsky the remedy of contract rescission against the seller, Ackley.

EPILOGUE
The case generated considerable publicity and area real estate agents had between 25 and 50 potential buyers calling within a week of the court's decision.

Among the prospective buyers to the house at 1 LaVeta Place on the Hudson River was Kreskin. Kreskin was a renowned mentalist interested in purchasing a haunted home in which to curate his collection of paranormal paraphernalia. Ackley sold the house to another buyer and moved to Florida in 1991. Helen Ackley died in 2003 and her son-in-law "lays odds" that her spirit has taken up residence back at 1 Ackley Place.[3]There have not been public reports of hauntings in recent years.

GHOST STORIES

The house had been vacant and was in disrepair when the Ackleys moved in to the waterfront home in the 1960's. Local children purportedly warned them that the house was haunted, though no prior paranormal incidents appear to have been published.

Helen Ackley claimed there were at least three ghosts in the residence. She described two as a married couple who lived in the 18th century, and the other as a Navy Lieutenant in the American Revolution. In 1993 she was contacted by paranormal researcher Bill Merrill, and medium Glenn Johnson who claimed to have already made contact with two of the spirits at 1 LaVeta Place.

The pair met with Helen and disclosed that the couple were likely the poltergeists of Sir George and Lady Margaret who lived in the region in the 18th century. In 1995 Merrill and Johnson published a book about their findings entitled Sir George, The Ghost of Nyack (Deer Publishing, Beaverton, Oregon) – still available on Amazon.

- Helen claimed to have seen Sir George:
  "sitting in midair, watching me paint the ceiling in the living room, rocking back and forth… I was on an 8-foot stepladder. I asked if he approved of what we were doing to the house, if the colors were to his liking. He smiled and he nodded his head."

- Helen's daughter, Cynthia, when she was a child, reportedly would be woken most mornings by one of the spirits shaking her bed. When Cynthia was out of school for spring break she announced loudly before going to bed that she did not have school in the morning and would like to sleep in. The next morning she was not awoken by a shaking bed.

- Helen reported to neighbors that they heard phantom footsteps and slamming doors.

- Helen's grandchildren allegedly received trinkets, such as rings, from the ghosts. These trinkets would later vanish.

- Helen's daughter-in-law was gifted disappearing coins in the same manner, and Cynthia as an adult, claimed to receive silver sugar tongs.

- Helen claimed that her son came "eyeball-to-eyeball" with the figure of the Revolutionary Navy Lieutenant.

- Mark Kavanagh lived in the home briefly while engaged to Cynthia, he purported hearing conversation from a vacant room.

- Later Kavanagh recounted another experience:
  "Cyn had already fallen asleep and I was drifting. Then I heard the bedroom door creak, and the floor boards squeak. My back was to the edge of the bed. Suddenly the edge of the bed by my mid-section depressed down, and I felt something lean against me. I went literally stone stiff! I was speechless and could hardly move. I was able to twist my neck around enough to see a womanly figure in a soft dress through the moonlight from the bay windows. I felt like she was

looking straight at me. After about minute, the presence got up and walked back out of the room. I finally relaxed enough to shake my wife out of sound sleep acting like a toddler who just had a nightmare.

All but Kavanagh's accounts were written by Helen and submitted to Reader's Digest magazine and published in its May, 1977 issue.

Despite these somewhat unnerving tales, the Ackleys said they had a peaceful coexistence with the poltergeists, and the only account of any terrorizing events is Kavanagh's tale reproduced above.

Kavanagh later reflected on the incidents that he experienced and came to the conclusion that the ghosts were evaluating him to make sure he was a good suitor for Cynthia.

Since the Ackleys moved from the home in the beginning of the 1990's there have not been any more accounts of paranormal activity reported by any of the subsequent owners of which there have been three.

However, Merrill and Johnson reported that Sir George and Lady Margaret expressed that the spirits were not as fond of the new owners and were thinking of moving on. It is also reported that after the judgment against Helen in the law-suit she claimed that she was moving and taking the ghosts with her.

THE HOUSE – HISTORY AND TODAY

The imposing Victorian waterfront home was built in 1890 with 5 bedrooms, 3 ½ baths, and approximately 4,628 square feet was. George and Helen Ackley purchased the home in the early 1960's and shared the home with their four children, Cynthia, George, Cara, and William.[9]

George died in 1978 at the age of 53, less than one year after the first accounts of paranormal activity appeared in Reader's Digest.[10] Though his death was not in the home, but at an area hospital after heart surgery, however there was a death in the home sometime after when a relatively young and otherwise healthy dinner guest died of an brain aneurysm.[7][10]

By 1990 the residents included Helen's grandchildren, daughter-in-law and future son-in-law, Mark Kavanagh.[1][8]

The Ghostbusters home sold on Jan 8, 2016 for more than $600,000 above comparable homes in Nyack according to Trulia, fetching $1,770,000.[11]

The exterior of the home was red for some time, though it has now been painted light blue.

RESPONDING TO NON-CLIENT INQUIRIES

Customers shall be given fair and honest dealings. A broker is responsible to disclose what he knows about the property even if he thinks it will affect the buyer's decision to purchase. An agent is not responsible to disclose latent defects. But, if he knows about a latent defect, he must disclose it. A latent defect is an unseen defect.

> A **ministerial relationship** is when an agent helps a non client with something related to the transaction.
>
> Examples: Help them get paperwork together. Give the phone number to several inspectors, etc.

PROPERTY OWNER'S ROLE REGARDING PROPERTY CONDITION

will provide the buyer with a written property condition disclosure. The Seller must identify all material facts relating to the property and its surrounding area.

> The agent must disclose what is readily seen.

LICENSEE'S ROLE REGARDING PROPERTY CONDITION

A licensee is not responsible to identify latent defects. If the agent is aware of a latent defect, he must disclose it.

RECORD KEEPING

Sellers and lessors must retain a copy of the disclosures for no less than three years from the date of sale or the date the leasing period begins.

Latent Defects

Unseen Defects

The most common latent lead defect is lead pipes.

LEAD-BASED PAINT DISCLOSURE

The Federal Residential Lead-based Paint Hazard Reduction Act applies to residential buildings built before 1978. The law requires that the seller, landlord or licensee provide the following before a buyer signs a contract:

- Lead hazard information pamphlet
- Disclosure of the presence of any know lead-based paint or lead-based paint hazard
- Ten-day period to conduct an inspection

A lead-based paint warning should be included as part of the contract and a lead-based paint disclosure form completed by the seller, should be attached to the contract for all properties built before 1978.

The "Lead-Based Paint" pamphlet should be presented to the purchaser and receipt acknowledged.

Types of Housing Covered?

Most private housing, public housing, federally owned housing, and housing receiving Federal assistance are affected by this rule.

Other Disclosures

Material Facts Related to Property Condition or Location

Disclose anything that adversely affects the property.

Seller and Seller's agent must disclose all known material defects. Examples: pest infestation, lead paint, radon, etc. Anything that affects the physical condition of the property and the surrounding area must be disclosed.

RADON – Radon is an odorless colorless radioactive gas that enters a house through the basement. Radon is easily mitigated for under $3000.

If a buyer asks an agent if there is radon on the property, the agent should tell the buyer to get an inspection because radon can cause lung cancer.

Roof, Gutters, downspouts, doors, windows foundation?

Electric, plumbing?

RESTRICTIVE COVENANTS
If restrictive covenants exist for the property being sold, the purchasers must be presented with a copy before the buyer signs the purchase contract.

PEST INFESTATION – An agent is responsible to look for animal feces, strange odors, dead bugs and anything that will indicate an infestation. The findings may create a red flag issue. In that case, a professional should be called to investigate.

TOXIC MOLD – Stachybotrys Chartarum is black mold. Check around toilets, windows and doors.

STRUCTURAL ISSUES such as roof, gutters, downspouts, doors, windows, and foundation – Disclose anything you find may constitute a material fact.

KNOWN ALTERATIONS OR ADDITIONS – disclose if alterations were permitted or not.

ZONING AND PLANNING INFORMATION – There are zoning maps available. It is the duty of the agent to investigate the zoning of a property.

BOUNDARIES OF SCHOOL/UTILITY/TAXATION DISTRICTS, FLIGHT PATHS – Disclose everything. Section 16 of every township is set aside for schools. Disclose any special assessments added to the tax base.

Accuracy of Representation of Lot or Improvement Size, Encroachments or Easements Affecting Use

Hire a professional to measure the property and its improvements. Information may be gained from recorded instruments.

ENCROACHMENTS must be disclosed. Hire a profession to survey the property or look toward public records for the measurement.

LOCAL TAXES AND SPECIAL ASSESSMENTS, OTHER LIENS neighborhoods in the same city may have different tax amounts due to special assessments.

A SPECIAL ASSESSMENT is an added tax to the property owner. An example of a special assessment would be if a school district needed a new school; the city would go ahead and build it and then tax the homes in that district with a special assessment. Only the people who benefit from an improvement will pay the special assessments.

EXTERNAL ENVIRONMENTAL HAZARDS – Disclose any impact to air, noise, flooding, leaking underground storage tanks, public health and safety. A NHD (Natural Hazard Disclosure Report may be purchased to identify local hazards.

Location within **natural hazard or specifically regulated area** may cause a potentially uninsurable property – earthquake zone, hurricane zone, next to a toxic dump???

MEGAN'S LAW ISSUES – A federal Law that requires the disclosure of convicted sex offenders into a community. There is a database that can be obtained online.

The national database can be found at this site. https://www.nsopw.gov

DISCLOSE

Structural Items
Termites, Ants ….
Roof and Site Data
Water Damage
Is Flood Insurance Required?
Wetlands area
Additions/Remodels
Structure/wall/windows
Mechanical Items: electrical system/plumbing system
Water/sewer/septic
Flood zone
Leasehold or Sixteenth Section Land
Homeowners Association
Tax bill
Latent Defects

> # To identify the lot or improvement size, encroachments or easements, hire a professional.

AGENT RESPONSIBILITY TO INQUIRE ABOUT "RED FLAG" ISSUES

Red Flag Issues
A defect which requires further investigation.

A red flag issue is "something wrong with the property that you would like to inspect further". Examples would be a brown spot on the ceiling, musty mold smells or several cracks in a driveway going up or down a hill. A professional should inspect all red flags.

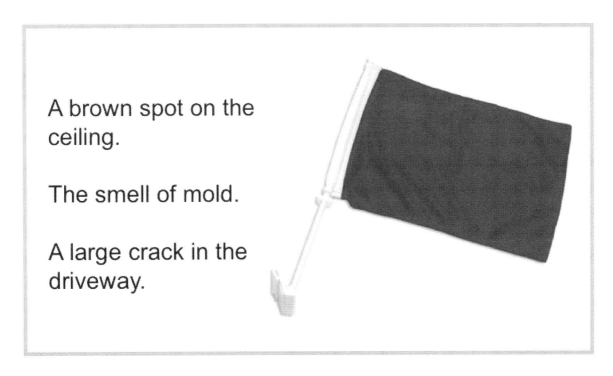

A brown spot on the ceiling.

The smell of mold.

A large crack in the driveway.

ENVIRONMENTAL ISSUES

Consumers are becoming more health-conscious and safety-concerned and are enforcing their rights to make informed decisions. Scientists are learning more about our environment, and consumers are reacting by demanding that their surroundings be free of environmental hazards. These developments affect not only sales transactions but also owners, buyers, sellers, contractors, appraisers, developers, lending institutions, and property managers.

NON-MATERIAL FACTS

Felonies, suicides, homicides are not material facts that need to be disclosed. The fact someone with HIV or Aides has lived or was living on the property is not a material fact that needs to be disclosed. HIV and AIDS are protected under handicapped status.

Non Material Facts

Felony on the property
Death
Suicide
Homicide
The fact that someone with HIV or aids has
lived on the property.

HOME WARRANTIES

Basic home warranty coverage includes the main systems of the home and certain appliances. Most companies cover plumbing, electrical, heating systems, as well as <u>refrigerators</u>, <u>dishwashers</u>, and ovens. Some charge additional coverage for appliances such as <u>clothes washers</u> and <u>clothes dryers</u>. A home warranty company will pay for the cost to repair or replace the system or appliance, as long as it has broken down from normal wear and tear. If the system or appliance failed because it wasn't maintained (the water heater was not flushed or the fridge's evaporative coils were not cleaned), most home warranty contracts will not cover the cost to repair or replace it. Home warranties exist to repair or replace old worn out systems that have been properly cared for by the homeowner. Buyers should read the home warranty contract carefully to understand coverages, limitations, and exclusions.[7]

---

[7] https://en.wikipedia.org/wiki/Home_warranty

Home warranties will include defects of major mechanical, plumbing, electrical, heating and appliances items.

Warranty programs could be an attractive selling point.

New Home Construction Warranties

Some states have mandatory statutes in which warranties must be offered by new homebuilders.

They usually cover limited defects.

Liability Ball

An inspection by a professional is not a warranty.

Throw the Liability Ball at the professional.

Chapter Thirteen

CONTRACTS

A "contract is a voluntary arrangement between two or more parties that is enforceable by law as a binding legal agreement. Contract is a branch of the law of obligations in jurisdictions of the civil law tradition. Contract law concerns the rights and duties that arise from agreements.

A contract arises when the parties agree that there is an agreement. Formation of a contract generally requires an offer, acceptance, consideration, and a mutual intent to be bound. Each party to a contract must have capacity to enter the agreement. Minors, intoxicated persons, and those under a mental affliction may have insufficient capacity to enter a contract. Some types of contracts may require formalities, such as a memorialization in writing."
Source: Contract - https://en.wikipedia.org

Requirements for a Valid Contract

Competent parties
Mutual assent
Legality of object - Seisen
Consideration
A legal description of the property
A written, signed and delivered contract

Valid

Contains all the elements of a valid contract.
Offer
Acceptance
Intention
Consideration
It's enforceable.
A contract signed by a married minor is valid.

NOVATION VS. ASSIGNMENT

In contrast to an <u>assignment</u>, which is generally valid as long as the other party is given notice (except where the obligation is specific to the obligor, as in a personal service contract with a specific ballet dancer, or where assignment would place a new and special burden on the counterparty), a novation is valid only with the consent of all parties to the original agreement.[2] A contract transferred by the novation process transfers all duties and obligations from the original obligor to the new obligor.

Novation - replacing an obligation to perform with another obligation; or
adding an obligation to perform; or replacing a party to an agreement with a new party.

Assignment - a transfer of rights between two parties. The transfer of rights held by one party—the **assignor**—to another party—the **assignee**.

Parties must be able to make a prudent and knowledgeable decision without undue influence. May be deprived by:
1. Mistake
2. Misrepresentation
3. Fraud
4. Undue influence, including chemical substances
5. Duress

Expressed Contract – A contract clearly spoken or in writing. (When I go to McDonalds and I am in the drive thru EXPRESS lane. I have to pay first, then they give me a receipt and my order.)

Implied Contract – A contract shown by actions. (When a person goes to a fancy restaurant, the hostess seats them, they order food, they eat and thru their actions they are implying that they will pay for the food.)

Executory Contract

Something still needs to be done.

Not complete.

An ongoing transaction.

Executed Contract

Completed

Finished

BILATERAL CONTRACT

Real estate contracts are typically bilateral contracts (i. e., agreed to by two parties) and should have the legal requirements specified by contract law in general and should also be in writing to be enforceable.

Source: Real estate contract - https://en.wikipedia.org

UNILATERAL CONTRACT

A contract in which only one party makes a promise.

VOIDABLE CONTRACT

"A voidable contract, unlike a void contract, is a valid contract which may be either affirmed or rejected at the option of one of the parties. At most, one party to the contract is bound. The unbound party may repudiate (reject) the contract, at which time the contract becomes void.

Typical grounds for a contract being voidable include coercion, undue influence, misrepresentation or fraud. A contract made by a minor is often voidable, but a minor can only avoid a contract during his or her minority status and for a reasonable time after he reaches the age of majority. After a reasonable period of time, the contract is deemed to be ratified and cannot be avoided. Other examples would be real estate contracts, lawyer contracts, etc.

When a contract is entered into without the free consent of the party, it is considered a voidable contract. The definition of the act states that a voidable contract is enforceable by law at the option of one or more parties but not at option of the other parties. A voidable contract may be considered valid if it is not cancelled by the aggrieved party within a reasonable time.

US Legal, Inc.,"
Source: Voidable contract - https://en.wikipedia.org

VOIDABLE

May lack a basic element but it could become void or valid at any time.
Example: A purchase contract with an unmarried minor who inherited real estate. The minor may cancel or change his mind at any time up to the actual transfer.

VOID

Lacks the basic elements for a valid contract.
Example: Trying to sell something a person doesn't own.

UNENFORCEABLE

Looks valid on the surface but unenforceable.

VOID CONTRACT

"A void contract cannot be enforced by law. Void contracts are different from voidable contracts, which are contracts that may be (but not necessarily will be) nullified. However, when a contract is being written and signed, there is no automatic mechanism available in every situation that can be utilized to detect the validity or enforceability of that contract. Practically, a contract can be declared to be void by a court of law. So the main question is that under what conditions can a contract be deemed as void?

An agreement to carry out an illegal act is an example of a void agreement. For example, a contract between drug dealers and buyers is a void contract simply because the terms of the contract are illegal. In such a case, neither party can go to court to enforce the contract. A void agreement is void ab initio, i e from the beginning while a voidable contract can be voidable by one or all of the parties. A voidable contract is not void ab initio, rather, it becomes void later due to some changes in condition. In sum, there is no scope of any discretion on the part of the contracting parties in a void contract. The contracting parties do not have the power to make a void contract enforceable.

A contract can also be void due to the impossibility of its performance. For instance, if a contract is formed between two parties A & B but during the performance of the contract the object of the contract becomes impossible to achieve (due to action by someone or something other than the contracting parties), then the contract cannot be enforced in the court of law and is thus void. A void contract can be one in which any of the prerequisites of a valid contract is/are absent for example if there is no contractual capacity, the contract can be deemed as void. In fact, void means that a contract does not exist at all. The law can not enforce any legal obligation to either party especially the disappointed party because they are not entitled to any protective laws as far as contracts are concerned.

An agreement may be void if any of the following:
Made by incompetent parties (e.g., under the age of consent, incapacitated)
Has a material bilateral mistake
Has unlawful consideration (e.g., promise of sex)
Concerns an unlawful object (e.g., heroin)
Has no consideration on one side
Restricts a person from marrying or remarrying
Restricts trade
Restricts legal proceedings
Has material uncertain terms
Incorporates a wager, gamble, or bet
Contingent upon the happening of an impossible event
Requires the performance of impossible acts

Cross, F.; Miller, R. (2011). The Legal Environment of Business. Cengage L"
Source: Void contract - _https://en.wikipedia.org_

ACKNOWLEDGMENT

In law, an acknowledgment is a declaration or avowal of one's own act, used to authenticate legal instruments, which may give the instrument legal validity, and works to prevent the recording of false instruments or fraudulent executions.

Acknowledgement involves a public official, frequently a notary public.

The party executing the legal instrument orally declares that the instrument is his or her act or deed, and the official prepares a certificate attesting to the declaration.

Source: Acknowledgment (law) - https://en.wikipedia.org

NOTARY PUBLIC

A notary public (or notary or public notary) is a public officer constituted by law to serve the public in matters usually concerned with estates, deeds, powers-of-attorney, and foreign and international business.

A notary's main function is to make sure the person signing is who he or she say they are.

Source: Notary public - https://en.wikipedia.org

STATUTE OF FRAUDS

The statute of frauds refers to the requirement that certain kinds of contracts be memorialized in a writing, signed by the party to be charged, with sufficient content to evidence the contract.

LACHES – FALLS UNDER STATUTE OF LIMITATIONS

Losing the right to be heard in court because of inaction. Laches falls under the Statute of Limitations.

INTOXICATED PERSONS

A contract made by an intoxicated person is voidable.

COMPETENT PARTIES

A natural person who agrees to a transaction has complete legal capacity to become liable for duties under the contract unless he or she is an infant, insane, or intoxicated.

UNDUE INFLUENCE

Involves one person taking advantage of a position of power over another person.

MISREPRESENTATION

a false statement of fact made by one party to another party, which has the effect of inducing that party into the contract.

A finding of misrepresentation allows for a remedy of rescission and sometimes damages depending on the type of misrepresentation

DURESS

Duress or coercion refers to a situation whereby a person performs an act as a result of violence, threat, or other pressure against the person.

JOINT AND SEVERAL LIABILITY

A claimant may pursue an obligation against any one party as if they were jointly liable and it becomes the responsibility of the defendants to sort out their respective proportions of liability and payment.

SEVERAL LIABILITY

The converse is several or proportionate liability, where the parties are liable for only their respective obligations.

JOINT LIABILITY

If parties have joint liability, then they are each liable up to the full amount of the relevant obligation. So if a married couple takes a loan from a bank, the loan agreement will normally provide that they are to be "jointly liable" for the full amount. If one party dies, disappears or is declared bankrupt, the other remains fully liable.

ILLETERACY

An illiterate person is capable of giving real consent to a contract; the person has a duty to ask someone to read the contract to him or her and to explain it, if necessary.

LIQUIDATED DAMAGES

Liquidated damages are damages whose amount the parties designate during the formation of a contract for the injured party to collect as compensation upon a specific breach (e.g., late performance).
Source: Liquidated damages - https://en.wikipedia.org

ACCELERATION CLAUSE

A provision that allows a lender to demand payment of the total outstanding balance or demand additional collateral under certain circumstances, such as failure to make payments, bankruptcy, nonpayment of taxes on mortgaged property, or the breaking of loan covenants.

Read more: http://www.investorwords.com/36/acceleration_clause.html#ixzz4gFz4qhzx

SUIT FOR SPECIFIC PERFORMANCE (USED WHEN THERE IS A BREACH OF CONTRACT)

An order of a court which requires a party to perform a specific act, usually what is stated in a contract.
Source: Specific performance - https://en.wikipedia.org

ESCAPE CLAUSE

Another example is the "Subject to 30-day due diligence" clause, which effectively gives the purchaser a 30-day buffer period to inspect any and all aspects of the property before having to commit to the purchase.

A 72-hour clause is an example of a seller's escape clause that frequently appears in real estate contracts.

The finance contingency clause:
Makes the purchase offer contingent upon the buyer and also the property qualifying for the loan the buyer will need.

A legal event involving a principle or the death of a principle can end a contract.

If the broker goes insane, the deal dies.

Bankruptcy can end a deal.

Other Ways to End a Contract

Expiration of the contract.

Mutual Agreement

Destruction of the property.

Death of the Buyer or Seller will end a contract.

ASSIGNMENT – The transfer in writing of a mortgage.

NOVATION – Novation is when the **New** person is assigned the contract.

Assignment
The transfer in writing of a mortgage.

Novation
The substitution of an old party with a new party in a mortgage.

BILATERAL CONTRACT – A promise for a promise. (A mutually agreeable Real Estate Purchase Agreement.)

UNILATERAL CONTRACT – Only one person will be doing something. (A rent to own. In a rent to own, the renter isn't forced into buying the property but if he does decide to purchase within the contract period, the seller is forced into selling. Listing Agreements are unilateral contracts.

Listing Agreements

Unilateral contracts

The listing agreement is between the seller and his/her agent.

GENERAL REQUIREMENTS FOR VALID LISTING – Listings must be in writing, state the exact rate or amount of commission, listing price or range, a description of the property, brokers name and be acknowledged by the seller.

Everything in real estate has to be in writing to be enforceable in court. A judge will not hear a complaint based on verbal agreements.

EXCLUSIVE RIGHT LISTING

An exclusive listing agreement whereas the agent will get paid no matter who procures the buyer. You always get paid even if the Seller sells it herself. (Thus, if it doesn't say RIGHT, then it's wrong for you.) The listing Agent will get paid no matter who brings the buyer.

EXCLUSIVE LISTING

The owner wants to hire one agent and have their property listed on the MLS but they also want to reserve the right to sell it themselves without paying a commission. The listing agent would need to prove they were the Procuring Cause to get paid. (Procured the Buyer) An agent may not be paid at all if the seller procures the buyer.

OPEN LISTING

The seller hires many agents. The agent that gets paid is the one that can prove they were the procuring cause.

In a listing, the broker will need to bring a ready, willing and able buyer to meet the terms of the listing agreement to earn his commission. A seller is not obligated to accept less than asking price. If the seller does accept less than asking price, the seller's agent has also earned a commission by bringing a ready, willing and able buyer.

Buyer/Broker Agreements

Broker Duties

The broker will locate and identify potential properties for the buyer to consider; disclose material facts, review paperwork, prepare purchase offers, conduct a visual inspection, among other obligations.

Buyer Duties

The buyer will consider the homes presented, act in good faith, qualify to purchase the property, read documents -- especially the buyer inspection advisory -- and cooperate with the broker, among other obligations.

Contracts: Landlord and Tenant

Estate for Years (tenancy for years)
It does not have to be for a year or years. It can be any amount of time.
There has to be a definite beginning and a definite ending.
No notice is required to terminate.
Does not automatically renew.

Estate from Period to Period (periodic tenancy)
Month to Month. A fixed period of time. Auto renewal.
Notice must be given by either party to terminate.

Holdover Tenancy
Landlord may evict or treat holdover tenant as one who has periodic tenancy.

Estate at Will (tenancy at will)
The consent of the landlord is mandatory.
Informal and usually oral.
Indefinite in length.
Notice must be given to terminate the lease.

Estate at Sufferance (tenancy at sufferance)
An eviction by the landlord or the landlord's representative is eminent. The tenant refuses to vacate.

Federal Fair Housing Act makes it illegal to discriminate on basis of physical disabilities.
Tenants may make reasonable modifications to property but must restore at end of lease term.

Types of Lease Contracts
Percentage Lease
Index Lease
Gross Lease
Net Lease
Lease with an Obligation to Purchase
Ground Lease
Graduated Lease
Oil and Gas Lease
Agricultural lease

OFFER

A promise made by one party (offeror) with the request for something in exchange for that promise

An Offer may be terminated by
1. Rejection, including a counteroffer
2. Failure to accept within prescribed time period
3. Revocation by the offeror before acceptance

A Counter Offer voids the original offer.

CONSIDERATION

Something of legal value; that which is "good or valuable" between the parties.

Consideration

Consideration is the concept of legal value in connection with contracts. It is anything of value promised to another when making a contract.

A valid contract requires some exchange of consideration.

Love and affection are not permissible forms of consideration.

Love and affection will support a deed and make it valid, but it is not sufficient Consideration.

In other words, a contract to transfer real estate upon love and affection is not enforceable.

One who takes property for a consideration of love and affection cannot be a bona fide purchaser for value, because the consideration is only good, it is not valuable.

COUNTEROFFER

A new offer which rejects the original offer.

A Buyer deposits an earnest money deposit to show his true intention to move forward with the deal.

Offer

A Counter Offer voids the original offer.

A client/customer must respond to one counter offer at a time.

LEGAL OBJECT - "SEISIN (OR SEIZIN)

Denotes the legal possession of an estate in land. The person holding such estate is said to be "seized of it".

STATUTE OF LIMITATIONS

The time limit in which to enforce rights; time varies for different legal actions, rights not enforced within time period are lost.

"LACHES

Refers to a lack of diligence and activity in making a legal claim, or moving forward with legal enforcement of a right, it is an unreasonable delay.

That is, "those who sleep on their rights]." Put another way, failure to assert one's rights in a timely manner can result in a claim being barred."

Source: Laches (equity) - https://en.wikipedia.org

IMPOSSIBILITY OF PERFORMANCE

Legally impossible to perform the required act.

> A person would like to buy a specific piece of land in order to open a casino in a non-casino state. Why will the contract fail? Impossibility of Performance.

> A person made an offer on a parcel of land. In the contract, it states that he must be approved for a liquor store before the contract is fully executed. He was denied the whisky store license. Why has the contract failed?
> Impossibility of Performance.

CONTRACT CAN ALSO FAIL BY:

Operation of law

As in the voiding of a contract by a minor, result of fraud, improper alteration of the contract, or expiration of statute of limitations

Rescission

One party may rescind the contract and return the parties to their original positions; monies that have been exchanged must be returned

Mutual Assent

Both parties agree to end the contract.

Performance of Contract

"Time is of the essence" means the contract must be performed within the stipulated time.

If no time is stipulated, it should be performed within a reasonable time.

Breach of Contract

A failure to perform without a legal excuse.

Performed or Discharged Contract – A contract that has been executed or discharged by law. Mutual agreement can cancel (mutual consent)

Breach of Contract

A Remedy for Breach - Specific Performance law suit

The property must be delivered to the buyer in the same condition as when there was the "meeting of the minds".

A Seller cannot go around and remove expensive features and replace them with inexpensive ones before the close.

The seller cannot remove the window boxes, dig up the rose bushes or remove fixtures unless there is a written agreement to do so.

REMEDIES FOR BREACH – SPECIFIC PERFORMANCE law suit – A suit for damages. A seller may collect liquidated damages from the buyer. If the seller takes out all the fancy ceiling lamps and other fixtures after an accepted offer, he is in breach of contract and may be sued for Specific performance.

Purchase Agreement: an agreement between a buyer and a seller of real estate property.

A contract is valid and binding when it has been signed, delivered and accepted.

CONTRACT CLAUSES – Contingencies – subject to clauses.
Something has to happen before the contract can move forward. (Examples: Bob will buy Ed's house if Bob can sell his house. Cindy will buy the property if it's zoned for a home-based business.

Contract Clauses – Contingencies – Subject to Clauses

Something has to happen before the contract can move forward.

"I will buy your house if I can sell my house."
"If the inspection is acceptable, I will purchase your home."
"If I can get financed, I will buy your home."

To avoid a lengthy transaction, an agent will put a time frame for the contingencies in the contract.

LEGALLY COMPETENT PARTIES

Of legal age
Sufficient mental capacity to understand the actions or consequences.

Everything in real estate has to be in writing to be enforceable in court. A judge will not hear a complaint based on verbal agreements.

Right of first refusal – The tenant is offered to purchase the property before the landlord puts the property up for sale on the open market.

BROKER COMPENSATION

Retainer Fee – An incentive to perform. A work for hire contract. Monies paid up front.

Flat or fixed -Flat fee brokers charge their clients a flat fee instead of commission.

Percentage Fee – This type of commission is the most popular. It's a percentage of the selling or rental amount.

A real estate licensee who is not a licensed attorney may not practice law, i.e., draw up a contract.

Preprinted forms are used.

> The **Purchase Agreement** is the most important document in a transaction, because it establishes the legal rights and obligations of the buyer and seller; it dictates the contents of a deed

A Counteroffer may be revoked at any time before it has been accepted.

An Offer may be revoked at any time before it has been accepted.

ACCEPTANCE / MEETING OF THE MINDS

There must be an acceptance to create a contract.

If accepted as written, the contract is created and a signed copy must be given to all parties.

Notification of acceptance must be given to the party who made the offer before the contract is considered created.

EARNEST MONEY DEPOSIT

Evidence of the buyer's intention to carry out the terms of the contract

All earnest money deposits are given to the responsible broker.

Earnest money deposits should be of a sufficient amount to discourage the buyer from defaulting, and compensate the seller for taking the property off the market.

EQUITABLE TITLE

After the contract is created but before the deed
is delivered, the buyer has an insurable interest in the property being purchased.

LEGAL TITLE

The seller has
legal title until the
deed is accepted
by the buyer.

LIQUIDATED DAMAGES

Commonly, the contract specifies that the earnest money will be used as liquidated damages, which is an amount agreed to by the parties to compensate one if the other breaches the contract. The amount of money set aside for liquidated damages is negotiable.

ADDENDUM
Add something

AMENDMENT
Amend or Change Something

OPTION AGREEMENTS

The optionee gives valuable consideration, and has the right to buy or lease the property or let the option expire.

The **optionor** must reserve the property for only the **optionee**.

The optionor must sell or lease the property if the optionee exercises the option.

Options = Unilateral Contract.

A fee is paid for the option.

LAND CONTRACT (CONTRACT FOR DEED, INSTALLMENT CONTRACT)

The seller/**vendor** retains legal title (fee simple ownership) of the property.

The buyer/**vendee** receives possession and **equitable title**.

The buyer becomes responsible for paying principal, interest, real estate taxes, hazard insurance premiums, and maintenance and repairs on the property, depending on terms of the contract.

The seller delivers the deed when the terms of the contract have been met.

Right of First Refusal

A contractual **right** that gives its holder the option to enter a business transaction with the owner of something, according to specified terms, before the owner is entitled to enter into that transaction with a third party.

Chapter Fourteen

TRANSFER OF TITLE

Title
The right to own and evidence of the ownership.

VOLUNTARY ALIENATION
the owner intentionally conveys the ownership during his or her lifetime using some form of deed; may be a gift or a sale.

INVOLUNTARY ALIENATION
Transfers without the owner's consent

TRANSFER BY OPERATION OF LAW

Eminent domain (through condemnation)
Escheat

Any type of foreclosure; for example delinquent real estate taxes or special assessments, mortgage or deed of trust laws, mechanic's liens, judgment liens.

TRANSFER BY NATURAL FORCES

Accretion

The slow accumulation of soil, rock, or other matter deposited on one's property by the movement of water. The opposite of erosion.

Erosion

The gradual wearing away of the land.

Avulsion

The sudden and violent tearing away of the land.

Other acts of nature such as earthquakes, hurricanes, etc.

Alluvium

The deposit of soil, rock, or other matter on one's property

Accession

The acquiring of property that is abandoned when a commercial tenant leaves trade fixtures behind and moves.

TRANSFER BY ADVERSE POSSESSION

Possession by the trespasser **must be open, notorious, continuous for a statutory number of years, hostile, and adverse** to the true owner.

Each jurisdiction has its own minimum requirements before an adverse possession claim can be filed.

Adverse possession is a situation when a person who does not have legal title to land (or real property) occupies the land without the permission of the legal owner.

The law allows the adverse possessor to acquire title to the land after a prescribed statutory period, which varies between jurisdictions, and depends on the type of land and other circumstances.

The laws of most jurisdictions do not permit claims of adverse possession against public land.

Squatting is a form of adverse possession. The adverse possessor is usually required to prove non-permissive use which is actual, open and notorious, exclusive, adverse, and continuous for the statutory period. If a claim to title by adverse possession is successful, title is acquired without compensation.

The required period of uninterrupted possession is governed by the statute of limitations.

Source: Adverse possession - https://en.wikipedia.org

TESTATE

Transfer of title by will.

Property passes by Devise

Divisor – The givor of the estate
Divisee – The "ee ee" gimmee of the estate

A will is a testamentary instrument that becomes effective only after the death of its maker.

Codicil

A modification of or an amendment to a will.

Holographic Will

A will is in its maker's own handwriting.

A **nuncupative** will is given verbally by its maker. Some states do not permit property to be conveyed by oral or handwritten wills.

INTESTATE

Transfer of title by descent

The laws of the state determine to whom ownership passes when a person dies intestate.

The laws of intestate succession vary from state to state.

Generally, there are primary heirs (spouse, children).

The closeness of one's relationship to the deceased determines the amount of the estate that will be received.

ESCHEAT – Property becomes owned by the state. Land cannot be ownerless

PROBATE

It is a legal process that proves or confirms the validity of the will.

Determines the precise assets of the deceased person.
Identifies the persons to whom the assets are to pass.
Takes place in the county where the decedent resided.

An administrator/administratrix (male/female) is appointed if there is no will designating an executor/executrix.

Legal procedures vary considerably from state to state
Decedent's debts must be satisfied before any property can be disbursed to the devisees or heirs.

Taxes are paid first.

Execution of Corporate Deeds

The deed must be signed by an authorized corporate officer.

IMPORTANCE OF RECORDING

Recording a deed gives **constructive notice to the world.** The first one to record a deed owns the property. An unrecorded deed is only valid between the parties and anyone who has actual notice about it.

Deeds must be recorded in the county where the real estate is located.

TRANSFER TAX STAMPS

Usually payable when the deed is recorded; also called "documentary stamps."

RESPONSIBILITIES OF ESCROW AGENT

(THE TRANSACTIONAL AGENT)

The escrow agent is a neutral third party who coordinates the activities and documents to transfer the property. They confirm that the obligations of the buyer and seller are fully executed before the transfer of the deed. They hold deposits, collect and hold loan and legal documents, prepare closing statements and make sure everything is in place and on occasion recording the deed. The closing attorney fills out a 1099S to send to the IRS. Information includes Seller's name, social security number and sold price.

Prorated items – Seller is responsible for the date of closing. Items included may be taxes, rents, mortgage interest, homeowner's association dues and other fees or dues in relation to the property,

Estimating closing costs - Include: loan application fee, loan originating fees, credit report, appraisal and property taxes.

PROPERTY TAX - Tax is administered at the local government level. The amount of tax is determined annually based on market value of each property. In some cases is expressed as a "millage" or dollars of tax per thousand dollars of assessed value

TAX DEDUCTIONS - Owners may deduct; some loan origination fees, real estate taxes, discount points, and prepayment penalties.

AD VALOREM - According to value. This is the property real estate tax.

Judicial Foreclosure
Legal event whereas the lender receives a court order. The sale of the property is approved by the court. Property is usually sold to the highest bidder.

Non-judicial Foreclosure
Standard in a Deed of Trust. Allows the Trustee to sell the property to the highest bidder for the lender. Seller financing often has a Deed of Trust because it's easier to foreclose on the property.

Strict Foreclosure
A decree orders the debt to be paid within a set time limit. If the payment is not met, the mortgagor's right of equitable redemption is forever lost. The lien holder takes possession when the court awards title to him.

Deed in Lieu of Foreclosure
A friendly foreclosure. The property usually reverts back to the lender in a better condition than other foreclosures. The borrower will attempt to surrender the deed. The lien holder is not forced into accepting it.
Banks sometimes will not take a Deed in Lieu of Foreclosure because they may have to pay off a second loan.

A legal foreclosure kills the relationship with the second lien holder's secured property. It becomes an unsecured loan that will follow the mortgagor.

> **Short Sale** – The lien holder negotiates to avoid foreclosure. The lien holder accepts less than the loan amount.

REDEMPTION – The action of saving your ownership of a property.

> **Equitable Redemption**
> Occurs prior to the sales. The borrower pays the stated amount and the mortgage is reinstated.

> **Statutory Redemption**
> After the public sale the borrower has a certain amount of time to redeem his property.

DEFICIENCY JUDGMENT – **If the lender is unable to recover the amount due on a defaulted loan, the lender may sue the borrower for the outstanding balance.**

REO – **Real Estate Owned. Bank ownership. The property has been foreclosed and is now owned by the bank.**

Capital Gains Exclusions – Available on a Personal Residence only. The owners must have lived in the property for two of the last five years.

A single person can make up to $250,000 profit on their personal residence before having to pay taxes.

A married couple can make up to $500,000.

1031 TAX DEFERRED EXCHANGE

Deferring the capital gains taxes on investment property. Exchange one property for a "like kind property. An intermediary is used to retain the money into a tax deferred exchange account.

A "Like Kind" property is very liberal. Example: You are allowed to transfer an apartment for land.

Once a property closes, the intermediary and not the seller receive the sales proceeds. Within 45 days the seller must identify in writing to the intermediary which property they wish to acquire. You can designate up to three properties so long as you eventually close on one of them.

You must close on the new property within 180 days of the close of the first property. (The first leg of the transaction)

Any money left in the account after the 180 days is sent to the transferor and that money is taxed. It is called boot.

Boot is money taken out of the 1031 tax deferred transaction. Taxes are paid on the boot portion.

Uniform Commercial Code (UCC)

Used when personal property is the collateral for a loan

Financing statement (UCC-1)—the short form of the security agreement which must be recorded

Chapter Fifteen

Title Insurance, Searches and Abstracts

TITLE INSURANCE

What it is insured against?

Title insurance insures against financial loss from defects in title to real property and from the invalidity or unenforceability of mortgage loans.

Insures the policyholder against loss due to defects in the title other than those exceptions identified in the policy.

Based on the title search.

Preliminary report of title (commitment to issue policy) contains:
1. Name of insured party
2. Legal description of property
3. Estate or interest covered
4. Conditions and stipulations
5. Schedule of exceptions

The title insurance premium is paid once, at the closing.

The insurer's liability cannot exceed the face amount of the policy unless an inflation rider is included.

Extent of Coverage

Standard Coverage Policy insures against:

Defects found in public records.

Forged documents.

Incompetent grantors.

Incorrect marital statements.

Improperly delivered deeds.

Extended Coverage Policy insures against:

All perils insured against by the standard coverage policy.

Property inspection, including unrecorded rights of persons in possession.

Examination of survey.

Unrecorded liens not known by the policyholder.

TYPICAL EXCLUSIONS

Defects and liens listed in the policy.
Defects known to the buyer.
Changes in land use brought about by changes in zoning ordinances.

TYPES OF POLICIES

Owner's policy
Issued for the benefit of the owner.

Lender's policy
issued for the benefit of the mortgagee; coverage commensurate with amount of loan; does not protect owner's interest.

TORRENS SYSTEM

The "Torrens title is a system of land registration.

Land ownership is transferred through registration of title instead of using deeds.

Its main purpose is to simplify land transactions and to certify to the ownership of an absolute title to realty.
Source: Torrens title - https://en.wikipedia.org

Title Searches

A search of the recorded documents on the property.

An examination of public records to determine what defects, if any, exist in the chain of title.

Search begins with present owner and traces back to the origin of title.

Length of search is usually between 40-60 years.

Abstract of title

A summary report of the items about a property that can be found in public record.

Prepared by an abstractor.

Does not reveal items that cannot be found in the public records.

Abstract and Attorney's Opinion

Attorney's opinion issued on basis of the abstract.

Chain of Title

Recorded history of all of the matters that affect the title.

Beginning with the original source of ownership and linking the passage of ownership to subsequent owners to form a chain.

A gap in the chain requires a **suit to quiet title** or **quitclaim deeds** to establish the ownership.

MARKETABLE TITLE

No serious defects

Does not depend on doubtful questions of law or fact to prove its validity.

Does not expose a purchaser to the hazard of litigation or threaten the quiet enjoyment of the property.

Convinces a reasonably well-informed and prudent person that he or she could, in turn, sell or mortgage the property.

UNMARKETABLE TITLE can still be transferred, but its defects may limit or restrict its ownership.

CLOUD ON TITLE
A defect found in the public records.

SUIT TO QUIET TITLE
A court action to remove a cloud on title.

Chapter Sixteen

DEEDS

PURPOSE OF DEED

Evidence of title ownership. Alienation of the seller. To show ownership from one person to another person.

TYPES OF DEEDS

Deeds show the covenants by which a grantor is bound to the buyer in the transaction

---

General Warranty Deed

The deed that gives the most protection to the buyer.

It has 5 covenants.

Seisen, covenant against encumbrances, quiet enjoyment, further assurance and the covenant of warranty forever.

May contain express written warranties; may state "convey and warrant" or "warrant generally" depending on state law.

May contain implied warranties according to state statutes.

Special Warranty Deed

The grantor is warranting that there are no encumbrances on the property during his ownership except for those things stated in the deed.

(Used often at auctions or tax sales)

Contains clause "remise, release, alienate, and convey"

Bargain and Sale Deed

Contains no warranties against encumbrances unless stated.

Only implies that the grantor holds title and is in possession.

Quitclaim Deed

Contains no warranties.

Usually transferred between people who know each other.

Used to clear up clouds/defects on title or relinquish an inchoate interest.

Least protection.

Carries no covenants or warranties whatsoever.

May be used to transfer an easement.

Trustee's Deed

Used to convey property out of a trust to anyone other than the trustor.

Executed by the authority granted to the trustee.

Reconveyance Deed

Executed by the trustee to return (reconvey) title to property held in trust.

Executor's Deeds, Administrator's Deeds, Sheriff's Deeds

A deed executed pursuant to a court order.

Used to convey title to property transferred by court order or by will.

WHEN TITLE PASSES
Ownership passes when the buyer accepts the delivered and signed deed.

ESSENTIAL ELEMENTS OF DEEDS

Grantor
Grantee
Consideration
Granting Clause (Habendum Clause)
Description of the property
Signature of the grantor
Delivery and Acceptance by the grantee

The first person to record their deed owns the property.

Recording the deed gives constructive notice to the world.

Deeds are valid to all those who have been notified about the deed whether they actually know about it or not. Recording the deed gives notice to the world.

An unrecorded deed is valid to the parties and anyone who knows about it.

WHAT IS A CLOSING DISCLOSURE?

A Closing Disclosure is a five-page form that provides final details about the mortgage loan you have selected. It includes the loan terms, your projected monthly payments, and how much you will pay in fees and other costs to get your mortgage (closing costs).

The Closing Disclosure is a new form. For most kinds of mortgages, borrowers who apply for a loan on or after October 3, 2015 will receive a Closing Disclosure.

The lender is required to give you the Closing Disclosure at least three business days before you close on the mortgage loan. This three-day window allows you time to compare your final terms and costs to those estimated in the Loan Estimate that you previously received from the lender. The three days also gives you time to ask your lender any questions before you go to the closing table.

Chapter Seventeen

PRACTICE OF REAL ESTATE

HOMEOWNERS INSURANCE

BASIC POLICY

provides coverage against fire or lightning, glass breakage, windstorm and hail, explosion, riot and civil commotion, damage by aircraft, damage from vehicles, damage from smoke, vandalism and malicious mischief, theft and loss of property removed from the premises when endangered by fire or other perils.

Also covers falling objects; weight of ice, snow, or sleet;
collapse of all or part of the building; bursting, cracking, burning, or bulging of a steam or hot water heating system; accidental discharge, leakage, or overflow of water or steam from within a plumbing, heating, or air conditioning system; freezing of plumbing, heating, or air conditioning system; injury to electrical appliances, devices, fixtures, and wiring from short circuits or other accidentally generated currents

HOME WARRANTY

A home warranty is a contractual agreement provided to an owner of a house by any of a number of different types of entities such as home builders, risk management groups, or others.

The home warranty industry was founded in 1971 by American Home Shield. In the strictest legal sense a warranty of any kind within the United States must adhere to guidelines set at the states' and federal government's levels.

A home warranty is not a warranty at all, but rather a home service contract that covers the repair and/or replacement costs of home appliances, major systems such as heating and cooling, and possibly other components of a home, structural or otherwise.

The home service contract generally covers home systems such as the home's plumbing or electrical, and appliances like dishwashers that fail from old age/normal wear and tear.

Coverage varies significantly across home warranty companies. Home warranty contracts do not cover all home repairs.

RENTER'S INSURANCE

It provides liability insurance and the tenant's personal property is covered against named perils such as fire, theft, and vandalism.

It also pays expenses, when the dwelling becomes uninhabitable.

TRUST / ESCROW ACCOUNT
Client and Customer Funds
Trust / Escrow money are not assets of the broker.
No moneys from this account may be used for the broker's business or personal expenses.
Money from this account may not be transferred to the broker's account. It is called commingling.

Earnest money deposits must be deposited into the Trust/escrow account (according to state laws) in a timely manner.

BUSINESS ACCOUNT
Business money
Broker's assets
Commissions come in and out of this account.
This account pays things like rent, electric, gas and other business related expenses.

IDX

AN INTERNET DATA EXCHANGE (IDX, ALSO KNOWN AS INFORMATION DATA EXCHANGE

A real estate property search site which allows the public to conduct searches of approved Multiple Listing Service properties in a certain area. The term may be defined in documents for real estate transactions, but also may loosely refer to any hypertext transfer protocol (http) telecommunication. This page describes the use of the term in the real estate industry.

Site users generally gain the benefit of anonymous property searching and review. IDX sites usually provide less detailed information than the full Realtor Multiple Listing Service, limiting the data to that which is deemed publicly accessible. This system benefits both parties. The benefit to realtors is that users of their IDX web site can search freely, establish some confidence, and qualify themselves before contacting the realtor. The benefits to clients is to save time and refine their targets.

This technology allows brokers and agents to put the MLS on their website

---

Technology in Advertising

IDX is the type technology allowing agents to put the MLS on their website.

HUD Fair housing issues in advertising – Guidelines cover race, color, national origin, religion, sex, disability, familial status and photographs or illustrations of people.

Use of human models. Human models in photographs, drawings, or other graphic techniques may not be used to indicate exclusiveness because of race, color, religion, sex, handicap, familial status, or national origin. If models are used in display advertising campaigns, the models should be clearly definable as reasonably representing majority and minority groups in the metropolitan area, both sexes, and, when appropriate, families with children. Models, if used, should portray persons in an equal social setting and indicate to the general public that the housing is open to all without regard to race, color, religion, sex, handicap, familial status, or national origin, and is not for the exclusive use of one such group.

```
┌─────────────────────────────────────────────────────────┐
│                                                           │
│   Uniform Electronic Transfer Act (UETA)                  │
│   A document cannot be voided of its legal effect         │
│   because of electronic format.                           │
│                                                           │
│   FTC / Federal Telemarketing Law – Do not call list      │
│   Telemarketers are limited to 18 months for follow up    │
│   calls.                                                  │
│                                                           │
└─────────────────────────────────────────────────────────┘
```

DO NOT CALL LIST

You can reduce the number of unwanted sales calls you get by signing up for the National Do Not Call Registry. It's free. Visit donotcall.gov to register your number.

```
┌─────────────────────────────────────────────────────────┐
│                                                           │
│   National Commerce Act (E-sign)                          │
│                                                           │
│   Electronic signatures are valid even if state laws      │
│   conflict.                                               │
│                                                           │
│   A consent process is required if persons would like to  │
│   substitute electronic documents for written documents.  │
│                                                           │
└─────────────────────────────────────────────────────────┘
```

ESIGN

THE ELECTRONIC SIGNATURES IN GLOBAL AND NATIONAL COMMERCE ACT

A law passed to facilitate the use of electronic records and electronic signatures in interstate and foreign commerce by ensuring the validity and legal effect of contracts entered into electronically.

UNIFORM ELECTRONIC TRANSACTIONS ACT (UETA)

It is the first comprehensive effort to prepare state law for the electronic commerce era.

Many states have already adopted legislation pertaining to such matters as digital signatures, but UETA represents the first national effort at providing some uniform rules to govern transactions in electronic commerce that should serve in every state.

The rules of UETA are primarily for "electronic records and electronic signatures relating to a transaction".

UETA applies only to transactions in which each party has agreed by some means to conduct them by electronically.

Nobody is forced to conduct to electronic transactions. Parties to electronic transactions come under UETA, but they may also opt out. They may vary, waive or disclaim most of the provisions of UETA by agreement, even if it is agreed that business will be transacted by electronic means.

Electronic commerce means, of course, persons doing business with other persons with computers and telephone or television cable lines. The Internet is the great marketplace for these kinds of transactions.

The most fundamental rule provides that a "record or signature may not be denied legal effect or enforceability solely because it is in electronic form."

The second most fundamental rule says that "a contract may not be denied legal effect or enforceability solely because an electronic record was used in its formation."

The third most fundamental rule states that any law that requires a writing will be satisfied by an electronic record.

And the fourth basic rule provides that any signature requirement in the law will be met if there is an electronic signature.

Blind Ads – An ad where one cannot identify the broker or brokerage firm.

Blind Ads are illegal.

1099 S

At the sale.

Closing attorney submits it to the IRS

Seller's name

Social security number

Sold price

FILER'S name, street address, city or town, state or province, country, ZIP or foreign postal code, and telephone number		1 Date of closing	OMB No. 1545-0997	Proceeds From Real Estate Transactions
		2 Gross proceeds	**2017**	
		$	Form **1099-S**	
FILER'S federal identification number	TRANSFEROR'S identification number	3 Address or legal description (including city, state, and ZIP code)		Copy A For Internal Revenue Service Center File with Form 1096.
TRANSFEROR'S name				For Privacy Act and Paperwork Reduction Act Notice, see the **2017 General Instructions for Certain Information Returns.**
Street address (including apt. no.)		4 Check here if the transferor received or will receive property or services as part of the consideration ▶		
City or town, state or province, country, and ZIP or foreign postal code		5 Check here if the transferor is a foreign person (nonresident alien, foreign partnership, foreign estate, or foreign trust) . . . . ▶		
Account or escrow number (see instructions)		6 Buyer's part of real estate tax $		

1099 Misc

The form the broker gives to his salespeople indicating the amount of commission made.

INDEPENDENT CONTRACTOR VS. EMPLOYEE

Employee

Broker can control and dictate exact job duties. Salespersons must follow rules such as work hours, dress code, lunch times, etc. Broker will deduct income and social security taxes from pay. Salespeople will receive a W9.

Independent Contractor

Most salespeople are independent contractors. Broker can control what the salesperson does but not how it's done. Broker cannot dictate office hours, dress codes or meetings. Independent Contractors pay their own taxes and receive a 1099misc.

The IRS instructs businesses to consider three categories of "facts that provide evidence of the degree of control and independence" in the relationship. The **three** categories are:

1. Behavioral: Does the company control or have the right to control what the worker does and how the worker does their job?

2. Financial: Are the business aspects of the worker's job controlled by the payer? (These include things like how the worker is paid, whether expenses are reimbursed, who provides tools/supplies, etc.)

3. Type of Relationship: Are there written contracts or employee-type benefits (i.e., pension plan, insurance, vacation pay, etc

INDEPENDENT CONTRACTOR

90% of income comes from Commission or sales.

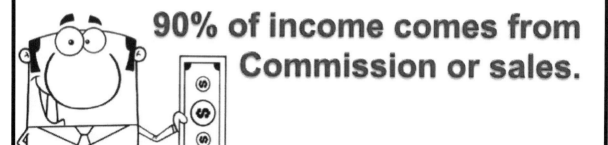

EMPLOYEE

90% of income comes from salary and wages.

Independent Contractor

Broker can't tell you how to do your job.

Employee

Broker can tell you exactly how to do your job.

INDEPENDENT CONTRACTOR

No employee benefits.

EMPLOYEE

Benefits

Withheld Taxes

Liability/responsibility for acts of associated licensees and employees

A broker is responsible for the real estate activities of their associated salespersons.

A broker is not responsible to make sure their agents license and schooling is up to date.

Antitrust Laws and Purpose

Fair competition for the benefit of consumers.

"Unfair or deceptive acts or practices." are illegal.

Sherman Antitrust Act

The mission is to enforce the rules of the competitive marketplace.

These include plain arrangements among competing individuals or businesses to fix prices, divide markets, or rig bids.

Commissions and fees are negotiated.   (More)

Illegal Activities

Allocate markets or customers
Price fix
Boycott

Tie In Arrangements

ANTITRUST LAWS

Brokers may not get together and allocate markets or customers, price fix or boycott another agent.

They can't divide markets, rig bids or price fix.

A local board of realtors cannot set commission fees. Everything is negotiated.

Tie In Arrangements – illegal practice. (Example: I will have my client buy your property if you have your client buy my swampland.)

> **The Sherman Act** imposes criminal penalties of up to $100 million for a corporation and $1 million for an individual, along with up to 10 years in prison.

FEDERAL EQUAL CREDIT OPPORTUNITY ACT

Protected Classes

> # Federal Equal Credit Opportunity Act
>
> ## Race – color – religion
>
> ## National origin
>
> ## Sex - marital status
>
> ## Age
> ## Dependency on public assistance

Federal Equal Credit Opportunity Act – prohibits discrimination based on race, color, religion, national origin, sex, marital status, age and dependency on public assistance. A rejected applicant must be informed within 30 days of the reasons for the rejection.

EQUAL HOUSING OPPORTUNITY

PURPOSE

To ensure that all persons have access to housing of their choice, including rentals, within their ability to pay, without differentiation in terms and conditions, because of their race, color, religion, sex, familial status, handicap, or national origin.

EQUAL HOUSING OPPORTUNITY POSTER (EHO POSTER)

EHO Poster – must be predominately displayed in every real estate off or it is considered prima facie discrimination.

U. S. Department of Housing and Urban Development

EQUAL HOUSING OPPORTUNITY

We Do Business in Accordance With the Federal Fair Housing Law

(The Fair Housing Amendments Act of 1988)

It is illegal to Discriminate Against Any Person Because of Race, Color, Religion, Sex, Handicap, Familial Status, or National Origin

---

- In the sale or rental of housing or residential lots
- In advertising the sale or rental of housing
- In the financing of housing

- In the provision of real estate brokerage services
- In the appraisal of housing
- Blockbusting is also illegal

Anyone who feels he or she has been discriminated against may file a complaint of housing discrimination:
1-800-669-9777 (Toll Free)
1-800-927-9275 (TTY)

U.S. Department of Housing and Urban Development
Assistant Secretary for Fair Housing and Equal Opportunity
Washington, D.C. 20410

Previous editions are obsolete

form HUD-928 1 (2/2003)

COVERED TRANSACTIONS

Fair housing discrimination laws are intended to protect buyers, renters and any person of a residential property from seller or landlord discrimination.

CIVIL RIGHTS ACT OF 1866

Prohibits discrimination based on race.

Licensees cannot disclose to the landlord or seller that the buyer or renter is a member of a protected class.

Unlawful to discriminate on the basis of race, color religion, national origin.

Title VIII of the Civil Rights Act of 1968 is commonly known as the Fair Housing Act.

1974 Housing and Community Development Act added gender.

1988 added Handicapped and Familial status.

Handicapped Status – Persons with AIDs and HIV are protected.

Drug addicts and alcohol addicted persons currently in treatment or have had treatment and are not currently addicted are protected.

A person convicted of illegal manufacturing or selling of illegal drugs is not protected.

ADA provides comprehensive guideline for making public facilities accessible. Protects landowner from extensive expenses to retrofit an existing building. New buildings must be accessible.

AMERICAN WITH DISABILITIES ACT / ADA – Rights of individuals with disabilities in employment / accessibility and public accommodations. Companies with 15 or more employees must make reasonable accommodations to enable a person with a disability to perform his job. Individuals must have full and equal access. Obstacles and barriers must be removed.

People diagnosed as mentally ill are protected. The mentally ill tenant may be evicted if he/she is acting inappropriately and counseling has not solved the problem.

> Example: A housing provider may not refuse to rent to an otherwise qualified individual with a mental disability because s/he is uncomfortable with the individual's disability. Such an act would violate the Fair Housing Act because it denies a person housing solely on the basis of their disability.

SERVICE ANIMALS ARE PROTECTED.

Support Animals are protected. A landlord must not refuse to rent to a person with a service or comfort pet if he has a pet free apartment or complex. The landlord must make accommodations.

> Persons with disabilities may request a reasonable accommodation for any assistance animal, including an emotional support animal
>
> An assistance animal is not a pet. It is an animal that works, provides assistance, or performs tasks for the benefit of a person with a disability, or provides emotional support that alleviates one or more identified symptoms or effects of a person's disability. Assistance animals perform many disability-related functions, including but not limited to, guiding individuals who are blind or have low vision, alerting individuals who are deaf or hard of hearing to sounds, providing protection or rescue assistance, **pulling** a wheelchair, fetching items, alerting persons to impending seizures, or providing emotional support to persons with disabilities who have a disability-related need for such support. For purposes of reasonable accommodation requests, neither the FHA act nor Section 504 requires an assistance animal to be individually trained or certified.
>
> While dogs are the most common type of assistance animal, other animals can also be assistance animals.

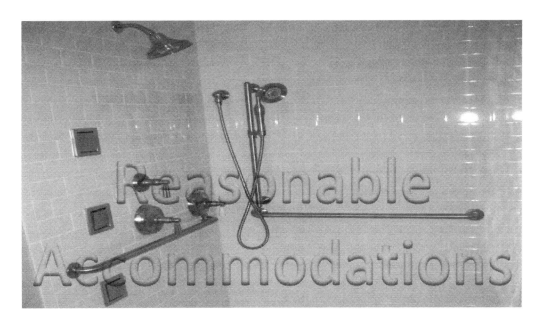

Reasonable Accommodations or Modifications – A tenant may modify existing premises that are necessary for full enjoyment. The tenant must bring the property back to its original condition upon vacating the property.

> **Reasonable Accommodations requires housing providers to allow persons with disabilities to make reasonable modifications**. A reasonable modification is a structural modification that is made to allow persons with disabilities the full enjoyment of the housing and related facilities. Examples of a reasonable modification would include allowing a person with a disability to: *install a ramp into a building, lower the entry threshold of a unit, or install grab bars in a bathroom.*
>
> Reasonable modifications are usually made at the resident's expense. However, there are resources available for helping **fund building modifications**.

Civil penalty – ADA – 50.000 first violation and 100,000 for subsequent violations. (up to)

FAMILIAL STATUS

Persons under the age of 18 are protected and persons who are pregnant. Housing specifically designed for older persons are excluded from familial status.

A Landlord may not charge higher rents to a family with children. A landlord may not segregate families with children into one area of the complex or building. A landlord may not advertise or maintain a "for ADULTS ONLY" complex.

62 years or older or housing intended for 55 years of age or older are exempt from Familial Status.

VIOLATIONS - A person who feels he has been discriminated against has one year to file a claim with HUD.

PENALTIES: Up to: 100,000 first offense
25,000 if another offense is within the past 5 years.
50,000 if two or more discriminatory practices within 7 years.

EXEMPTION FROM FEDERAL FAIR HOUSING – Sale or rental of a home by an owner who does not have 3 such homes operating at the same time and a broker is not used, discriminatory advertising is not used and of the owner is not living in the property and only one such exempt sale has been made within 2 years.

Rental units in an owner-occupied one to four family dwelling units are exempt.

Religious organizations and private clubs may be exempt.

Private Clubs can be excluded from Fair housing laws as long as they don't operate commercially. (They don't advertise or hire a real estate broker.)
A religious organization may be excluded from fair housing laws.

GENERAL ETHICS

Realtor® Code of Ethics
Training must be done every two years.

PUFFING

An opinion or exaggeration. Puffing can lead to misrepresentation.

An example would be when a salesperson tells a couple that he is showing them the best house in the best neighborhood. When the couple got to the property, they knew it was a nice neighborhood and house but they know of other neighborhoods and homes just as nice or nicer.

> Intentional Fraud is illegal.
>
> Puffing is an exaggerated opinion.
>
> Puffing can lead to misrepresentation.

PUFFING CAN LEAD TO MISREPRESENTATION

An agent told the buyers that they were buying a home with the best tasting water well. After the buyers purchased the property, they found out that the water well was tainted. Or, another example would be when the salesperson told buyers that they are buying a house in a neighborhood with the lowest tax rates. After the buyers closed on the property, they found out they bought a house in the highest taxed area.

FRAUD is an intentional misrepresentation.

> Practice within your area of competence.
>
> A first year agent should **not** accept a listing with a complicated transaction.
>
> Avoid unauthorized practice of law.
>
> Attorneys are Conveyancers.

Practicing within area of competence - Licensees should practice within their area of competency. For example, a first-year agent should most likely not accept a listing for a large residential apartment complex. It would be sufficient to refer that transaction to a professional in that area of expertise and earn a referral fee or split commission.

MISREPRESENTATION

Misrepresentation is one of several vitiating factors that can affect the validity of a contract. A misrepresentation occurs when one party makes a false statement, inducing another party to contract. For an action to be successful, some criteria must be met in order to prove a misrepresentation. These include:

- A false statement of past or existing fact has been made,
- The statement was directed at the suing party and
- The statement had acted to induce the suing party to contract.

FIDUCIARY RELATIONSHIPS

A fiduciary relationship is one of trust and confidence; it involves one party acting for the benefit of another.

CONFLICT OF DUTIES

A fiduciary's duty must not conflict with another fiduciary duty.

Conflicts between one fiduciary duty and another fiduciary duty arise most often when an agent, such as a real estate agent, represent more than one **client**, and the interests of those **clients** conflict.

Fiduciary Duties

Confidentiality
Obedience
Loyalty
Disclosure
Accountability
Care

Dual Agency

Dual agency has to be accepted by both seller and buyer in writing.

NEGLIGENT MISREPRESENTATION

Negligent misrepresentation occurs when the agent carelessly makes a representation while having no reasonable basis to believe it to be true.

> If a professional, who has or professes to have special knowledge or skill, makes a representation by virtue thereof to another…with the intention of inducing him to enter into a contract with him, he is under a duty to use **reasonable care** to see that the representation is correct, and that the advice, information or opinion is reliable

SCENARIO ONE

A woman wanted to purchase a historic home. Her real estate broker found one and made an appointment for the buyer to view.

While walking the property, the broker made a comment about the beautiful antique features of the interior. The broker pointed toward the fireplace and commented on how beautiful it was and how having a fire at the holidays will add such a nice ambiance for her family.

The buyer purchased the home.

In November, the buyer was getting ready for her family dinner on Thanksgiving. She went to purchase her groceries and included wood to burn in the fireplace on the grocery list.

A few days later, she put the wood in the fireplace and attempted to open the flue.

At that moment, she realized the fireplace was just a fake fireplace front only. She walked out of the house to see if there was a chimney. There was no chimney.

What is the real estate broker guilty of?

Answer: Negligent Misrepresentation

What didn't the real estate broker not do?

She did not practice care.

What is the real estate broker's financial liability?

Actual Damages

What will help the broker pay for her mistake?

Errors and Omissions Insurance (E & O Insurance)

Errors and Omission Insurance – Protects an agent for accidental negligent acts. It will help the agent pay any penalties. E and O Insurance does not cover intentional acts.

A form of liability insurance that helps protect professional advice- and service-providing individuals and companies from bearing the full cost of defending against a negligence claim made by a client, and damages awarded in such a civil lawsuit.

SCENARIO TWO

Hairdresser Holly asked her friend, real estate salesperson Sally is she could find Holly a home.

Holly was very specific about how large the garage needed to be. Holly told Sally that she planned on putting her hair salon in the garage. Holly state that she has enough clientele that will follow her wherever she has her salon therefore she wanted the salon to be a home based business.

Sally found a lovely home in a quiet neighborhood that fit the stipulations her friend Holly requested.

Sally showed Holly the house. Holly loved it and proceeded to make an offer to purchase. After several counteroffers between Holly and the Seller, there was a meeting of the minds. Holly purchased the property.

Holly moved into her new home six week later. The day she was having her salon equipment delivered into her new garage, the city code enforcer vehicle pulled up. The code enforcer requested to inspect the garage.

The code enforcer handed Holly a copy of the neighborhood code. The property and neighborhood were not zoned for home based business.

What is real estate salesperson Sally guilty of?

Answer: Negligent Misrepresentation

What didn't real estate salesperson Sally not do?

She did not practice care.

What is real estate salesperson Sally's financial liability?

Actual Damages

What will help Sally pay for her mistake?

Errors and Omissions Insurance (E & O Insurance)

> **Steering**
> Directing clients and customers into areas
> you believe they belong in.
>
>
> **Blockbusting – Panic Peddling**
> Inducing fear to make money.

STEERING

A salesperson who steers clients or customers into neighborhoods that he/she believes that they belong in.

BLOCKBUSTING

Panic Peddling.

This is when a salesperson canvasses a neighborhood and tells all the residents that people of a protected class is moving into an area. He is trying to scare people into selling so that he can make commissions.

Redlining – Banks

The practice of not lending in a block or neighborhood when the bank doesn't like the population of protected individuals.

REDLINING

A bank deciding not to loan in a particular neighborhood because of a heavy population of a protected class.

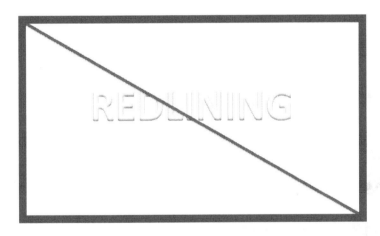

Can three individual banks decide to independently refuse to grant a loan to a minority (or anyone) in a particular neighborhood because the crime rate and deteriorating factors are extremely detrimental to the property?

YES

Their decision was not based on factors noted in Fair Housing Laws.

Business' are allowed to protect their investments.

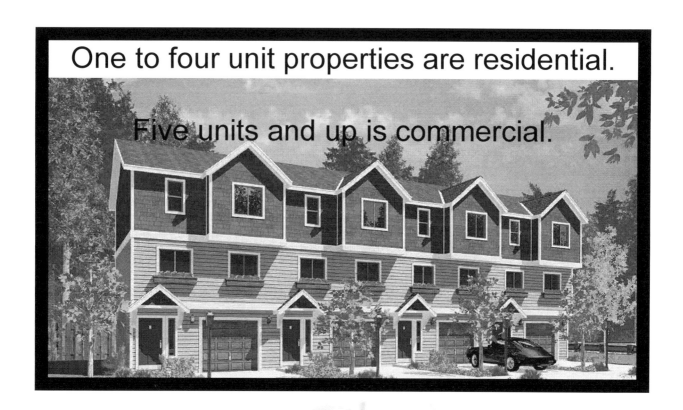

One to four unit properties are residential.

Five units and up is commercial.

Practicing within area of competence - Licensees should practice within their area of competency. For example, a first-year agent should most likely not accept a listing for a large residential apartment complex. It would be sufficient to refer the transaction to a professional in that area of expertise and earn a referral fee or split commission.

Practice within your area of competence.

A first year agent should **not** accept a listing with a complicated transaction.

Avoid unauthorized practice of law.

Attorneys are Conveyancers.

Avoiding unauthorized practice of law – Licensees are not attorneys. Agents are not allowed to give legal or accounting advice. A licensee cannot change legal documents. They may add an amendment or addendum on behalf of their client or customer.

Real Estate professionals are not allowed to give any legal advice or accounting advice.

A real estate agent may not be a Conveyancer. (A Conveyancer is an attorney who tells someone how to title to his or her property.)

Real Estate Investment Trust – A syndication of investors who pool their money to make investments.

A REIT is a company that owns, and in most cases, operates income-producing real estate. REITs own many types of commercial real estate, ranging from office and apartment buildings to warehouses, hospitals, shopping centers, hotels and even timberlands.

Some REITs also engage in financing real estate. The REIT structure was designed to provide a real estate investment structure similar to the structure mutual funds provide for investment in stocks.

Desk Cost- Even though it's called "Desk Cost or Desk Fee", it is not based on the number of desks in the office. It is based on the number of salespeople. The broker divides the operating expenses (rent, gas, electric, business license etc.) by the number of active salespeople.

A 100% commission paid to agent's compensation plan would most likely be found in a Landlord Broker Office. Landlord Brokers make their money on desk fees.

UCC- Uniform Commercial Code regulates the sale of personal property apart from the real estate being sold when a business transfers ownership.

Personal property is transferred with a **Bill of Sale**.

Real Estate Brokerage payment can be in many forms.
Commission
Flat fee
Retainer
Advisor fee
There is no set commission. Commission and payment is negotiable.

Referrals and Finders Fees
Licensees commonly will pay referral fees to other licensees. Most states do not allow for salespeople to pay a non-licensed person a referral fee or finder's fee.

Chapter Eighteen

CALCULATIONS
Real Estate Calculations

Basic Math Concepts

Area= length x width

Basic Math Concepts

Area = length x width

Loan-to-value ratios - the ratio of a loan to the value of the real property. The equity.

Discount points

Down payment

Amount to be financed

Loan-to-value ratios - the ratio of a loan to the value of the real property.

Equity - The difference between the value of the asset and the cost of the liabilities

---

Down payment - The initial amount that's paid on something that is to be financed.

Amount to be financed - The amount of credit made available to a borrower in a loan.

Points

1 point equals one percent of the loan.

Bob's purchased a property for $200,000.

His down payment is $20,000.

He will be paying **three points** at the close.

How much will he pay for points?

Answer:

Purchase Price: $200,000
Down Payment: $20,000
Loan Amount: $180,000

One point equal one percent of the loan.

$180,000 x **.03** = $5400

Prorations (utilities, rent, property taxes, insurance, etc.) –

Prorations in escrow are the fair division of property expenses between the Seller and Buyer. Each party is responsible only for those days, which he actually owns the

Proration's are based on a **360-day** year with each month having 30 days. Unless stated otherwise. The 365-day year requires the actual number of days in each month.

Prorations
360-day year with each month having 30 days

Loan Assumptions – credit buyer and debit seller (ABC Question)

Loan Assumptions – credit buyer and debit seller.

When there is a question referring to the assumption of a loan, look for **ABC.** The correct answer is going to seem backwards to most people.

Bob assumed Carol's loan. The property sold for $180,000. The loan amount is $150,000. What are the prorations?

1. Credit Buyer $150,000, debit Seller $150,000 ***** Correct answer always finish it up with the opposite. (debit seller)
2. Credit Seller $150,000, debit Buyer $150,000
3. Debit Buyer
4. Credit Seller

Property Taxes – Credit to buyer and debit to seller

When you get the property tax proration question, it goes like this:

Sally sold her property for $200,000. She will be closing on Oct. 3rd. She has pre-paid (for the year), her property taxes of $2780.

What is the proration at closing?

Think about this: SHE PAID TOO MUCH. BUT Taxes have to be paid. She is due a refund of the unused amount and then the buyer has to pay for his amount.

ANSWER: Credit Sally (for what she didn't use) Debit Buyer (for the rest of the year) Credit Seller, Debit Buyer

Property tax calculations – Prorated. Based on the actual ownership time. Unless otherwise noted, the seller is responsible for the closing date.

Broker Commission – Usually Debit to Seller

Commission and commission splits – Brokers may share commission with other brokers or their salespeople. Commission amounts are always negotiated.

Listing Broker

Salesperson Sally

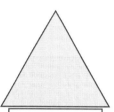

Listing Price: $300,000 Seller's commission is 4%

2% to the Selling Broker

Selling Broker

Salesperson Ed

Broker Commission – Usually Debit to Seller

Commission and commission splits – Brokers may share commission with other brokers or their salespeople. Commission amounts are always negotiated.

Listing Broker

Selling Broker

Salesperson Sally

Salesperson Ed

Listing Price: $300,000

Seller's commission is 4%

2% to the Selling Broker

Commission paid by seller $12.000

2% to each broker $6.000

Salesperson Ed has an employment agreement with his broker that he will be paid 70% of everything he brings in but he does have a $100 a month desk fee. What is salesperson Ed' commission?

Salesperson Sally has an employment contract with her broker stating that she will be paid 50% of everything she takes into the office.

What is Sally's commission?

Sally will receive $3,000
Ed will receive $4,200

Broker Commission – Usually Debit to Seller

Transfer tax/conveyance tax/revenue stamps are one time charges

Transfer tax/conveyance tax/revenue stamps - one-time charges based on the price of the transaction.

Credited to Seller / Debited From Buyer – Sales price, taxes and insurance reserves on assumed loan, prepaid taxes and fuel remaining in storage tanks

Credited to Buyer / Debited from Seller – Rents collected in advance, unpaid utility bills and the buyer's earnest money.

Seller's proceeds of sale – The net amount the seller receives at closing.

Competitive/comparative market analyses (CMA)

A broker tool to help a seller identify a selling price range.

Unlike an appraisal, the Broker will not make adjustments to the comparable properties.

A CMA takes into account recent sales in the same neighborhood.

Location and square footage are usually the most important factors the broker will consider.

Competitive/comparative market analyses (CMA)

A broker tool to help the seller find a price range for listing their property.

A CMA benefits the seller.

Broker Price Opinion (BPO)

A BPO is popularly used in situations where a financial institution believes the expense and delay of an appraisal is unnecessary.

Broker's price opinions are initiated by financial institutions.

Examples are banks, mortgage companies, and loss mitigation companies.

The BPO is performed by a real estate professional who is acting on behalf of the financial institution.

Through BPOs, agents can improve their skills in property inspection, market evaluation, and property pricing.

At a price of US$50–150 per BPO, the work can provide side income or steady income for real estate agents.

Agents may also create working relationships and a rapport with financial institutions.

Some BPO agents work through a BPO company that provides a single point of contact to the client and oversight of agents and their reports.

Net operating income - Used to find the value of an income producing property. Income minus Operating Expense equals Net Operating Income. (Income – Operating Expenses = NOI)

Net operating income – income property
The Bottom Line
(Income – Operating Expenses = NOI)

Depreciation – Wasting assets
Loss in value can be due to internal or external factors.

Depreciation

Depreciation is a method of reallocating the cost of a tangible asset over its useful life span of it being in motion. Businesses depreciate long-term assets for both tax and accounting purposes.

Land Does Not Depreciate

Purchase: $800,000
Deduct Land Value of $200,000
Depreciated Value $600,000

$600,000 divided by (the useful life) 27.5 years = 21,818.18 can be depreciated that year.

Tax depreciation on income property.

Recover the investor's costs.

Adjusted basis divided by the useful life of a property.

Tax depreciation

Depreciation is allowed on income producing property. It allows an investor to recover his costs. Straight-line method of depreciation allows for periodic amounts of deductions over the useful life of a property. Land cannot be depreciated.

Buyer Qualification Ratios

Front End Ratio
Identifies what the buyer can afford for a monthly payment.

Back End Ratio
Identifies what the buyer can afford including his monthly debt.

Interest rate
The charge for money borrowed

Interest amounts
The total interest paid over the life of the loan.

Interest rates - The rate at which interest is paid by borrowers for the use of money that they borrow from lenders.

Interest amounts – The total interest paid over the life of the loan.

An amortization schedule is a table detailing each periodic payment on an amortizing loan

AMORTIZATION TABLE - MONTHLY PAYMENT PER $1000 OF LOAN

Rate Per Year	5 years	10 years	15 years	20 years	25 years	30 years	35 years	40 years
5	18.88	10.61	7.91	6.6	5.85	5.37	5.05	4.83
5 1/2	19.11	10.86	8.18	6.88	6.15	5.68	5.38	5.16
6	19.34	11.11	8.44	7.17	6.45	6	5.71	5.51
6 1/2	19.57	11.36	8.72	7.46	6.76	6.32	6.05	5.86
7	19.81	11.62	8.99	7.76	7.07	6.66	6.39	6.22
7 1/2	20.04	11.88	9.28	8.06	7.39	7	6.75	6.59
8	20.28	12.14	9.56	8.37	7.72	7.34	7.11	6.96
8 1/2	20.52	12.4	9.85	8.68	8.06	7.69	7.47	7.72
9	20.76	12.67	10.15	9	8.4	8.05	7.84	7.72
9 1/2	21.01	12.94	10.45	9.33	8.74	8.41	8.22	8.11
10	21.25	13.22	10.75	9.66	9.09	8.78	8.6	8.5
10 1/2	21.5	13.5	11.06	9.99	9.45	9.15	8.99	8.89
11	21.75	13.78	11.37	10.33	9.81	9.53	9.37	9.29
11 1/2	22	14.06	11.69	10.67	10.17	9.91	9.77	9.69
12	22.25	14.35	12.01	11.02	10.54	10.29	10.16	10.09
12 1/2	22.5	14.64	12.33	11.37	10.91	10.68	10.56	10.49
13	22.76	14.94	12.66	11.72	11.28	11.07	10.96	10.9
13 1/2	23.01	15.23	12.99	12.08	11.68	11.46	11.36	11.31
14	23.27	15.53	13.32	12.44	12.04	11.85	11.76	11.72
14 1/2	23.53	15.83	13.66	12.8	12.43	12.25	12.17	12.13
15	23.79	16.14	14	13.17	12.81	12.65	12.57	12.54
15.5	24.06	16.45	14.34	13.54	13,20	13.05	12.98	12.95

Go to the top to find the years of the loan.

Go to the left-hand side to find the interest amount quoted.

YEARS

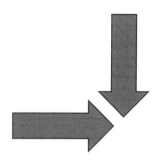

Interest Rate

Where do they meet?

That is the number to use.

Towana was offered a loan of $150,000 with a 7% interest rate for 15 years. What is her monthly payment?

Step One: Loan of $150,000 divided by 1000 = **150**
Step Two: Find 15 years at the top
Step Three: Find 7% on the left side

Where does 15 years and 7% meet?

8.99

8.99 X 150 = **$1,348 is her payment.**

Carl and Sandy are attempting to purchase their first home together. They have been told by the lender that they can afford $1,000 a month. They found a property that they would like to buy. After their down payment of $2,500, the loan amount is $150,000.

Should they get a 15-year loan at 6%
Or a 30-year loan at 7%?

15-year loan at 6% = 8.44

Amortization Table - Monthly Payment per $1000 of loan

Rate Per Year	5 years	10 years	15 years	20 years	25 years	30 years	35 years	40 years
5	18.88	10.61	■	6.6	5.85	5.37	5.05	4.83
5 1/2	19.11	10.86	■	6.88	6.15	5.68	5.38	5.16
6	■	■	★	7.17	6.45	6	5.71	5.51
6 1/2	19.57	11.36	8.72	7.46	6.76	6.32	6.05	5.86
7	19.81	11.62	8.99	7.76	7.07	6.66	6.39	6.22
7 1/2	20.04	11.88	9.28	8.06	7.39	7	6.75	6.59
8	20.28	12.14	9.56	8.37	7.72	7.34	7.11	6.96
8 1/2	20.52	12.4	9.85	8.68	8.06	7.69	7.47	7.72
9	20.76	12.67	10.15	9	8.4	8.05	7.84	7.72
9 1/2	21.01	12.94	10.45	9.33	8.74	8.41	8.22	8.11
10	21.25	13.22	10.75	9.66	9.09	8.78	8.6	8.5
10 1/2	21.5	13.5	11.06	9.99	9.45	9.15	8.99	8.89
11	21.75	13.78	11.37	10.33	9.81	9.53	9.37	9.29
11 1/2	22	14.06	11.69	10.67	10.17	9.91	9.77	9.69
12	22.25	14.35	12.01	11.02	10.54	10.29	10.16	10.09
12 1/2	22.5	14.64	12.33	11.37	10.91	10.68	10.56	10.49
13	22.76	14.94	12.66	11.72	11.28	11.07	10.96	10.9
13 1/2	23.01	15.23	12.99	12.08	11.68	11.46	11.36	11.31
14	23.27	15.53	13.32	12.44	12.04	11.85	11.76	11.72
14 1/2	23.53	15.83	13.66	12.8	12.43	12.25	12.17	12.13
15	23.79	16.14	14	13.17	12.81	12.65	12.57	12.54
15.5	24.06	16.45	14.34	13.54	13,20	13.05	12.98	12.95

30-year loan at 7% = 6.66

Amortization Table - Monthly Payment per $1000 of loan

Rate Per Year	5 years	10 years	15 years	20 years	25 years	30 years	35 years	40 years
5	18.88	10.61	7.91	6.6	5.85	■	5.05	4.83
5 1/2	19.11	10.86	8.18	6.88	6.15	■	5.38	5.16
6	19.34	11.11	8.44	7.17	6.45	■	5.71	5.51
6 1/2	19.57	11.36	8.72	7.46	6.76	■	6.05	5.86
7	■	■	■	■	■	★	6.39	6.22
7 1/2	20.04	11.88	9.28	8.06	7.39	7	6.75	6.59
8	20.28	12.14	9.56	8.37	7.72	7.34	7.11	6.96
8 1/2	20.52	12.4	9.85	8.68	8.06	7.69	7.47	7.72
9	20.76	12.67	10.15	9	8.4	8.05	7.84	7.72
9 1/2	21.01	12.94	10.45	9.33	8.74	8.41	8.22	8.11
10	21.25	13.22	10.75	9.66	9.09	8.78	8.6	8.5
10 1/2	21.5	13.5	11.06	9.99	9.45	9.15	8.99	8.89
11	21.75	13.78	11.37	10.33	9.81	9.53	9.37	9.29
11 1/2	22	14.06	11.69	10.67	10.17	9.91	9.77	9.69
12	22.25	14.35	12.01	11.02	10.54	10.29	10.16	10.09
12 1/2	22.5	14.64	12.33	11.37	10.91	10.68	10.56	10.49
13	22.76	14.94	12.66	11.72	11.28	11.07	10.96	10.9
13 1/2	23.01	15.23	12.99	12.08	11.68	11.46	11.36	11.31
14	23.27	15.53	13.32	12.44	12.04	11.85	11.76	11.72
14 1/2	23.53	15.83	13.66	12.8	12.43	12.25	12.17	12.13
15	23.79	16.14	14	13.17	12.81	12.65	12.57	12.54
15.5	24.06	16.45	14.34	13.54	13.20	13.05	12.98	12.95

Loan: $150,000 divided by 1000 - 150

15-year loan at 6% = 8.44 X 150 = 1266

30-year loan at 7% = 6.66 X 150 = 999

Which loan should Carl and Sandy take?
*They can only afford $1,000 a month

Pre-Qualification Letter
ABC Bank of Mississippi
Gopher Toes, Mississippi

1. **Sale Price: $300,000.00**
2. **Down Payment: 20%**
3. **Interest Rate: 6.5%**
4. **Terms: 30 years**
5. **Homeowner's Insurance: $1850.00 per year**
6. **Property Tax: Assessed at 70% of its purchase price and $2.84 per $100.00. (mill rate)**
7. **What is the monthly payment?**

$300,000 x .8 = $240,000 * Loan Amount
(Use Amortization Table) 6.5 at 30 years = 6.32
$240,000 divided by 1000 = 240
240 x 6.32 = **$1516.80** * monthly loan payment
1850 divided by 12 months = **154.16** * insurance per month
300,000 x .70 = 210,000
210,000 divided by 100.00 = 2100
2100 x 2.84 = 5964 divided by 12 months = **497**
Add: $1516.80 + 154.16 + 497 = 2167.96

Straight Line Method of Depreciation

Depreciation is a method of reallocating the cost of a tangible asset over its useful life span. Land value is deducted. Land does not depreciate.

EXAMPLE:

Purchase price of a four-plex: $800,000
Subtract the land value: -200,000
amount you can depreciate:--------------------------
                                            $600,000
The IRS uses 27.5 years for the four-plex.
600,000 divided by 27.5 = 21,818.18
$21,818.18 is what an investor can depreciate on taxes.

FOR THOSE WHO WANT MORE DETAIL

Calculations for Valuation
HOW TO DETERMINE MARKET VALUE FOR YOUR HOME
http://www.wikihow.com/Determine-Market-Value-for-Your-Home

SALES COMPARISON APPROACH
Learning Where to Find Information

When planning to sell your home, coming up with the right price can seem like a very difficult process. There is a lot of data to sift through and you might feel a little lost. With some careful investigation and calculations, however, you can come up with a good estimate of your property's market value — or the price your house can be expected to bring — without too much trouble. With this information, you can come up with the right price for your house.

1

Do an internet search for recently-sold homes in your area. Some local governments and realty sites publish this information on their websites. Using an online search engine is a good first step to take before you make any phone calls or visit any offices. That way, you can get an idea of what information is available without a lot of inconvenience for yourself.[1]

- Some of the most popular sites for real estate research are Realtor, Trulia, and Zillow. Start here when searching for information about recent sales or other real estate data for your area. Keep in mind that this information isn't always 100% accurate, which is why you should gather information from multiple sources.

2

Contact your local tax assessment office. Local governments keep records of recent property sales, which are usually held in the tax assessment office. Contact the office and ask for records of recent sales in your neighborhood or zip code. See if they can give you a list with all the details of each property, including selling price, date of sale, square footage, year built, and number of bedrooms and bathrooms. You'll need all of this information to make an educated guess on the market price for your home.[2]

- This data has the advantage in that it is real sales data and is in your local market (real estate value is based on location), but very seldom is a home exactly like yours sold in the recent past, so some adjustments will need to be made.

3

Contact a local real estate agent. Realtors will have plenty of experience in your area and be aware of recent sales, even if their office didn't make the sale. Contact the realty office and see if any agents are willing to talk about recent sales. Remember to get all the necessary information about the sale, including at least the selling price, date of sale, square footage, year built, and number of bedrooms and bathrooms.[3]

- It would probably make the realtor more willing to share information with you if you mention that you're looking for information because you plan on selling your house. When the realtor sees you as a potential client, he may be more open with you.

- If you do hire a realtor, he should perform a comparative market analysis. This report covers many data points including comparable sales of other properties and estimates of market value.

4

Ask for a property profile from an insurance company. Insurance companies keep data on real estate sales in a given area. Some will provide you with a property profile for free, hoping you'll buy insurance from them. The property profile will contain a list of comparable properties to your own, and the specific aspects of these properties.[4]

- Not all companies will do this for free, but you might still be able to obtain a property profile for a fee.

5

Look in local newspapers. Town, city, and county newspapers often publish information on local property sales. You can scan the real estate section for information on recent sales. Bear in mind that you might not get all of the information you need solely from a newspaper. You'll probably still have to contact a tax assessor or real estate agent for all of the necessary information.[5]

Putting Information Together

1

Make a spreadsheet on your computer. You'll have to organize a lot of information once you get a list of recent sales, and the most efficient way to do this is with a spreadsheet. Make a separate column for all the information about properties, including address, lot size, square footage, home style, year built, garage size, number of bedrooms and bathrooms, condition of the property, and selling price. Start by plugging in your own house's information, though of course leaving the selling price section blank for now. You'll then plug in other properties as you asses the list of recent sales you've acquired.[6]

- If you've never made a spreadsheet before, read Make a Spreadsheet in Excel.

- If you're unaware of the square footage of your own home, look at your real estate documents like closing papers. It will probably be included somewhere on these papers.
- If you can't find your home's square footage, you can get a rough estimate by measuring the outside of the house. In feet, measure the length and width of the house and multiply these two numbers. This will give you a larger number than the actual square footage, because professional appraisals subtract non-liveable space inside like hallways and closets. You could get a more accurate estimate by finding the area (length x width, just like with the outside) of each interior room, excluding the basement. Then add these numbers together.[7]

2

Look for homes that have sold within the last six months. When you've acquired the necessary information about sales, you have to start sorting the properties. Start by rejecting any sales that occurred over six months ago. The real estate market changes quickly, and sales more than six months old could be too outdated to be useful. Only use older sales if you can't find any data on a more recent sale.[8]

3

Find at least three homes that are most like yours. After finding the most up to date sales that have occurred in your area, you can start assessing the information to find comparable properties. Remember that you probably won't find properties exactly like yours. The aim is just to find properties that are most like yours out of the list of sales. Using the following criteria, find comparable properties to get the best idea of what your home will sell for. Then plug them into your spreadsheet to compare them to your own home.[9]

- Lot size.
- Square footage.
- Home style.
- Number of bedrooms and bathrooms. Also include whether these are full bathrooms, with a shower and toilet, or half, with just a toilet.
- Age.
- Location.
- Whether or not there is a finished basement.

4

Adjust the sales price if necessary. This is where a good deal of estimation comes in. Since it's unlikely that all of the homes you'll put on your list will be identical to yours, you'll have to make them fit yours and then adjust the sales price accordingly. Adjusting the market price is a difficult process. It would help if you consulted a realtor or someone else who is experienced in the real estate market. She will know the value of certain specifications for properties.

- For example, say you find a house that is exactly like yours that sold for $200,000, except it has two bathrooms and yours has one. Try to estimate what it would have sold for without that extra bathroom. A bathroom can add over $10,000 to the market price. You therefore estimate that the home would have sold for $190,000 if it had the exact specifications of your house.[10]

- A realtor will be able to provide the comparative market analysis and has experience in making the estimates and adjustments based on differences. Make sure that you consult an experienced realtor with a large number of sales in your market.

5

Use the adjusted sales prices of comparable prices to estimate your home's market value. Once you've adjusted the sales price of comparable homes, you should be able to make an educated guess on your home's market price. For example, if you chose 4 homes and they had sales prices of $240,000, $248,000, $255,000, and $257,000, you can make a good estimate that your house will sell somewhere between $240,000 and $257,000.[11]

- When coming up with adjusted sales prices, only use the final selling price of a home. The asking price of a home doesn't tell you anything; sellers can ask anything they want, but it doesn't mean they'll get it. Use only prices that houses actually sold for. This will tell you the market value of the area you live in.

6

Increase the market value to find your asking price. After you find the expected market price of your home, you should increase this number for your asking price. This will give you room to negotiate with a buyer and hopefully end up at the market price. The specific amount you should add will vary. You might be able to add $20,000 or more. If you plan on putting your home on the market, talk this over with your realtor to find the ideal asking price.

VALUE PER SQUARE FOOT

1

Figure out the price of comparable homes per square foot. If adjusting the prices of comparable properties seems too imprecise, you could also figure out how much comparable homes sold for based on square footage.[12]

- Start by dividing sales prices by the homes' square footage. You should end up with a price per square foot for each home on your list.
- Then arrange the list in order from highest to lowest.
- If you have a large gap between the highest or lowest number, cross it off the list. There are various reasons a house's price per square foot is lower or higher: it could have been foreclosed on, it might be in a more expensive area, or the price may have just been too high or low for that house. For example, say your price per square foot range is like this: 40, 55, 57, 60, 62. The amount of $40/sq. foot seems very out of sync with the others. There may have been something wrong with that house that wasn't reported on the data you found. Cross it off your list so it doesn't artificially pull down your price.
- Average out the remaining numbers. From the previous example, we're left with 55, 57, 60, and 62. The average of these numbers is 58.5 (55+57+60+62=234; 234/4=58.5). This means your house has a price per square foot of $58.50.
- Multiply the price per square foot by your home's square footage. If your home has 2,000 sq. feet, than the estimated market value would be $117,000.

2

Compute the price it would take to replace your home. Another technique for estimating your property value is to add up all the costs necessary for completely rebuilding your home as it is. Find out how much it would take to construct every part of your home and property. This will probably entail talking to contractors and getting price quotes. When you've done so, you can add up the estimates to come to a final estimate of your home's market price.[13]

- Beware that this method, while it is used, tends to be inaccurate. The price comparison method is usually much more accurate because it pays attention to current trends in the housing market.

•

HOW TO FIGURE CAP RATE

http://www.wikihow.com/Figure-Cap-Rate

Real estate investors rely upon a variety of types information when negotiating for income producing properties - for instance, the desirability of the property's current location and/or any prospective changes in the neighborhood are two common factors. One crucial piece of information that helps investors make their decision is called the capitalization rate (or "cap rate"). The cap rate (expressed as the **ratio of the property's net income to its purchase price**) allows investors to compare properties by evaluating a rate of return on the investment made in the property. See Step 1 below to calculate the cap rate for your home!

1

Calculate the yearly gross income of the investment property. The gross income of a piece of investment property will mainly be in terms of rent rolls. In other words, when a real estate investor buys a home, s/he usually makes money from it primarily by renting it out to tenants. However, this isn't the sole possible source of income - miscellaneous income can also accrue from the property in the form of coin operated vending or washing machines, etc.

- For example, let's say that we've just purchased a house we intend to rent to tenants at a rate of $750/month. At this rate, we can expect to make $750 \times 12 =$ **$9,000** per year in gross income from the property.

2

Subtract the operating expenses associated with the property from the gross income. Any piece of real estate comes with operating costs. Usually, these are in the form of maintenance, insurance, taxes, and property management. Use accurate estimates for these numbers and subtract them from the gross income you found above. This will find the property's net income.

- For example, let's say that, after having our rental property appraised, we find that we can expect to pay $900 in property management, $450 in maintenance, $710 in taxes, and $650 in insurance per year for our property. 9,000 - 900 - 450 - 710 - 650 = **$6,290**, our property's net income.

- Note that the cap rate doesn't account for the property's business expenses - including the purchase costs of the property, mortgage payments, fees, etc. Since these items reflect the investor's standing with the lender and are variable in nature, they adversely affect the neutral comparison that the cap rate is meant to deliver.

3

Divide the net income by the property's purchase price. The cap rate is the ratio between the net income of the property and its original price or capital cost. Cap rate is expressed as a percentage.

- Let's assume we purchased our property for $40,000. Given this information, we now have everything we need to know to find our cap rate. See below:

- $9000 (gross income)

- -$900 (property management)
- -$450 (maintenance)
- -$710 (taxes)
- -$650 (insurance)
- =$6290 (net income) / $40000 (purchase price) = 0.157 = **15.7% cap rate**

Using Cap Rates Wisely

1

Use cap rates to quickly compare similar investment opportunities. The cap rate basically represents the estimated percent return an investor might make on an all-cash purchase of the property. Because of this, cap rate is good statistic to use when comparing a potential acquisition to other investment opportunities of a similar nature. Cap rates allow quick, rough comparisons of the earning potential of investment properties and can help you narrow down your list of choices.

- For example, let's say that we're considering buying two pieces of property in the same neighborhood. One has a cap rate of 8%, while the other has a cap rate of 13%. This initial comparison favors the second property - it is expected to generate more money for each dollar you spend on it.

2

Don't use cap rate as the sole factor when determining an investment's health. While cap rates offer the opportunity to make quick, easy comparisons between two or more pieces of property, they're far from the only factors you should consider. Real estate investment can be quite tricky - seemingly straightforward investments can be subject to market forces and unforeseen events beyond the scope of a simple cap rate calculation. At the very least, you'll also want to consider the growth potential of your property's income as well as any likely changes in the value of the property itself.

- For example, let's say that we buy a piece of property for $1,000,000 and we expect to make $100,000 per year from it - this gives us a cap rate of 10%. If the local housing market changes and the value of the property increases to $1,500,000, suddenly, we have a less-lucrative cap rate of 6.66%. In this case, it may be wise to sell the property and use the profits to make another investment.

3

Use the cap rate to justify the income level of the investment property. If you know the cap rate of properties in the area of your investment property, you can use this information to determine how much net income your property will need to generate for the investment to be "worth it". To do this, simply multiply the property's asking price by the cap rate of similar properties in the area to find your "recommended" net income level. Note that this is essentially solving the equation (Net income/Asking price) = cap rate for "net income".

- For example, if we bought a property for $400,000 in an area where most similar properties have about an 8% cap rate, we might find our "recommended" income level by multiplying 400,000 × .08 = **$32,000**. This represents the amount of net income the property would need to generate per year to get an 8% cap rate, so we would set the rental rates accordingly.

- The cap rate doesn't reflect future risk. The investor cannot rely on the cap rate to assume that the property will sustain its current income or value. The property and rents associated with it can depreciate or appreciate. The expenses can simultaneously rise. The cap rate offers no prediction about future risk.

Gross rent (GRM)

Gross Rent Multiplier is the ratio of the price of a <u>real estate</u> investment to its annual rental income before accounting for expenses such as property taxes, insurance, utilities, etc.[1] To sum up **Gross Rent Multiplier**, it is the number of years the property would take to pay for itself in gross received rent.

For the investor looking to purchase, a higher GRM (perhaps over 12) is a poorer opportunity, whereas a lower one (perhaps under 8) is better.

The monthly (or annual) rent divided into the selling price.
Gross Income Multiplier (GIM)

Calculating the GIM requires that you divide the property value by the total income from the property, <u>after</u> accounting for expenses.

Chapter Nineteen

SPECIALTY AREAS

Real Estate Specializations

Brokerage
the business of bringing people together in a real estate transaction

Appraisal
the process of estimating the market value of real property

Property Management
the business of managing real estate to protect the owner's investment and maximize the owner's return
Trust fund accounts for income property must be maintained.

Financing
the business of arranging for or providing funds for real estate transactions

Subdivision and Development
the activities of splitting a large parcel of real estate into smaller ones and constructing improvements on the land.

Plottage: Assemblage creates Plottage

Subdivisions
A builder or sub-divider breaks up a large parcel of land into plats

PUD
Planned Unit Development
The4 development of an entire community.

Subdivisions
A Tract of land divided by the sub-divider. The new legal description will be recorded and contain lots, blocks and street addresses.

Deed Restrictions
Deed restrictions are listed in the deed. Often, developers restrict the parcels of property in a development to maintain a homogeneous neighborhood. A deed restriction is a clause in a deed that limits the use of land. The restrictions stay with the deed. The community enforces deed restrictions.

Commercial

The term **commercial property** (also called **commercial real estate**, investment or income property) refers to buildings or land intended to generate a profit, either from capital gain or rental income.[1]

Income Property – Multi Family Unit

Multifamily residential (also known as **multidwelling unit** or **MDU**) is a classification of housing where multiple separate housing units for residential inhabitants are contained within one building or several buildings within one complex. A common form is an apartment building.

Home inspection
the activities involved in conducting a visual survey of a property's site conditions, structure, and systems and preparing an analytical report useful to both buyers and homeowners

Counseling
the activity of providing clients with competent and independent information and advice to assist in their real estate investment decisions

Education
the provision of real estate education opportunities both to practitioners and consumers

Others
settings in which real estate expertise is required, such as the practice of law, corporations with extensive land holdings, and government agencies

Real Estate Investment Trust

REITs were designed to provide a real estate investment structure similar to the structure of mutual funds. They invest in real estate such as commercial real estate, offices, apartment buildings, shopping centers and other real estate investments.

Errors and Omission Insurance – Covers unintentional acts only

Desk Cost – Divided by the number of salespeople to cover office expenses.

UCC - Uniform Commercial Code - Bill of Sale – The transfer of personal property when a business is sold.

Chapter Twenty

Practice Exams

Electronic Exams are available at www.goretionline.com

Quizlet Flash Cards and Games

https://quizlet.com/_2ucddw

https://quizlet.com/_1s1rpt

https://quizlet.com/_1s1rpt

https://quizlet.com/_1s1r2q

https://quizlet.com/_1s1rm1

Exam One

1. A written agreement or contract between a buyer and seller when the buyer wants to buy and the seller wants to sell, after a meeting of the minds is called?
1. A BPO.
2. An appraisal.
3. A contract.
4. A disclosure agreement.

2. An appraiser must be licensed or certified to handle federally related work on residential, residential income, commercial and all other real estate properties valued at
1. $1,000,000.
2. $550,000.
3. $250,000.
4. $525,000.

3. Which of the following homeownership costs and expenses may be deducted on Federal Income Taxes?
1. Repairs to the exterior building, assessments and purchasing fees.
2. Cost of purchase including commissions paid premiums on title insurance and deed encumbrances.
3. Mortgage loan origination fees, mortgage loan interest and local property taxes.
4. Repairs, insurance premiums and interest.

4. Which type of ownership is most often used for a timeshare?
1. Stock Cooperative.
2. Tenancy in common.
3. Tenancy in severalty.
4. Joint.

5. How is title held when a person owns a cooperative?
1. Tenancy in common.
2. Tenancy by the entirety.
3. Joint tenancy.
4. Stock.

6.   The sellers and buyers have a contract in which the seller will convey title to the buyer if the buyer comes up with $35,000 before February 1st. What type of contract is this?

1.   Installment.
2.   Option contract.
3.   Variable.
4.   A buy - sell contract.

7.   The closing agent must give information as to the sales price and seller's social security number to the

1.   Bank in which the new mortgage is.
2.   HUD office.
3.   National Home Mortgage Association.
4.   IRS.

8.   A broker has supplied the money for a developer to build a new neighborhood with the stipulation that the broker becomes the sole agent for the builder when the properties are ready for sale. This is a

1.   Specific agency.
2.   Riparian rights.
3.   Agency coupled with an interest.
4.   Open agency.

9.   A Real Estate Broker has given a developer the money to build a new community in return for the developer to give the broker an Exclusive Right to Sell Agreement. This is a/an

1.   open agency coupled with financing.
2.   agency coupled with financing.
3.   open Listing Agreement.
4.   agency coupled with an interest.

10.   In a transaction what type of legal description is used in most cases?

1.   The street address only.
2.   The same one used in prior transactions, verified by a surveyor.
3.   The metes and bounds if the property is west of the Mississippi River.
4.   The one the seller guesses are correct.

11.   Assuming all factors are the same, which location would probably bring the highest price for a parking lot for sale?

1.   Business district zoned for one story small businesses.
2.   Recreational area.
3.   Residential area zoned for single-family homes.
4.   Business zoned for 20 story high rises.

12.	An arrangement in which an elderly homeowner borrows against the equity in his home and in return receives a regular monthly tax free payment from the lender is a
1.	Back Load Mortgage.
2.	Front Load Mortgage.
3.	Reverse Annuity.
4.	Inverse Annuity.

13.	A mentally disabled person that was declared incompetent can't enter into a contract unless
1.	a person appointed by a parent can sign legal contracts for the disabled person.
2.	a disabled person can under no circumstances enter into a contract without the written certification acquired while in school.
3.	a person appointed by the court may enter into the contract on the disabled person's behalf.
4.	All of the above under certain conditions.

14.	In a situation where state water rights are automatically conveyed with property is (*hint- best answer answer)
1.	prior appropriation.
2.	prior subjective conditions.
3.	a condition stated on all loan documents.
4.	alluvial.

15.	A client would like to sell his house after owning it for one year. The client let the agent know that the property was treated for termites 14 months ago. What should the agent do?
1.	Tell the client not to disclose the information so the agent's husband can re - treat the property and make money.
2.	Tell the client to keep his car out of the garage so not to attract any new termites.
3.	Tell the client that radon is nothing to be afraid of.
4.	Tell the client to disclose that information.

16.	Radon
1.	enters the house through the roof vents.
2.	is nothing to be concerned about?
3.	enters the house through the basement floor.
4.	is caused by friable asbestos.

17.	Radon is
1.	a colorless, odorless and tasteless gas occurring naturally from the decay of substances.
2.	colorless, odorless and tasteless friable asbestos.
3.	a lead by product.
4.	a black mold infestation that has become airborne.

18.   Friable asbestos
1.   airborne asbestos.
2.   airborne asbestos coupled with lead.
3.   is addictive and must be avoided.
4.   can be found in paint on windowsills.

19.   When a judgment on a property has been properly recorded. The world has been given
1.   substantive written notice.
2.   construed notice.
3.   construction notice.
4.   constructive notice.

20.   Two lots owned by the same seller and of the same size were sold two days apart. The lot directly on the sand beach was sold for $100,000 more than the lot across the highway which will have a peek a boo look at the water. What characteristic was taking effect?
1.   Permanence.
2.   Streetus.
3.   Situs.
4.   Situational indestructability.

21.   The FHA is best associated with
1.   a qualifying tool for mortgages.
2.   a banking entity with assets.
3.   a secondary market mortgage based interest indicator.
4.   an insurance company.

22.   Ana, a property manager, may legally refuse to rent to
1.   a person unable to live alone without help.
2.   a person convicted of selling drugs.
3.   a person who wants to adjust the apartment and pay for it in order to fit her wheelchair.
4.   Both 1 and 2.

23.   Discount points
1.   are the points paid on the sales price in order to reduce the price of a property.
2.   are the points paid on the full price offer with a 20% down payment in order to reduce a loan.
3.   are points paid on the amount of the loan in order to buy down interest rate.
4.   Can be any of the above.

24. **Each discount point is**
1. based on 1% of the loan.
2. based on 1% of the purchase price.
3. based on 1% of the cost of repairs made by the seller.
4. based on 1% of each friable asbestos particle inhaled.

25. **Ana, a property manager and who under usual circumstances would not have to give notice to vacate to a person whose one-year lease will be coming to an end in 10 days. Ana has discovered that the tenant whose situation is mentioned above has been convicted of illegal drug dealing and knows she can legally not rent to the convicted drug dealer. Ana decided to give the convicted drug dealer a Notice to Vacate just in case. The drug dealer stayed in the property for 45 more days after the expiration of the lease and attempted to pay rent in which Ana refused. The tenant has**
1. a periodic tenancy.
2. tenancy in common with other tenants.
3. a tenancy in sufferance.
4. a radar problem.

26. **A foremost reason for buying a condo over a luxury single family home on the ocean is**
1. the back yard.
2. price.
3. loan terms.
4. discount points.

27. **A woman bought a house subject to her getting approval to run her beauty shop from the city. The city refused her request. The contract was canceled because of**
1. inability to pay.
2. financing based on homes rather than businesses.
3. impossibility of performance.
4. her mother.

28. **A woman bought a house subject to her getting approval to run her business from her home. The city rejected her request. The woman was able to get her deposit money back because of a**
1. noncompliance clause.
2. liquidated damages contingency.
3. contingency in the offer.
4. noncompliance of zoning.

29. **When taking a listing, the agent should verify**
1. radon.
2. lead.
3. square footage.
4. the original purchase price.

30. For federal tax purposes, the form a broker will give an agent to file their taxes is a

1. 5024 – misc.
2. 1099 misc.
3. 1099 – s.
4. 940.

Answers Exam One

1. A written agreement or contract between a buyer and seller when the buyer wants to buy and the seller is wanting to sell, after a meeting of the minds is called?
3. A contract.

2. An appraiser must be licensed or certified to handle Federally related work on residential, residential income, commercial and all other real estate properties valued at
3. $250,000.

3. Which of the following costs of homeownership may be deducted on Federal Income Taxes?
3. Mortgage loan origination fees, mortgage loan interest and local property taxes.

4. Which type of ownership is most often used for a timeshare?
2. Tenancy in common.

5. How is title held when a person owns a cooperative?
4. Stock.

6. The sellers and buyers have a contract in which the seller will convey title to the buyer if the buyer comes up with $10,000 before July 1st. What type of contract is this?
2. Option contract.

7. The closing agent must give information as to the sales price and seller's social security number to the
4. IRS.

8. A broker has supplied the money for a developer to build a new neighborhood with the stipulation that the broker becomes the sole agent for the builder when the properties are ready for sale. This is a
3. agency coupled with an interest.

9. A Real Estate Broker has given a developer the money to build a new community in return for the developer to give the broker an Exclusive Right to Sell Agreement. This is
4. agency coupled with an interest.

10. In a transaction what type of legal description is used in most cases?
2. The same one used in prior transactions, verified by a surveyor.

11. Assuming all factors are the same, which location would probably bring the highest price for a parking lot for sale?

4. Business zoned for 20 story high rises.

12. An arrangement in which an elderly homeowner borrows against the equity in his home and in return receives a regular monthly tax-free payment from the lender is

3. reverse annuity.

13. A mentally disabled person that was declared incompetent can't enter into a contract unless

3. a person appointed by the court may enter into the contract on the disabled person's behalf.

14. In a situation where state water rights are automatically conveyed with property is

1. prior appropriation.

15. A client would like to sell his house after owning it for one year. The client let the agent know that the property was treated for termites 14 months ago. What should the agent do?

4. Tell the client to disclose that information.

16. Radon

3.   enters the house through the basement floor.

17. Radon is

1. a colorless, odorless and tasteless gas occurring naturally from the decay of substances.

18. Friable asbestos

1. airborne asbestos.

19. When a judgment on a property has been properly recorded. The world has been given

4. constructive notice/eviction.

20. Two lots owned by the same seller and of the same size were sold two days apart. The lot directly on the sand beach was sold for $100,000 more than the lot across the highway which will have a peek a boo look at the water. What characteristic was taking effect?

3. Situs.

21. The FHA is best associated with

4. an insurance company.

22. Ana, a property manager, may legally refuse to rent to

2. a person convicted of selling drugs.

23. Discount points

3. are points paid on the amount of the loan in order to buy down interest rate.

24. Each discount point is
1. based on 1% of the loan.

25. Ana, a property manager and who under usual circumstances would not have to give notice to vacate to a person whose one-year lease will be coming to an end in 10 days. Ana has discovered that the tenant whose situation is mentioned above has been convicted of illegal drug dealing and knows she can legally not rent to the convicted drug dealer. Ana decided to give the convicted drug dealer a Notice to Vacate just in case. The drug dealer stayed in the property for 45 more days after the expiration of the lease and attempted to pay rent in which Ana refused. The tenant has
3. a tenancy in sufferance.

26. A foremost reason for buying a condo over a luxury single family home on the ocean is
2. price.

27. A woman bought a house subject to her getting approval to run her beauty shop from the city. The city refused her request. The contract was canceled because of
3. impossibility of performance.

28. A woman bought a house subject to her getting approval to run her business from her home. The city rejected her request. The woman was able to get her deposit money back because of a
3. Contingency in the offer.

29. When taking a listing, the agent should verify
3. square footage.

30. For federal tax purposes, the form a broker will give an agent to file their taxes is a
2. 1099 misc.

1. The escrow agent or attorney at the close of escrow will file which tax form to be sent to the IRS?
   1. 1099 - misc.
   2. 1099 - s
   3. 1040
   4. 360

2. When a "trigger term" is used in an ad, The Truth in Lending Act requires the following disclosures except
   1. amount of loan or cash price.
   2. pre-payment penalties.
   3. number, amount and frequency of payments.
   4. amount of the down payment required.

3. Earnest money deposits should be
   1. deposited into the broker's business account.
   2. deposited into a safe deposit box.
   3. deposited into a trust account by the end of the next business day.
   4. be given to the agent to hold.

4. When a borrower defaults on a loan which has an acceleration clause it permits the lender
   1. seize the personal assets of the borrower.
   2. force the borrower to vacate his home immediately.
   3. demand the entire note be paid immediately.
   4. All of the above.

5. When a buyer of a four-plex refers to the property renting for 1000 dollars a month therefore the property is worth $100,000, the buyer is using the
   1. IRS.
   2. HUD.
   3. GRM.
   4. NOAA.

6. An Environmental Impact Statement
   1. projects the dollar amount of an entire project.
   2. summarizes the neighborhood in general terms.
   3. projects the impact on the environment of a proposed project.
   4. is used only for state projects.
   5.

7. A buyer wants to make an offer based on complex financing. The agent should
1. give legal advice.
2. call his broker at home.
3. suggest the buyer consult an attorney to furnish the wording.
4. drop the client.

8. The purpose of collecting an earnest money deposit is to
1. display the buyer has intention to carry out the deal.
2. insure a commission will be paid.
3. set aside funds for prorated taxes.
4. All of the above.

9. Usury laws are
1. intended to protect an agent from his broker.
2. intended to supply fair housing information.
3. intended to provide the FHA with down payment assistance.
4. intended to regulate interest charged by lenders.

10. Real Property is converted to personal property by
1. annexation.
2. severance.
3. novation.
4. laches.

11. Inducing panic selling in a neighborhood is
1. redlining.
2. steering.
3. friable asbestos.
4. blockbusting.

12. One day after a broker's listing on a property expired, the seller hired a new agent and that agent put the property on the MLS. A third agent called the broker with the expired listing and asked to see the property. The broker should respond by
1. telling the third agent who called to see the property that he no longer is the agent for the seller.
2. setting up an appointment with the seller to show the property.
3. hanging up.
4. talking bad about the seller's property.

13. Which of the following investors would like a property manager that emphasizes income and cash flow over maintenance?
1. The Dept. of Housing and Urban Development.
2. A bank owning foreclosed property.
3. An entrepreneur who owns several apartment buildings.
4. All of the above.

14. **A buyer depended on his agent's information that the property the buyer is considering making an offer on is in a tax area of the lowest taxes in the city. Based on that information, an offer was made. Before the transaction closed the buyer found out the taxes in that area are some of the highest in the state. The buyer may seek to rescind the contract based on**
    1. redlining.
    2. blockbusting.
    3. misrepresentation.
    4. puffing.

15. **The document the buyer and seller sign to establish their legal rights is the**
    1. deed.
    2. purchase contract.
    3. listing agreement.
    4. buyer's agreement.

16. **Ownership of common stock in a corporation**
    1. can be real estate.
    2. is a deed.
    3. is considered personal property.
    4. is required to purchase a home.

17. **A homeowner paid his neighbor $10,000 in order to have access to cross over the southeast portion of his property to reach a new road. This is an easement**
    1. by prescription.
    2. in gross.
    3. appurtenant.
    4. for safety.

18. **Which of the following would cancel a listing agreement?**
    1. salesperson transferring to a new broker.
    2. property owner's divorce.
    3. property owner's marriage.
    4. property owner's death.

19. **A competitive market analysis (CMA) considers**
    1. demographics.
    2. unknown friable asbestos.
    3. original price of the property.
    4. square footage of the subject property.

20. Under the Comprehensive Environmental Response, Compensation and Liability Act (CERCLA) who is liable for damages from the dumping hazardous waste on the property being sold?
1. The state government.
2. The federal government.
3. The buyer.
4. The seller.

21. Methods to calculate the reproduction or replacement cost of a building include all of the following except
1. quantity survey method.
2. straight line method.
3. unit in place method.
4. square foot method.

22. The best example of a buffer zone is
1. a warehouse between a neighborhood and strip mall.
2. garden homes between a single-family residential neighborhood and a shopping center.
3. an office building between a commercial strip mall and a school.
4. All of the above.

23. Antitrust Laws prohibit all except
1. dual representation.
2. setting commission fees with other brokers.
3. boycotting other brokers.
4. restricting competition.

24. Private homes built before 1978 may contain potentially dangerous levels of lead. The FHA
1. will not lend money on these properties.
2. require the buyer to acknowledge a disclosure of the presence of any known lead paint.
3. require the seller to remove the lead before selling.
4. require testing before the property can be sold.

25. Inverse (Reverse) Condemnation may be brought by
1. the city government.
2. the homeowner.
3. the federal government.
4. the state government.

26. **The responsible broker is responsible for**
    1. all actions of salespeople.
    2. all actions of unlicensed salespeople.
    3. real estate activities of associated salespeople.
    4. no acts of employees.

27. **A salesperson told a customer that his listing has the best view of the ocean. The customer noticed that the property has a peek a boo view of the ocean. This is an example of**
    1. blockbusting.
    2. a violation of Truth in Lending Laws.
    3. puffing.
    4. intentional fraud.

28. **When does a lender require flood insurance?**
    1. When the property was flooded by a busted water line.
    2. When the property is located in a Flood Hazard Zone.
    3. When the seller puts down more than 20%.
    4. When the buyer is using an out of state lender.
    1. None of the above.

Answers Exam Two
1. **The escrow agent or attorney at the close of escrow will file which tax form to be sent to the IRS?**
2. 1099 – s

2. . **When a "trigger term" is used in an ad, The Truth in Lending Act requires the following disclosures except**
2. pre-payment penalties.

3. **Earnest money deposits should be**
3. deposited into a trust account by the end of the next business day.

4. **When a borrower defaults on a loan that has an acceleration clause it permits the lender**
3. demand the entire note be paid immediately.

5. **When a buyer of a four-plex refers to the property renting for 1000 dollars a month therefore the property is worth $100,000, the buyer is using the**
3. GRM.

6. **An Environmental Impact Statement**
3. projects the impact on the environment of a proposed project.

7. **A buyer wants to make an offer based on complex financing. The agent should**
3. suggest the buyer consult an attorney to furnish the wording.

8. The purpose of collecting an earnest money deposit is to

1. display the buyer has intention to carry out the deal.

9. Usury laws are

4. intended to regulate interest charged by lenders.

10. Real Property is converted to personal property by

2. severance.

11. Inducing panic selling in a neighborhood is

4. blockbusting.

12. One day after a broker's listing on a property expired, the seller hired a new agent and that agent put the property on the MLS. A third agent called the broker with the expired listing and asked to see the property. The broker should respond by

1. telling the third agent who called to see the property that he no longer is the agent for the seller.

13. Which of the following investors would like a property manager that emphasizes income and cash flow over maintenance?

3. An entrepreneur who owns several apartment buildings.

14. A buyer depended on his agent's information that the property the buyer is considering making an offer on is in a tax area of the lowest taxes in the city. Based on that information, an offer was made. Before the transaction closed the buyer found out the taxes in that area are some of the highest in the state. The buyer may seek to rescind the contract based on

3. misrepresentation.

15. The document the buyer and seller sign to establish their legal rights is the

2. purchase contract.

16. Ownership of common stock in a corporation

3. is considered personal property.

17. A homeowner paid his neighbor $10,000 in order to have access to cross over the southeast portion of his property to reach a new road. This is an easement

3. appurtenant.

18. Which of the following would cancel a listing agreement?

4. Property owner's death.

19. A competitive market analysis (CMA) considers

4. square footage of the subject property.

20. Under the Comprehensive Environmental Response, Compensation and Liability Act (CERCLA) who is liable for damages from the dumping hazardous waste on the property being sold?
4. The seller.

21. Methods to calculate the reproduction or replacement cost of a building include all of the following except
2. straight line method.

22. The best example of a buffer zone is
2. garden homes between a single-family residential neighborhood and a shopping center.

23. Antitrust Laws prohibit all except
1. dual representation.

24. Private homes built before 1978 may contain potentially dangerous levels of lead. The FHA
2. require the buyer to acknowledge a disclosure of the presence of any known lead paint.

25. Inverse (Reverse) Condemnation may be brought by
2. the homeowner.

26. The responsible broker is responsible for
3. real estate activities of associated salespeople.

27. A salesperson told a customer that his listing has the best view of the ocean. The customer noticed that the property has a peek a boo view of the ocean. This is an example of
3. puffing.

28. When does a lender require flood insurance?
2. when the property is located in a Flood Hazard Zone.

1. Under a land contract who retains equitable title?
1. Vendee.
2. Vendor.
3. Grantee.
4. Grantor.

2. Under a land contract who retains fee ownership of the property? (Title)
1. Vendor
2. Vendee
3. Grantor
4. Grantee

3.   A buyer made an offer and the seller responded with a counter offer. When the buyer was reviewing the counter offer the seller received a better offer from another buyer. The seller can accept the second offer
1. if the second offer is coupled with a higher down payment.
2. if the seller withdraws the counter offer before the buyer accepts it.
3. if the first buyer has been informed in writing that the seller is going to accept the second offer.
4. the seller is forced to wait for the response of the first buyer.

4.   A broker received a commission of 6% of the selling price from his client. The commission was $9720. The sales price of the property was
1. $160,000.
2. $158,000.
3. $162,000.
4. None of the above.

5.   John listed his property with sales agent Tracy. John sold his own home to his cousin. John did not have to pay a commission to Tracy. The type of listing most likely was a/an
1. net listing.
2. gross listing.
3. exclusive Right to sell listing.
4. exclusive listing.

6.   A broker has decided to buy his client's house, which the broker has listed. The broker should
1. wait six weeks.
2. buy the property through a straw man.
3. not accept any offers on the property to protect his interest.
4. make his true intention known to his client.

7.   The gross rent multiplier for a duplex is calculated by dividing the sales price by
1. its gross yearly rent.

2. its gross monthly payment.
3. its gross monthly rent.
4. its net yearly income.

8. **Depreciation is based on**
   1. land and the building.
   2. land only.
   3. building only.
   4. economic obsolescence.

9. **A minority couple asked a salesperson to find them a property worth around $500,000. The salesperson showed the couple lower priced property in integrated neighborhoods only. This may be an example of**
   1. blockbusting.
   2. redlining.
   3. steering.
   4. puffing.

10. **Mary died without a will. She has one daughter and three granddaughters. Mary's estate will be distributed by**
    1. statute of novation.
    2. statute of reverse condemnation.
    3. statute of escheat.
    4. statute of descent.

11. **Real Estate transactions are reported to the IRS. Required information includes**
    1. sales price and buyer's name and social security number.
    2. seller's name, social security number(s) and price.
    3. buyer's name and method of payment.
    4. seller's name and address only.

12. **If conditions for purchase are included in the deed and those conditions are violated**
    1. the violator may face jail and a fine.
    2. the violator will serve jail time.
    3. an injunction can be placed on the property.
    4. the property reverts back to the original grantor/owner.

13. **When a seller gives her broker authorization to perform a single act, it causes**
    1. special agency.
    2. dual agency.
    3. universal agency.
    4. uncommon lawful agency.

14.   When the government establishes legislation to preserve order, protect the public health and safety and promotes the general welfare of the public, it is called

1.   lawful power.
2.   police power.
3.   inverse condemnation.
4.   All of the above.

15.   If one party in a contract does not live up to their part of the contract there is money set aside that will serve as full compensation to the aggrieved party. This is called

1.   earnest money.
2.   liquidated damages.
3.   arbitration clause.
4.   agreement pay.

16.   When two parties have a verbal and a written contract and the contracts conflict, which contract takes precedent?

1.   The oral agreement if it was made first.
2.   The written contract.
3.   Neither, new contracts must be drawn.
4.   The oral agreement in all cases.

17.   Usury Laws protect

1.   the lender.
2.   the seller.
3.   the borrower.
4.   the agent.

18.   Which is the best method to appraise a single-family home?

1.   Cost comparison.
2.   Depreciated method.
3.   Market data.
4.   Tax assessment method.

19.   A single woman has applied to rent an apartment in a community where 95% of the residents are over the age of 55. She has two children. One is eight and the other is three. The Federal Fair Housing Law

1.   makes it mandatory that she be rented to.
2.   protects the apartment owner from being forced to rent to her because over 80% of the residents are over the age of 55.
3.   protects the children for familiar status.
4.   All of the above could happen.

20. **An agent told the buyer that the property the buyer wanted was connected to the city's sewer system. After the purchase the buyer found out that the property had a septic tank and was not connected to the city's sewer system. What protects the agent from financial loss?**
    1. The National Association of Realtors national protection fund.
    2. E and O insurance coverage.
    3. The homeowner's insurance policy.
    4. Title insurance.

21. **A position of trust and confidence a client puts into an agent is called**
    1. implied or expressed.
    2. fiduciary.
    3. customer loyalty.
    4. It can be any of the above.

22. **The owner of the property you have listed is**
    1. the customer.
    2. the subagent.
    3. the prospect.
    4. the client.

23. **The following is considered prima facie evidence of discrimination by a broker;**
    1. Failure for a customer to qualify for a loan.
    2. Failure of the lender not to grant.
    3. Failure to display the equal opportunity poster at the broker's office.
    4. Failure to keep appointments.

24. **Termination of an easement can happen**
    1. with a fire on the dominant property.
    2. when the owner of the easement dies.
    3. with the merger of titles.
    4. when one property sells.

25. **A contract to purchase that has not closed is**
    1. null.
    2. void.
    3. an executory contract.
    4. an implied assessment.

26. **An adjustable mortgage contains all of the following except**
    1. life of loan cap.
    2. margin.
    3. depreciation.
    4. index.

27.   **Zoning Ordinances primarily**
   1.   implements a city master plan.
   2.   implement the quality of workmanship.
   3.   control business.
   4.   control water quality.

28.   **Economic characteristics of land include**
   1.   the metes and bounds.
   2.   situs or area preference, scarcity and durability.
   3.   the plot plan.
   4.   palm trees.

29.   **A tenant's lease expired last week. The tenant went ahead and paid next month's rent and the landlord gave him a receipt. This is a**
   1.   net lease.
   2.   tenancy in common.
   3.   holdover tenancy.
   4.   tenancy at sufferance.

30.   **A neighbor allowed his next-door neighbor to fish from his pond in the month of July only. The neighbor with the lake granted**
   1.   an easement appurtenant.
   2.   a restriction.
   3.   a gross easement.
   4.   a license.

Answers Exam Three

1.   **Under a land contract who retains equitable title?**
1. Vendee

2.   **Under a land contract who retains fee ownership of the property? (Title)**
1. Vendor

3.   **A buyer made an offer and the seller responded with a counter offer. When the buyer was reviewing the counter offer the seller received a better offer from another buyer. The seller can accept the second offer if**
2. the seller withdraws the counter offer before the buyer accepts it.

4.   **A broker received a commission of 6% of the selling price from his client. The commission was $9720. The sales price of the property was**
3. $162,000.

5.   **John listed his property with sales agent Tracy. John sold his own home to his cousin. John did not have to pay a commission to Tracy. The type of listing most likely was a/an**
4. exclusive listing.

6. A broker has decided to buy his client's house that the broker has listed. The broker should
4. make his true intention known to his client.

7. The gross rent multiplier for a duplex is calculated by dividing the sales price by
3. its gross monthly rent.

8. Depreciation is based on
3. building only.

9. A minority couple asked a salesperson to find them a property worth around $500,000. The salesperson showed the couple lower priced property in integrated neighborhoods only. This may be an example of
3. steering.

10. Mary died without a will. She has one daughter and three granddaughters. Mary's estate will be distributed by
4. statute of descent.

11. Real Estate transactions are reported to the IRS. Required information includes
2. seller's name, social security number(s) and price.

12. If conditions for purchase are included in the deed and those conditions are violated
4. the property reverts back to the original owner.

13. When a seller gives her broker authorization to perform a single act, it causes
1. special agency.

14. When the government establishes legislation to preserve order, protect the public health and safety and promotes the general welfare of the public, it is called
2. police power.

15. If one party in a contract does not live up to their part of the contract there is money set aside that will serve as full compensation to the aggrieved party. This is called
2. liquidated damages.

16. When two parties have a verbal and a written contract and the contracts conflict, which contract takes precedent?
2. The written contract.

17. Usury Laws protect
3. the borrower.

18. Which is the best method to appraise a single-family home?
3. Market data.

19. A single woman has applied to rent an apartment in a community where 95% of the residents are over the age of 55. She has two children. One is eight and the other is three. The Federal Fair Housing Law

2. protects the apartment owner from being forced to rent to her because over 80% of the residents are over the age of 55.

20. An agent told the buyer that the property the buyer wanted was connected to the city's sewer system. After the purchase the buyer found out that the property had a septic tank and was not connected to the city's sewer system. What protects the agent from financial loss?

2. E and O insurance coverage.

21. A position of trust and confidence a client puts into an agent is called

2. fiduciary.

22. The owner of the property you have listed is

4. the client.

23. The following is considered prima facie evidence of discrimination by a broker.

3. Failure to display the equal opportunity poster at the broker's office.

24. Termination of an easement can happen

3. with the merger of titles.

25. A contract to purchase that has not closed is

3. an executory contract.

26. An adjustable mortgage contains all of the following except

3. depreciation.

27. Zoning Ordinances primarily

1. implements a city master plan.

28. Economic characteristics of land include

2. Situs, scarcity and durability.

29. A tenant's lease expired last week. The tenant went ahead and paid next month's rent and the landlord gave him a receipt. This is a

3. holdover tenancy.

30. A neighbor allowed his next-door neighbor to fish from his pond in the month of July only. The neighbor with the lake granted

4. a license.

1.   A violation of The Federal Fair Housing law can be heard by either within the Dept. of Housing and Urban Development or by a Federal Judge. The Federal Court hearing has an advantage to the complaining party because
    1.   it's faster.
    2.   there is no dollar limit on damages paid.
    3.   it's fairer.
    4.   there is no advantage.

2.   When a property owner dies without a will or heirs, the property
    1.   become at sufferance.
    2.   is executory.
    3.   becomes the property of the closest neighbor.
    4.   escheats to the state.

3.   Ana, John and Jim bought together a property worth $675,000. John put up $337,500, Ana put up 25%. How much ownership interest does Jim have?
    1.   15%
    2.   25%
    3.   35%
    4.   45%

4.   Ana, John and Jim bought together a property worth $675,000. John put up $337,500, Ana put up 25%. How much money did Jim have to come up with?
    1. $172,564.
    2. $158,943.
    3. $168,750.
    4. $89,500.

5.   The amount of commission is
    1.   set by the Board of Realtors.
    2.   negotiable.
    3.   set by multiple brokers.
    4.   set by law.

6.   A doctor built a five-bedroom house with five bathrooms on a lot in a neighborhood where all the homes are three bedrooms and one bath. The doctor's home will most likely suffer from
    1.   subrogation.
    2.   novation.
    3.   progression.
    4.   regression.

7. **Which of the following owners of an apartment building would emphasize maintenance of value over income?**
    1. An entrepreneur who owns several income properties.
    2. HUD
    3. FCC
    4. Dept. of the Interior

8. **When several approaches of value are applied to a property, the appraiser will do which of the following?**
    1. Plottage
    2. Reconciliation
    3. Ascension
    4. Round off to the highest value

9. **Elevation Benchmark?**
    1. A seat in the community park zoned recreational.
    2. Horizontal Plain used to find the legal description in high rises.
    3. A mark used in a rectangular survey system measurement.
    4. The measurement point as the point of beginning.

10. **Jim wants to open a grocery store on a lot that is zoned for residential. Jim**
    1. will need to obtain a variance or a conditional use permit.
    2. will need to petition the local courts to change the zoning.
    3. will be able to open if the people in the neighborhood write letters to the mayor.
    4. All of the above can happen.

11. **The Equal Credit Opportunity Act does not address**
    1. factors for borrower's analysis.
    2. written credit denial letters.
    3. interest rates.
    4. discrimination in lending.

12. **A property went into foreclosure with a first mortgage of 158,000 and a second mortgage of 33,000. The second mortgagee most likely will receive**
    1. the entire 33,000.
    2. whatever is left over after paying off all other property liens.
    3. one half of the amount owed.
    4. nothing .

13. **The government survey system is not generally used in**
    1. states west of the Mississippi River.
    2. the southern states.
    3. the original 13 states.
    4. the northern states.

14. Violating Fair Housing practices, an agent
1. will lose their license only.
2. will get probation.
3. will get arrested immediately.
4. will have his license revoked and will be criminally prosecuted.

15. A very old oak tree!
1. Metes and Bounds
2. Rectangular Survey
3. Straight Line Method
4. North America

16. A CMA benefits?
1. The Buyer
2. The Seller
3. The Agent
4. The Broker

17. A contour map is used for which of the following locations?
1. Flat low-lying areas
2. Desert towns
3. A very hilly location
4. They are never used.

18. A Trustee may?
1. Sell the property
2. Lien the property
3. Do whatever is permitted in the trust agreement
4. Keep the deed after final payment

19. Prior Appropriation will most likely be found in what type of area?
1. Mountains
2. Deserts - Dry areas
3. Islands
4. Jungles

20. An Environmental Impact Statement is used for?
1. A proposed project
2. An outdated project
3. A private company
4. A quitclaim deed

21. An environmental Impact Statement is considered police power because it deals with which of the following?

1. Fish
2. Boats
3. Health and Safety
4. Pets

22. When a person dies without a will and no heirs can be found, the property

1. escheats to the state.
2. gets condemned.
3. gets reverted.
4. becomes part of the heir's estate.

23. Escheat happens

1. because property – land cannot be ownerless.
2. when the heirs reject the property.
3. land reverts back to the original grantor.
4. All of the above.

24. Inverse – Reverse Condemnation may be brought by the

1. state.
2. county.
3. feds.
4. homeowner.

25. Deed restrictions pertain to

1. the seller only.
2. the buyer only.
3. the future and current owners.
4. the previous grantee only.

26. Determinable and defeasible are best described as

1. ownership with a condition.
2. ownership with a deed.
3. dual representation.
4. single representation.

27. When a condition is violated in a deed

1. it becomes a brownfield.
2. the property becomes unusable.
3. the property reverts back to the original grantor.
4. the owner gets escheated.

28. **All of the following terms deal with appraisal except?**
   1. Reproduction costs
   2. Replacement costs
   3. Straight line method of depreciation
   4. Valuation

29. **Usury laws**
   1. protect the lender.
   2. protects the borrower.
   3. protects the bank.
   4. protects trade.

30. **The clause in a contract that allows the bank to call the entire note due and payable is?**
   1. Acceleration Clause
   2. Protection Clause
   3. Defeasible Fee Clause
   4. Santa Clause

Answers Exam Four

1.   A violation of The Federal Fair Housing law can be heard by either within the Dept. of Housing and Urban Development or by a Federal Judge. The Federal Court hearing has an advantage to the complaining party because
2. there is no dollar limit on damages paid.

2.   When a property owner dies without a will or heirs, the property
4. escheats to the state.

3.   Ana, John and Jim bought together a property worth $675,000. John put up $337,500, Ana put up 25%. How much ownership interest does Jim have?
2. 25%

4.   Ana, John and Jim bought together a property worth $675,000. John put up $337,500, Ana put up 25%. How much money did Jim have to come up with?
3. $168,750.

5.   The amount of commission is
2. negotiable.

6.   A doctor built a five-bedroom house with five bathrooms on a lot in a neighborhood where all the homes are three bedrooms and one bath. The doctor's home will most likely suffer from
4. regression.

7. Which of the following owners of an apartment building would emphasize maintenance of value over income?

2. HUD

8. When several approaches of value are applied to a property, the appraiser will do which of the following?

2. Reconciliation

9. Elevation Benchmark?

2. Horizontal Plain used to find the legal description in high rises.

10. Jim wants to open a grocery store on a lot that is zoned for residential. Jim

1. will need to obtain a variance or a conditional use permit.

11. The Equal Credit Opportunity Act does not address

3. interest rates.

12. A property went into foreclosure with a first mortgage of 158,000 and a second mortgage of 33,000. The second mortgagee most likely will receive

4. nothing.

13. The government survey system is not generally used in

3. The original 13 states.

14. Violating Fair Housing practices, an agent

4. will have his license revoked and will be criminally prosecuted.

15. A very old oak tree!

1. Metes and Bounds

16. A CMA benefits?

2. The Seller

17. A contour map is used for which of the following locations?

3. A very hilly location

18. A Trustee may?

3. Do whatever is permitted in the trust agreement.

19. Prior Appropriation will most likely be found in what type of area?

2. Deserts - Dry areas

20. An Environmental Impact Statement is used for?

1. A proposed project

21. An environmental Impact Statement is considered police power because it deals with which of the following?

3. Health and Safety

22. When a person dies without a will and no heirs can be found, the property
1. escheats to the state.

23. Escheat happens
1. because property – land can-not be ownerless.

24. Inverse – Reverse Condemnation may be brought by the
4. homeowner

25. Deed restrictions pertain to
3. the future and current owners

26. Determinable and defeasible are best described as
1. ownership with a condition.

27. When a condition is violated in a deed
3. the property reverts back to the original grantor.

28. All of the following terms deal with appraisal except?
3. straight line method of depreciation

29. Usury laws
2. protect the borrower.

30. The clause in a contract that allows the bank to call the entire note due and payable is?
1. Acceleration Clause

1. Who would have the most options for loans and loan programs?
  1. Mortgage Banker
  2. Mortgage Broker
  3. Mortgage Servicer
  4. Mortgage Repo Guy

2. An agent brought a ready, willing and able buyer that met the terms of the contract. The broker has earned her commission
  1. when the seller gives a counter offer.
  2. when the buyer gives a counter offer.
  3. when the seller accepts the offer.
  4. when the buyer accepts the counteroffer.

3. The term "Remainder" is most like?
  1. When an owner conveys a life estate to one party and the remainder to another.
  2. When the owner conveys ½ the estate to a relative and the remainder to a friend.
  3. The remainder of the Offer to Purchase that needs to be completed.
  4. The remainder of the rejected offers.

4. Tenancy for years is?
  1. A leasehold for at least 5 years.
  2. A lease for at least two years with a definite end.
  3. A lease with a definite beginning and a definite ending.
  4. A lease for the remainder of a person's life.

5. Real estate contracts must be in writing to be enforceable in court according to
  1. prima facie laws.
  2. statue of frauds.
  3. moveable chattel.
  4. because Jim says so.

6. The term "Duress" is most like;
  1. Durability
  2. Attainability
  3. Undue Influence
  4. Escheat

7. When a renter finds the rental to be dangerous or unsafe to live in and the landlord refuses to make repairs needed to bring the property to a safe condition, the tenant may vacate and not be responsible for the remainder of the lease. When the tenant moves, the tenant has given the landlord
   1. condemnation.
   2. association.
   3. constructive notice/eviction.
   4. construction notice.

8. A lease on an apartment has ended yet the tenant keeps paying a monthly rent and the landlord keeps accepting the rent. This type of leasehold would be considered
   1. a holdover tenancy.
   2. an illegal contract.
   3. unacceptable.
   4. void.

9. The Civil Rights Act of 1968 was meant as a follow-up to the Civil Rights Act of 1964. It is called the
   1. Fair Act.
   2. Fair Housing Act.
   3. Fair Housing Enactment.
   4. Fair Rental Housing Act.

10. The Civil Rights Act of 1866 prohibited discrimination based on?
   1. National Origin
   2. Familial Status
   3. Race
   4. Pregnancy

11. The definition of subletting is most like?
   1. The leasing of a premise by a lessee to a third party.
   2. The lease leasing to the lessor.
   3. The lessor leasing to a relative.
   4. The least lease the lessor leased to the lease.

12. Which of the following is true for both VA Loans and FHA Loans?
   1. They are both insured.
   2. Both are guaranteed.
   3. The buyer is insured by FHA with both.
   4. Both loans could have discount points to buy down the loan.

13. Public Assistance is considered
1. lawful income.
2. income not used in calculating income for a mortgage.
3. income not used in calculating income for a rental.
4. All of the above.
5.

14. When a landlord owns a four-plex in a FEMA designated flood plain and decides not to buy insurance but instead raise the air conditioners and heaters on high platforms, the owner
1. has forced insurance companies to accept his decision and pay him for new equipment in case of flood.
2. violated FEMA laws.
3. is said to be "Controlling his Risk".
4. is said to be "eliminating his risk".

15. A liquor store on the main highway was enjoying brisk business and substantial profits. The county decided to move the main highway ¼ mile away to the north of the store. This caused traffic to be re-routed and profits dropped significantly. This would be an example of?
1. Substantial misrepresentation
2. External or Economic obsolescence
3. Interior obsolescence
4. Functional Obsolescence

16. Which term describes a loan with the loan payment is less than the interest charged resulting in the outstanding balance of the loan increasing?
1. Straight Mortgage
2. Fully Amortized
3. Negative Amortization
4. Partial Payment and Interest

17. An Abstract of Title is
1. the history of the property.
2. the future recorded documents of the property.
3. the history of the recorded documents on a property.
4. an ownership title.

18. Into which bank account would a broker deposit commissions?
1. personal account
2. business account
3. escrow account
4. cash account

19. The cheapest way to handle asbestos is
1. to pull it from the floor with no protection.
2. scrap it off a building.
3. hire someone to take it out of a building.

4. encapsulation.

20. Radon
1. is an odorless colorless (radioactive) gas that may cause lung cancer.
2. is easily mitigated.
3. should be inspected and verified by a real estate broker before taking a listing.
4. Both one and two.

21. A buyer is purchasing a home in a neighborhood that has a homeowner's association. At the closing, what additional documents should the buyer receive?
1. The Neighborhood CC and R's (The covenants, conditions and restrictions) and bylaws.
2. The neighborhood nuisance disclosures.
3. The city tax disclosure and 6-month retroactive bill.
4. All of the above.

22. After the close of an escrow, who would keep for three years the Listing Agreement?
1. The customer and the client
2. The buyer and the Selling Agent
3. The Seller and the customer
4. The Client and the Seller's Agent

23. After the close of escrow, who would for three years keep the Purchase Agreement?
1. The Client
2. The Client, the Customer, the Selling Agent and the Seller's Agent
3. The Seller and the Buyer
4. The Customer and the Buyer's Agent

Answers: Exam Five

1. Who would have the most options for loans and loan programs?
2. Mortgage Broker

2. An agent brought a ready, willing and able buyer that met the terms of the contract. The broker has earned her commission
3. when the seller accepts the offer.

3. The term "Remainder" is most like?
1. When an owner conveys a life estate to one party and the remainder to another.

4. Tenancy for years is?
3. A lease with a definite beginning and a definite ending.

5. Real estate contracts must be in writing to be enforceable in court according to
2. Statue of Frauds.

6. The term "Duress" is most like
3. undue influence.

7. When a renter finds the rental to be dangerous or unsafe to live in and the landlord refuses to make repairs needed to bring the property to a safe condition, the tenant may vacate and not be responsible for the remainder of the lease. When the tenant moves, the tenant has given the landlord

3. constructive notice/eviction.

8. A lease on an apartment has ended yet the tenant keeps paying a monthly rent and the landlord keeps accepting the rent. This type of leasehold would be considered

1. a holdover tenancy.

9. The Civil Rights Act of 1968 was meant as a follow-up to the Civil Rights Act of 1964. It is called the

2. Fair Housing Act.

10. The Civil Rights Act of 1866 prohibited discrimination based on?

3. Race

11. The definition of subletting is most like?

1. The leasing of a premise by a lessee to a third party

12. Which of the following is true for both VA Loans and FHA Loans?

4. Both loans could have discount points to buy down the loan

13. Public Assistance is considered

1. lawful income.

14. When a landlord owns a four-plex in a FEMA designated flood pain and decides not to buy insurance but instead raise the air conditioners and heaters on high platforms, the owner

3. is said to be "Controlling his Risk".

15. A liquor store on the main highway was enjoying brisk business and substantial profits. The county decided to move the main highway ¼ mile away to the north of the store. This caused traffic to be re-routed and profits dropped significantly. This would be an example of?

2. External or Economic obsolescence

16. Which term describes a loan with the loan payment is less than the interest charged resulting in the outstanding balance of the loan increasing?

3. Negative Amortization

17. An Abstract of Title is

3. the history of the recorded documents on a property.

18. Into which bank account would a broker deposit commissions?

2. Business account

19. The cheapest way to handle asbestos is

4. encapsulation.

20. Radon
4. Both one and two.

21. A buyer is purchasing a home in a neighborhood that has a homeowner's association. At the closing, what additional documents should the buyer receive?
1. The Neighborhood CC and R's (The covenants, conditions and restrictions) and bylaws.

22. After the close of an escrow, who would keep for three years the Listing Agreement?
4. The Client and the Seller's Agent

23. After the close of escrow, who would for three years keep the Purchase Agreement?
2. The Client, the Customer, the Selling Agent and the Seller's Agent

1. An Environmental Impact Statement is used for what?
1. A proposed project.
2. An outdated project.
3. A private company project only.
4. A governmental project only.

2. An Environmental Impact Statement is considered a Police Power because it deals with
1. bridges.
2. boat docks.
3. health and safety.
4. animals.

3. When a person dies without a will and no heirs can be found, the property
1. escheats to the state.
2. condemnation occurs.
3. a suit for specific non-action is filed.
4. inverse condemnation occurs.

4. Escheat happens
1. because property can - not be ownerless.
2. because there are more than two people involved.
3. because local governments want to build a real estate portfolio.
4. All of the above.

5. Inverse (Reverse) Condemnation may be brought by
1. the state.
2. the city.
3. the seller.
4. the homeowner.

6. Which of the following persons would most likely seek a Conditional Use Permit or Variance?
1. A person wanting to build an addition to their home.
2. A school.
3. A property owner whose property is zoned for single family residences but wants to open a small grocery store on the property.
4. A government agency.

7. **Which of the following pertain to the present and the future owners?**
   1. Family size.
   2. Home Designs.
   3. Deed Restrictions.
   4. All of the above.

8. **Determinable Fee or Defeasible Fee are**
   1. ownership with a condition.
   2. ownership without any conditions.
   3. fee Simple Ownership.
   4. a property owned by a corporation.

9. **When a condition in a deed is violated, what happens to the property?**
   1. Nothing.
   2. It reverts back to the original grantor.
   3. The deed gets given to a public party.
   4. All of the above.

10. **All of the following deal with appraisal except**
    1. reproduction cost.
    2. replacement cost.
    3. straight line method of depreciation.
    4. valuation.

11. **Usury Laws**
    1. protects the lender.
    2. protects the borrower.
    3. protects the government.
    4. protects China.

12. **When a borrower defaults on a payment, the lender will call the entire note due and payable. The clause in the contract that allows for this is called**
    1. Acceleration Clause.
    2. Protection Clause.
    3. Defeasible Fee Clause.
    4. Santa Claus.

13. **Who would have the most options for loans and loan programs?**
    1. Mortgage Banker.
    2. Mortgage Broker.
    3. Mortgage Servicer.
    4. Mortgage Repo Guy.

14. Another term for a Straight Mortgage (interest only) is a
1. variable mortgage.
2. amortized mortgage.
3. term mortgage.
4. reverse negative mortgage.

15. An agent brought a ready, willing and able buyer to the seller. The agent has earned her commission when which of the following happens?
1. The seller gives a counter offer.
2. The buyer withdraws the offer.
3. The seller accepts the offer.
4. The broker withholds all other offers.

Answers Exam Six

1. An Environmental Impact Statement is used for what?
1. A proposed project.

2. An Environmental Impact Statement is considered a Police Power because it deals with
3. health and safety.

3. When a person dies without a will and no heirs can be found, the property
1. escheats to the state.

4. Escheat happens
1. because property can - not be ownerless.

5. Inverse (Reverse) Condemnation may be brought by
4. the homeowner.

6. Which of the following persons would most likely seek a Conditional Use Permit or Variance?
3. A property owner whose property is zoned for single family residences but wants to open a small grocery store on the property.

7. Which of the following pertain to the present and the future owners?
3. Deed Restrictions.

8. Determinable Fee or Defeasible Fee are
1. ownership with a condition.

9. When a condition in a deed is violated, what happens to the property?
2. It reverts back to the original grantor.

10. All of the following deal with appraisal except
3. straight line method of depreciation.

11. Usury Laws

2.   protects the borrower.

12. When a borrower defaults on a payment, the lender will call the entire note due and payable. The clause in the contract that allows for this is called

1.   Acceleration Clause.

13. Who would have the most options for loans and loan programs?

2.   Mortgage Broker.

14. Another term for a Straight Mortgage (interest only) is

3.   term mortgage.

15. An agent brought a ready, willing and able buyer to the seller. The agent has earned her commission when which of the following happens?

3.   The seller accepts the offer.

1. In trying to find the value of a subject home, if the subject home has a fireplace worth $5000. and the comparable doesn't, where would an appraiser make an adjustment?
1. Add $5000 to the comparable property.
2. Add $5000 to the subject property.
3. Add $2500 to the comparable.

2. Allen was making payments of principle and interest but at the end of the term, he will be paying a balloon payment to pay off the outstanding balance. What type of loan does Allen have?
1. Straight
2. Negative
3. Partially Amortized

3. The term that best describes the effect on a property when there are six bedrooms on the second story and one bathroom of the first floor would most closely be?
1. Functional Obsolescence
2. External Obsolescence
3. Economic Obsolescence

4. Bob, a professional truck driver has been granted a right of way over Dwayne's property for ingress and egress so that he can park his large commercial truck on his own property when he is not working. Which of the following could terminate the easement?
1. When Dwayne sells his property to Samuel.
2. When Dwayne installs a fence to block Bob from using it.
3. When Bob sells his truck and retires.

5. Broker Sally has an Exclusive Buyer Agreement with potential buyer Towana. Broker Sally would like to show Towana a property listed by another company. What does Sally owe the Seller?
1. Fair and Honest Dealings
2. The seller is your client.
3. You are the subagent of the seller.

6. If Broker Tommy has an Exclusive Listing Agreement with his seller, he may have a relationship with the buyer in all of the following ways except
1. A dual agency
2. Exclusively represent the Buyer
3. The buyer may be your customer.

7. **Which of the following would be a violation of federal fair housing laws?**
    1. Refusing to rent to a person who has a comfort dog because you own a non-pet building.
    2. A 55+ community refused to rent to a woman with under-aged children based on familial status.
    3. The owner lives in his four-unit apartment building and refuses to rent to families.

8. **A landlord may do which of the following without being in violation of federal fair housing laws?**
    1. Demand that a vacating tenant remove the wheelchair ramp they installed before they move out.
    2. Segregating families with children into specific areas of his complex.
    3. Refusing to rent to a person because he does not want to install a wheel chair ramp.

9. **A very old oak tree or a very large boulder**
    1. Lots and Blocks
    2. Rectangular Survey System
    3. Metes and Bounds

10. **Who do Usury Laws protect?**
    1. Banks
    2. The consumer
    3. Mortgage Brokers

11. **Bob is selling his mid-century modern home. He has built a free-standing wall with bookshelves on one side to separate the dining room from the living room. When Bob sells the property, this free-standing wall will be considered?**
    1. Personal property
    2. Real property
    3. Trade Fixtures

12. **Billy and Scott were recently married. Both of them have never owned real estate. They decided to purchase their home with a FHA loan. What would be the advantage for them in choosing the FHA loan?**
    1. Buyer insurance with the FHA.
    2. Their down payment could be as low as 3.5%.
    3. FHA insuring the bank will get their money.

13. **It is meant to protect an owner's or a lender's financial interest in real property against loss due to title defects.**
    1. FHA Insurance
    2. Homeowners Insurance
    3. Title Insurance

14. To what date does title insurance insure up to?
   1. The date that it's issued.
   2. The date of the transaction.
   3. The date the purchase agreement was accepted.

15. An agent was showing a potential buyer a home. As they were walking up the driveway, the agent noticed that the property has nine missing roof tiles. The agent notified the Seller's Agent. The Seller's Agent and the Client denied there were missing tiles. What should they agent do?
   1. Inform the buyer that you were wrong about the missing tiles.
   2. Inform the buyer that the seller said tiles were not missing.
   3. Disclose in writing to the Buyer that there are tiles missing.

16. Two months after a buyer moved into his new home, he noticed there were several roof tiles missing. The missing tiles allowed rain to damage the interior walls. He asked his agent to repair the damage. Would his agent be allowed to keep his commission?
   1. No, because he is responsible for damages after the transfer.
   2. Yes. The purchase agreement is between the Seller and buyer.
   3. Yes but he is obligated to help the new owner make repairs.

17. An agent knowingly misleads the purchaser of a property as to where his property lines were. The new owner discovered the misrepresentation when he hired a contractor to build a fence on his property line. What could the agent be responsible for?
   1. Actual Damages or Financial Damages.
   2. Nothing. The buyer should have hired a surveyor before he made the offer to purchase.
   3. He will be forced to buy the property.

18. The listing broker failed to disclose to the buyer's agent that a felony was committed on the property. Is he required to disclose that information?
   1. No because the property has been renovated
   2. Yes because a felony is a material fact.
   3. No because a felony is not a material fact.

19. Brokers from Lazy Realty were in their weekly meeting. They were discussing how Ripped Realty charges a fee for a service that both companies do at a much higher price. What should the brokers do?
   1. Reduce their fee to match Ripped Realty
   2. Nothing
   3. Raise their fee.

20. Sellers and landlords must disclose known lead - based paint and lead - based paint hazards and provide available reports to buyers or renters for homes built before what year?
   1. 1978
   2. 1866
   3. 1986

21. The Lead Based Paint Disclosure Act allows a buyer or renter of a property built before 1978 to inspect the property in ten days. What else is the buyer or renter required to be given?
   1. A three day right of rescission.
   2. The government booklet "Protect Your Family From Lead Based Paint.
   3. Estoppel Certificates.

22. What is the most prevalent latent lead product found on a property?
   1. Lead paint.
   2. Lead based cleaners.
   3. Lead pipes.

23. During the final inspection, the buyer noticed that the seller had removed the built in stereo speakers in the den. There are now large holes in the walls. Was the seller allowed to remove them?
   1. Yes because they were connected to the seller's stereo which was not annexed onto the real property.
   2. No because the property must be delivered to the buyer in the same condition as when the contract was signed. (in place)
   3. Yes because it was the seller's personal property.

24. While moving her furniture into her new home, Suong realized that the seller had removed the window boxes containing perennial roses. Is the seller responsible for returning them?
   1. Yes, because they were fixtures attached to the home.
   2. No, because they were personal property.
   3. No, because her agent told her to take them.

25. Bob and Rick owned a liquor store and were experiencing brisk business. The county built a main highway diverting traffic away from their store. What term best describes this situation?
   1. Internal obsolescence
   2. Depreciation
   3. External obsolescence

26. What is the best example of a "Less Than Arm's Length" transaction?
1. A conveyance between two strangers.
2. A broker purchased a listing he had with a client.
3. A mother sold her daughter the family home for 75% of the true market value.

Answers Exam Seven

1. In trying to find the value of a subject home, if the subject home has a fireplace worth $5000. and the comparable doesn't, where would an appraiser make an adjustment?
1. Add $5000 to the comparable property.

2. Allen was making payments of principle and interest but at the end of the term, he will be paying a balloon payment to pay off the outstanding balance. What type of loan does Allen have?
3. Partially Amortized

3. The term that best describes the effect on a property when there are six bedrooms on the second story and one bathroom of the first floor would most closely be?
1. Functional Obsolescence

4. Bob, a professional truck driver has been granted a right of way over Dwayne's property for ingress and egress so that he can park his large commercial truck on his own property when he is not working. Which of the following could terminate the easement?
3. When Bob sells his truck and retires.

5. Broker Sally has an Exclusive Buyer Agreement with potential buyer Towanda. Broker Sally would like to show Towanda a property listed by another company. What does Sally owe the Seller?
1. Fair and Honest Dealings

6. If Broker Tommy has an Exclusive Listing Agreement with his seller, he may have a relationship with the buyer in all of the following ways except
2. Exclusively represent the Buyer at the detriment to the seller

7. Which of the following would be a violation of federal fair housing laws?
1. Refusing to rent to a person who has a comfort dog because you own a non-pet building.

8. A landlord may do which of the following without being in violation of federal fair housing laws?
1. Demand that a vacating tenant remove the wheelchair ramp they installed before they move out.

9. A very old oak tree or a very large boulder
3. Metes and Bounds

10. Who do Usury Laws protect?

2. The consumer

11. Bob is selling his mid-century modern home. He has built a free-standing wall with bookshelves on one side to separate the dining room from the living room. When Bob sells the property, this free-standing wall will be considered?
1. Personal property

12. Billy and Scott were recently married. Both of them have never owned real estate. They decided to purchase their home with a FHA loan. What would be the advantage for them in choosing the FHA loan?
2. Their down payment could be as low as 3.5%.

13. What is meant to protect an owner's or a lender's financial interest in real property against loss due to title defects.
3. Title Insurance

14. To what date does title insurance insure up to?
1. The date that it's issued.

15. An agent was showing a potential buyer a home. As they were walking up the driveway, the agent noticed that the property has nine missing roof tiles. The agent notified the Seller's Agent. The Seller's Agent and the Client denied there were missing tiles. What should they agent do?
3. Disclose in writing to the Buyer and Seller's Agent that there are tiles missing.

16. Two months after a buyer moved into his new home, he noticed there were several roof tiles missing. The missing tiles allowed rain to damage the interior walls. He asked his agent to repair the damage. Would his agent be allowed to keep his commission?
2. Yes. The purchase agreement is between the Seller and buyer.

17. An agent knowingly misleads the purchaser of a property as to where his property lines were. The new owner discovered the misrepresentation when he hired a contractor to build a fence on his property line. What could the agent be responsible for?
1. Actual Damages or Financial Damages.

18. The listing broker failed to disclose to the buyer's agent that a felony was committed on the property. Is he required to disclose that information?
3. No because a felony is not a material fact.

19. Brokers from Lazy Realty were in their weekly meeting. They were discussing how Ripped Realty charges a much higher fee for the same services. What should the brokers do?
2. Nothing Brokers cannot price fix.

20. Sellers and landlords must disclose known lead - based paint and lead - based paint hazards and provide available reports to buyers or renters for homes built before what year?

1. 1978

21. The Lead Based Paint Disclosure Act allows a buyer or renter of a property built before 1978 to inspect the property in ten days. What else is the buyer or renter required to be given?

2. The government booklet "Protect Your Family from Lead Based Paint.

22. What is the most prevalent latent lead product found on a property?

3. Lead pipes.

23. During the final inspection, the buyer noticed that the seller had removed the built in stereo speakers in the den. There are now large holes in the walls. Was the seller allowed to remove them?

2. No because the property must be delivered to the buyer in the same condition as when the contract was signed. (in place)

24. While moving her furniture into her new home, Al realized that the seller had removed the window boxes containing perennial roses. Is the seller responsible for returning them?

1. Yes, because they were fixtures attached to the home.

25. Bob and Rick owned a liquor store and were experiencing brisk business. The county built a main highway diverting traffic away from their store. What term best describes this situation?

3. External obsolescence

26. What is the best example of a "Less Than Arm's Length" transaction?

3. A mother sold her daughter the family home for 75% of the true market value.

1. A CMA is based on which appraisal technique?
1. Market Data
2. Cost Approach.
3. GRM

2. A CMA is predominately utilized by an agent to help a seller determine a listing range. What do the initials CMA stand for?
1. Complementary Market Analysis
2. Complete Monetary Action
3. Comparative Market Analysis

3. What are the four stages of a neighborhood?
1. growth, stability, decline, revitalization.
2. stability, growth, decline, revitalization.
3. growth, decline, revitalization, stability.

4. Outdated cabinets and fixtures would be an example of which of the following?
1. Incurable functional obsolescence.
2. Curable functional obsolescence.
3. Curable external obsolescence.

5. Which of the following would be used as a comparable when an appraiser is determining the value of a single-family residence?
1. The home that just closed yesterday and located one street over.
2. The same home floor plan built by the same contractor using the same materials three towns over.
3. The home for sale next door.

6. What is a deed restriction?
1. A police power
2. A zoning ordinance.
3. A limitation on use.

7. What is a good example of a buffer zone?
1. A large park between an office building and a single-family residence neighborhood.
2. A coffee shop between office buildings and a park.
3. A subway station between a city and the suburbs.

8. Which of the following is a material popular in the 1970's and 1980's used for insulation? It was pumped between the walls.
1. Pesticides
2. UFFI Urea Formaldehyde Foam Insulation (UFF or UFFI)
3. Brownfields

9. **Which of the following is not a police power?**
   1. deed restrictions
   2. eminent domain
   3. environmental protection laws

10. **How many square feet in an acre?**
    1. 43,560
    2. 55,000
    3. 640

11. **A developer would like to arrange for a loan on a large piece of land he plans to subdivide, record and develop.**
    1. Subdivision Mortgage
    2. Blanket Mortgage
    3. Package Mortgage

12. **A commercial tenant has a triple net lease. What expenses will he be paying?**
    1. The landlord's property taxes.
    2. His rent and the landlord pays all of his electric and gas payments.
    3. His rent plus some of the landlord expenses.

13. **Is a Judicial Foreclosure a legal event?**
    1. No
    2. It depends on factors leading to the foreclosure.
    3. Yes

14. **An agent told an older couple that he would show them the most beautiful house in the best neighborhood. When the couple got to the property, they felt it was nice but there were also equally nice properties in the area. What was the agent doing?**
    1. Puffing
    2. Negligent Misrepresentation.
    3. He was not practicing Care.

15. **What antitrust law would Tran and Bob be guilty of if they got together and decided not to do business with Arthur to stamp out the competition?**
    1. CERCLA.
    2. RESPA
    3. Antitrust – Sherman Antitrust.

16. **An agent showed a couple with 10 children properties only in neighborhoods where a bunch of other large families lived. The couple requested to see other neighborhoods as well but the agent declined their request. The agent may be guilty of what fair housing law?**
    1. Blockbusting
    2. Steering
    3. Redlining

17. **What is the minimum amount of time that a person or married couple needs to live in their primary residence in order to qualify for a capital gains exclusion?**

1. Three out of the last six years.
2. Two of the last five years.
3. Three out of the last five years.

18. What is the capital gains exclusion on a primary residence for a single person and a married couple?
1. $250,000 for a single person and $500,000 for a married couple.
2. $250,000 for both singles and married couples.
3. $100,000 for a single person and $250,000 for a married couple.

19. Toyota will be opening an auto factory in Small Town, USA within 12 months and will be creating 3000 new jobs. Several sellers decided to wait and sell their homes after the construction is complete because they believe their value will increase. What real estate theory do they believe?
1. Anticipation
2. Alienation
3. Novation

20. An investor wished to sell one of his town homes. What type of account should be set up for him to be able to reinvest his profit while deferring taxes?
1. 1099 misc. account
2. 1031 tax deferred exchange
3. **Capital Gains Exclusion Account**

21. When an attorney reads and interprets a Chain of Title, what is it called?
1. Abstract and Testimonial
2. Opinion and Guarantee
3. Abstract and Opinion

22. It protects an owner of a property or the mortgagee's financial interest in real estate against loss due to title defects, blemishes and liens.
1. Title Insurance
2. FHA Insurance
3. VA Guarantees

23. What is the recorded history of a property called?
1. Title Insurance
2. Chain of Title
3. Abstract and Opinion

24. What is the legal concept that gives the owner of real estate all legal rights such as possession, disposition and exclusion?
1. Power of Attorney
2. Reverse Condemnation
3. Bundle of Rights

25. If the closing attorney and both agents disagree as to where an earnest money deposit should go, who is it given to?
1. It's turned over to the court to decide.
2. It always goes back to the buyer.
3. It's split three ways.

26. Bob the Broker is a laissez faire manager. Instead of training his new agents, he provides them with manuals. An agent in Bob's office accidently disclosed some wrong information to a potential buyer. Whose responsible for the mistakes?
1. The agent
2. Bob the Broker and the agent
3. Bob the Broker only.

27. An agent and her client noticed mold around the plumbing at several locations on the property. Who should disclose this to potential buyers?
1. The buyer's agent.
2. The Seller, his agent and the buyer's agent.
3. The Seller's Agent.

28. A buyer gave an earnest money check to his Broker on Friday and the Broker deposited the check into his personal bank account on Saturday. What did the broker do?
1. Comingling
2. Negligent Misrepresentation
3. Arbitration

29. Which of the following may not necessarily cancel a contract?
1. Death of the Broker
2. The property burns down.
3. Insanity of the Broker

30. Sam and Al were in escrow. Sam was to buy Al's home. After the contract was executed and before the transaction was completed, Al's Broker called Sam's Broker to inform Sam that the property had a terrible fire last night and the entire structure is destroyed. Will Sam be forced into completing the contract to purchase Al's now destroyed property?
    1. No, when the deed is conveyed everything with the property must be "in place" as it was when the offer was accepted.
    2. No, because Al didn't have insurance on the home since there was no mortgage. Insurance will not replace the home before closing.
    3. Yes, because Sam already started paying a pre-insurance on the property.

31. What antitrust law would Tran and Bob be guilty of if they got together and both brokers decided not to do business with Arthur?
    1. Laches
    2. Sherman Antitrust Act.
    3. Regulation Z.

32. Carol represented Derrick in the purchase of Derrick's 20-unit apartment building. When the transaction was completed, Derrick asked Carol if she would like to manage the property for him. Carol accepted. What type of agent is Carol?
    1. Special
    2. General
    3. Universal

33. Bob could not afford a mortgage payment presented by his loan banker. The loan banker suggested that Bob should buy down the interest rate. What was the banker suggesting Bob to pay?
    1. Principle and Commission Only
    2. P & I
    3. Discount Points

34. Alice gave a small loan to Betty and recorded the note. After two years, Betty decided she would like to take out a larger mortgage. Betty asked Alice if she would sign a document to put her smaller loan into a second (junior lien position) position so that the bank would lend her $200,000. What document was Betty asking Alice to sign?
    1. Superfund - CERCLA – Brownfield Agreement
    2. Subordination Agreement.
    3. Purchase Agreement

35. What is the secondary mortgage market?
    1. Banks buying and selling loans to each other.
    2. A Consumer who applies for a loan at a credit union.
    3. FHA lending a consumer a guaranteed loan.

36. Which of the following could be considered a balloon payment?
1. Party Payments
2. The largest payment is paid as points.
3. A large balance due on a mortgage at a predetermined future date.

37. To find the value of a library, an appraiser would use which of the following to determine value?
1. Research the market data of sold buildings within a ten-mile radius of the library.
2. Find the replacement cost of the building and then add in the value of the land.
3. Find a comparable library that sold in the last six Months.

38. Which approach to value would an appraiser use to determine the value of Graceland?
1. Replacement Cost with new materials and add in the land.
2. Comparable Method.
3. Market Data and Reconciliation

39. In which of the following would the Cost Approach likely to be used?
1. A six-year-old SFR within a gated Community.
2. A five-year-old condo.
3. New construction.

40. An older woman decided not to list her home with Broker Carl because she believes the value of her home will increase when the new proposed highway is expanded into her area. What best describes her decision?
1. Alienation
2. Anticipation
3. Reverse Condemnation.

41. What does not contribute to value?
1. locations, situs and area preference
2. supply and demand and permanence.
3. Performance.

42. A developer built a new home community where the demand for his homes was great. Which home would most likely be sold for the least?
1. The last one.
2. The first one.
3. The one best negotiated

43. What does a home warranty cover?
1. Quality of workmanship.
2. It covers the seller against any latent defects that may show up to the new owner.
3. Plumbing and heating.

Answers Exam Eight

424

1. A CMA is based on which appraisal technique?
1. Market Data

2. A CMA is predominately utilized by an agent to help a seller determine a listing range. What do the initials CMA stand for?
3. Comparative Market Analysis

3. What are the four stages of a neighborhood?
1. growth, stability, decline, revitalization.

4. Outdated cabinets and fixtures would be an example of which of the following?
2. Curable functional obsolescence.

5. Which of the following would be used as a comparable when an appraiser is determining the value of a single-family residence?
1. The home that just closed yesterday and located one street over.

6. What is a deed restriction?
3. A limitation on use.

7. What is a good example of a buffer zone?
1. A large park between an office building and a single-family residence neighborhood.

8. Which of the following is a material popular in the 1970's and 1980's used for insulation? It was pumped between the walls.
2. UFFI Urea Formaldehyde Foam Insulation (UFF or UFFI)

9. Which of the following is not a police power?
1. deed restrictions

10. How many square feet in an acre?
1. 43,560

11. A developer would like to arrange for a loan on a large piece of land he plans to subdivide, record and develop.
2. Blanket Mortgage

12. A commercial tenant has a triple net lease. What expenses will he be paying?
3. His rent plus some of the landlord expenses.

13. Is a Judicial Foreclosure a legal event?
3. Yes

14. An agent told an older couple that he would show them the most beautiful house in the best neighborhood. When the couple got to the property, they felt it was nice but there were also equally nice properties in the area. What was the agent doing?
1. Puffing

15. What antitrust law would Tran and Bob be guilty of if they got together and decided not to do business with Arthur to stamp out the competition?

3. Antitrust – Sherman Antitrust.

16. An agent showed a couple with 10 children properties only in neighborhoods where a bunch of other large families lived. The couple requested to see other neighborhoods as well but the agent declined their request. The agent may be guilty of what fair housing law?

2. Steering

17. What is the minimum amount of time that a person or married couple needs to live in their primary residence in order to qualify for a capital gains exclusion?

2. Two of the last five years.

18. What is the capital gains exclusion on a primary residence for a single person and a married couple?

1. $250,000 for a single person and $500,000 for a married couple.

19. Toyota will be opening an auto factory in Small Town, USA within 12 months and will be creating 3000 new jobs. Several sellers decided to wait and sell their homes after the construction is complete because they believe their value will increase. What real estate theory do they believe?

1. Anticipation

20. An investor wished to sell one of his town homes. What type of account should be set up for him to be able to reinvest his profit while deferring taxes?

2. 1031 tax deferred exchange

21. When an attorney reads and interprets a Chain of Title, what is it called?

3. Abstract and Opinion

22. It protects an owner of a property or the mortgagee's financial interest in real estate against loss due to title defects, blemishes and liens.

1. Title Insurance

23. What is the recorded history of a property called?

2. Chain of Title

24. What is the legal concept that gives the owner of real estate all legal rights such as possession, disposition and exclusion?

3. Bundle of Rights

25. If the closing attorney and both agents disagree as to where an earnest money deposit should go, who is it given to?

1. It's turned over to the court to decide.

26. Bob the Broker is a laissez faire manager. Instead of training his new agents, he provides them with manuals. An agent in Bob's office accidently disclosed some wrong information to a potential buyer. Whose responsible for the mistakes?

2. Bob the Broker and the agent

27. An agent and her client noticed mold around the plumbing at several locations on the property. Who should disclose this to potential buyers?

2. The Seller, his agent and the buyer's agent.

28. A buyer gave an earnest money check to his Broker on Friday and the Broker deposited the check into his personal bank account on Saturday. What did the broker do?

1. Comingling

29. Which of the following may not necessarily cancel a contract?

2. The property burns down.

30. Sam and Al were in escrow. Sam was to buy Al's home. After the contract was executed and before the transaction was completed, Al's Broker called Sam's Broker to inform Sam that the property had a terrible fire last night and the entire structure is destroyed. Will Sam be forced into completing the contract to purchase Al's now destroyed property?

1. No, when the deed is conveyed everything with the property must be "in place" as it was when the offer was accepted.

31. What antitrust law would Tran and Bob be guilty of if they got together and both brokers decided not to do business with Arthur?

2. Sherman Antitrust Act.

32. Carol represented Derrick in the purchase of Derrick's 20-unit apartment building. When the transaction was completed, Derrick asked Carol if she would like to manage the property for him. Carol accepted. What type of agent is Carol?

2. General

33. Bob could not afford a mortgage payment presented by his loan banker. The loan banker suggested that Bob should buy down the interest rate. What was the banker suggesting Bob to pay?

3. Discount Points

34. Alice gave a small loan to Betty and recorded the note. After two years, Betty decided she would like to take out a larger mortgage. Betty asked Alice if she would sign a document to put her smaller loan into a second (junior lien position) position so that the bank would lend her $200,000. What document was Betty asking Alice to sign?

2. Subordination Agreement.

35. What is the secondary mortgage market?

1. Banks buying and selling loans to each other.

36. Which of the following could be considered a balloon payment?

3. A large balance due on a mortgage at a predetermined future date.

37. To find the value of a library, an appraiser would use which of the following to determine value?

2. Find the replacement cost of the building and then add in the value of the land.

38. Which approach to value would an appraiser use to determine the value of Graceland?

1. Replacement Cost with new materials and add in the land.

39. In which of the following would the Cost Approach likely to be used?

3. New construction.

40. An older woman decided not to list her home with Broker Carl because she believes the value of her home will increase when the new proposed highway is expanded into her area. What best describes her decision?

2. Anticipation

41. What does not contribute to value?

3. Performance.

42. A developer built a new home community where the demand for his homes was great. Which home would most likely be sold for the least?

2. The first one.

43. What does a home warranty cover?

3. Plumbing and heating.

Exam Nine

1. Bob and Patty have a verbal long term lease. According to the statute of frauds, If Bob breaches the agreement, Patty
1. Could not sue Bob in court because verbal agreements are unenforceable.
2. Would be successful in a court of law because Bob breached the contract.
3. Could sue Bob but an arbitration board would hear the case.
4. Could not sue Bob because the arbitration committee would refer the case to HUD.

2. At closing, which fees are prorated between the Seller and the Buyer?
1. Homeowners insurance.
2. Repair fees
3. Taxes
4. The mortgage late payments.

3. Patty acquired a loan from Mega Bank USA. The loan was secured on her new home and the furniture that was inside. The type of loan that Patty has is an?
1. Blanket Loan
2. Balloon payment loan.
3. Equity loan
4. Package loan.

4. Broker Bob received an offer on Seller Carl's home. The offeror gave Carl six days to decide if he would accept the offer. On day four, the offer wasn't accepted and the offeror instructed Broker Bob to withdraw his offer. In this case.
1. The offeror is entitled to his earnest money deposit because he withdrew the offer before the seller accepted the offer.
2. The offeror is not entitled to a refund of his earnest money deposit because the seller had planned to accept the offer later that afternoon.
3. The offeror's earnest money deposit is given to the seller because the offeror breached the contract.
4. Under no circumstances is the offeror entitled to an earnest money deposit once the offer is made.

5. Real Property includes all of the following except
1. water rights.
2. oak trees.
3. chattel.
4. rose bushes.

6. Two years ago the market was hot in City Ville. Homes were selling as fast as builders could build them. Several developers purchased land, got the required permits and built as many homes as they felt the market could handle. Now there are complete communities of vacant homes. The price of new homes in City Ville most likely will
   1. Increased in value.
   2. Decreased in value.
   3. Values will remain the same.
   4. Older home values will increase.

7. What section in a township is set aside for schools?
   1. section 6
   2. section 12
   3. section 16
   4. section 14

8. Metes and Bounds is associated with
   1. point of beginning.
   2. Meridians.
   3. Baselines
   4. Rectangles.

9. The family of an established farm is afraid the new farm upstream will divert water away from their farm. What water right may the established farm owners have?
   1. littoral
   2. riparian
   3. encroachment
   4. prior appropriation.

10. Bob, a truck driver, has an easement where he benefits. It allows him to have a wide ingress and egress so that he can store his very large truck when he is not driving it. How could this easement be terminated?
   1. The servient tenement holder rejects Bob's right for ingress and egress.
   2. Bob retires from truck driving, sells his truck and wants to end the easement.
   3. When the servient tenement holder buys a bigger truck and access for Bob's truck is narrowed.
   4. When Bob sells his truck.

11. Sally wants to have the highest protection of ownership when she purchases a new home. Sally should request what type of deed?
   1. General Warranty Deed
   2. Special Warranty Deed
   3. Quitclaim Deed
   4. Title Insurance

12. From the first day of ownership, four college students could not agree how to proceed the best way for their 400-unit apartment complex they purchased as Joint Tenants. They would like to divide the property so that each of them can do what they think is best. The four college students could go to court to dissolve the Joint Tenancy by requesting a?
    1. Manager
    2. Home Owners Association
    3. Trustor
    4. Partition

13. What are the two most important duties of a notary public?
    1. To make sure the person signing is not a felon and to report to the police if the signer has a criminal record.
    2. To make sure that the person signing is who they are and that the document is properly dated.
    3. To make sure the person is who they are and to make sure they have a witness to their signing.
    4. To make sure the person is who they claim to be and that their signing is voluntary.

14. The type of ownership known for double taxation is which of the following?
    1. LLC
    2. S Corporation
    3. Corporation
    4. REIT

15. When no specific type of co-ownership is stated in a deed, what type deed is presumed to be granted?
    1. General Warranty Deed
    2. Joint Tenancy
    3. Tenant in Common
    4. Tenants by the Entirety.

16. Investor have decided to create a limited partnership. What would be the benefit?
    1. Their losses are limited up to their investment.
    2. They would like to actively participate in the venture.
    3. The tax consequences are favorable.
    4. All of the above.

17. Corporations may take title in which of the following ways?
    1. Tenants by the Entirety or Joint Tenants
    2. Joint tenants and tenants in common
    3. In Severalty or joint Tenants
    4. in Severalty

18. Three Tenants in Common would like to dissolve their relationship on the ownership of a large commercial property. The best way to dissolve their ownership relationship would be to?
   1. Go to court and obtain a partition.
   2. Will their interests to their heirs?
   3. Write up a codicil.
   4. Turn the property over to a trustee.

19. What is the effect of recording a deed into public record?
   1. Letting the world acknowledge a warranty forever.
   2. Giving the world constructive notice.
   3. Title certification
   4. Intentional Notice

20. When a potential buyer inspects the recorded documents of a property and inspects the actual property, what type notice is he given?
   1. Constructive notice
   2. Intentional notice
   3. Accrued Notice.
   4. Actual Notice

Answers Exam Nine

1. Bob and Patty have a verbal long term lease. According to the statute of frauds, If Bob breaches the agreement, Patty
1. Could not sue Bob in court because verbal agreements are unenforceable.

2. At closing, which fees are prorated between the Seller and the Buyer?
3. Taxes

3. Patty acquired a loan from Mega Bank USA. The loan was secured on her new home and the furniture that was inside. The type of loan that Patty has is an?
4. Package loan.

4. Broker Bob received an off on Seller Carl's home. The offeror gave Carl six days to decide if he would accept the offer. On day four, the offer wasn't accepted and the offeror instructed Broker Bob to withdraw his offer. In this case.
1. The offeror is entitled to his earnest money deposit because he withdrew the offer before the seller accepted the offer.

5. Real Property includes all of the following except
3. chattel.

6.. Two years ago the market was hot in City Ville. Homes were selling as fast as builders could build them. Several developers purchased land, got the required permits and built as many homes as they felt the market could handle. Now there are complete communities of vacant homes. The price of new homes in City Ville most likely will

2. Decreased in value.

7. What section in a township is set aside for schools?
3. section 16

8. Metes and Bounds is associated with
1. point of beginning.

9. The family of an established farm is afraid the new farm upstream will divert water away from their farm. What water right may the established farm owners have?
4. prior appropriation.

10. Bob, a truck driver, has an easement where he benefits. It allows him to have a wide ingress and egress so that he can store his very large truck when he is not driving it. How could this easement be terminated?
2. Bob retires from truck driving, sells his truck and wants to end the easement.

11. Sally wants to have the highest protection of ownership when she purchases a new home. Sally should request what type of deed?
1. General Warranty Deed

12. From the first day of ownership, four college students could not agree how to proceed the best way for their 400-unit apartment complex they purchased as Joint Tenants. They would like to divide the property so that each of them can do what they think is best. The four college students could go to court to dissolve the Joint Tenancy by requesting a?
4. Partition

13. What are the two most important duties of a notary public?
4. To make sure the person is who they claim to be and that their signing is voluntary.

14. The type of ownership known for double taxation is which of the following?
3. Corporation

15. When no specific type of co-ownership is stated in a deed, what type deed is presumed to be granted?
3. Tenants in Common

16. Investor have decided to create a limited partnership. What would be the benefit?
1. Their losses are limited up to their investment.

17. Corporations may take title in which of the following ways?
4. in Severalty

18. Three Tenants in Common would like to dissolve their relationship on the ownership of a large commercial property. The best way to dissolve their ownership relationship p would be to?

1. Go to court and obtain a partition.

19. What is the effect of recording a deed into public record?
2. Giving the world constructive notice.

20. When a potential buyer inspects the recorded documents of a property and inspects the actual property, what type notice is he given?
4. Actual Notice

Chapter Twenty-One

Student Gifts to Students

Part One

1. **Avulsion**- a tearing away of land due to an earthly violent event. It's sudden.

> Example; a sweeping swollen river swept away an outcropping of land or an earthquake tore away some land. The exam may say that the two ends of a barrier island got washed away during a hurricane.

2. **A Specific lien** is specifically attached to the property. A **voluntary specific lien** would be financing a swimming pool. An **involuntary specific lien** would be taxes or a mechanics lien.

3. An example of a right, improvement or privilege that belongs to and conveys with a property is an **appurtenance**.

> **"In addition to"**. (Example an **easement appurtenant** is ownership of a property with a **right of way** over someone else's property. Example: Tom owns his homestaed in addition to a right away over Bob's property. Appurtenant may also be the percentage ownership of a parking structure owned by a condominium owner. You own the condo "in addition to" a portion of the parking structure

4. The last entities to receive money after **probate** are the **heirs**. The first **liens** to be paid are taxes. (Taxes include **Ad Valorem** and **Special Assessments**.)

5. **Private Restriction**: vs. **Public Restriction**

Private Restrictions
A Deed Restriction
A Limitation on Use
An example would be purchasing a home in a town that doesn't allow the owner to cut down any oak trees on his property. Even though the owner holds the title to the property, he is limited or restricted on his own land.

Public Restrictions
Zoning
Home Owners Association Rules
Environmental Hazards (what materials can be stored on the real property)
Public Easements and Rights of Way

6. **General lien vs. specific lien**. – need to know the difference

Specific Liens
Specific liens are liens specifically on a single property.
Mortgage liens and Trust Deeds
Property taxes are also liens
Ad Valorem taxes, meaning according to value.
Special Assessments: A special assessment is an added tax that is paid for by the people who benefit from an improvement.
Taxes take priority.
Mechanics liens

General Liens
General liens are liens on everything you own.
A judgment
Inheritance taxes
Income tax
Debts due of a deceased person
A General lien could be a lien on several properties one person owns.

7. **Testate vs. Intestate**

Testate with will – two syllables His will passes by **devise**. Executor's deed	**Intestate** with out will – three syllables His property passes by descent and distribution. Administrator's deed

8. If a person dies intestate and the state cannot find any living heirs, his property will escheat to the state. Land cannot be ownerless.

9. **Divisor** is the giver of the property when he testate. Devisee is the one inheriting the property. (OR OR is the GIVOR......EE EE is the Gimmee the Propertee.)

10. **Land**- Real Estate,. Land does not depreciate.

11. When **title** is granted in a **life estate** the person will own the property until he dies.

12. **Adverse Possession** - open, notorious, hostile and continuous possession. It's a taking of legal title from another person by meeting the statutory amount of time of open, notorious, hostile and continuous possession.

13. When the seller can furnish title insurance, the buyer can be assured he is getting fee simple title. (highest form of ownership)

14. If a homeowner is concerned that the construction project next door is encroaching on her property, she should hire a surveyor.

15. Paintings and furniture are personal property and are transferred by Bill of Sale.

16. The four unities of joint tenancy are time, title, interest and possession. The only unity for **Tenancy In Common** is possession.

17. The last surviving person owning as joint tenants owns the property themselves. JTWROS – Joint Tenancy with Rights of Survivorship.

18. When a husband and wife own property as **Tenant by the Entirety**, they both need to sign the listing agreement even if one spouse has a large amount of unpaid debt. With **Tenancy by the Entirety** the husband is a ½ person and the wife is a ½ person. The listing agreement needs at least one full person to sign.

19. If a tenant wants to sell his interest in the property and his partners do not, he can get a **suit to partition** and sell his interest only.

20. If a joint tenant is granted a **suit to partition**, the owners are now tenants in common.

21. A Tenancy by the Entirety cannot be partitioned.

22. A limited partner's liability is limited to his investment. General partners run the business.

23. Timeshare owners hold title as Tenants in Common. Several people own one unit.

24. You can will your interest in real estate if you own as **Tenancy in Common**.

25. Ownership in a resort condominium which allows the owner a specific amount of occupancy each year is a timeshare.

26. If your buyer wants to get a divorce before her and her husband complete a transaction to purchase a home, you should tell her to go see an attorney.

27. Common elements in a condominium do not include the owner's assigned parking spot.

28. In a Cooperative (Co-op) or (stock cooperative) a person owns stock in a corporation that owns the building in which he lives. The amount of stock could identify the square footage of his unit. They look very similar to a condo. A Cooperative is considered personal property because the residents own the stock and not the building. Stock is chattel. If a stockholder doesn't pay his mortgage, the other stock holders will have to pay his shares in order for the corporation to avoid loan default.

29. A condominium cannot eminent domain the three homes adjacent to their parking lot in order to expand the condo's parking lot.

30. A water company may lay pipes upon private property through an **easement in gross**. Easement in gross is for utility companies. An easement in gross does not have a dominant tenement.

31. Bob allowed Tom to hunt on his farm during hunting season. This is a **license**. A license is a revocable right that is temporary.

32. A judgment is not necessarily an **encumbrance**.

33. All property liens are encumbrances.

34. An **easement by necessity** is important to a land locked property.

35. **Condominium- Fee-simple** (the highest form of ownership) Ownership includes a share in the common elements. It's a condo. You own your unit and what's in it. You also own a portion of the common areas like the pool, elevators, hallways, and entryway. The ownership interest in the common area are appurtenances.

36. A corporation pays double taxation. An "S Corporation" is considered a pass thru company.

37. File Form IRS 8300 for cash transfers of $10,000 or over

38. Caveat Emptor vs. Caveat Venditor

Caveat Emptor Buyer beware	**Caveat Venditor** Seller beware

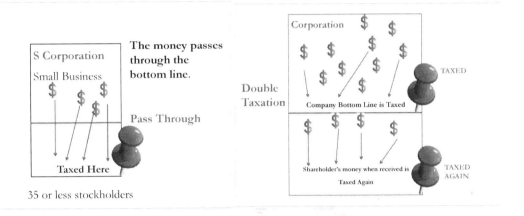

39. **Home Owners Association– CC and R's**. At the close the buyer will receive additional paperwork.

40. The homeowners enforce the CC and Rs in a Neighborhood Association.

41. The wall on the outside patio between two townhomes (garden homes) is called a **party wall.**

42. A husband and wife took ownership of their real estate in Joint tenants to avoid probate.

43. A landowner who sells his farm must specifically reserve the mineral rights or they will automatically pass to the buyer.

44. **Emblements** - Crops that require annual planting and harvesting. Examples are corn, peas, beans, tomatoes, cucumbers, and squash. They are personal property. If a tenant farmer has planted his yearly crops and then gets evicted before the crops are ready for harvest, the landlord cannot touch the crops. The crops of the evicted

439

farmer tenant are his personal property. The farmer is allowed to maintain the crops and harvest them. A farmer is entitled to the fruits of his labor

45. The furniture in your house is **personal property.**

46. **Real property** is land and the area below and above the surface to infinity and all of the improvements thereon. **Service, Subsurface and air rights**.

47. The intention of the party who annexed a **fixture** to real property is the most important factor in determining if something is real or personal. (Example: Was the freestanding refrigerator enclosed into the cabinets meant to be a permanent fixture? The intention of the owners who moved it into place and installed it will determine the answer.

48. The price of a fixture does not determine if it is real or personal.

49. Standing timber is **real property**. A vineyard is **real property**.

50. When lumber or bricks are left on a driveway in order for the homeowner to build a new fence, they are considered **personal property.** They are still movable. Once the lumber or bricks are built into a wall, it is now annexed and become real property. They are fixtures.

51. Once planted oranges and apple trees are real estate. If an orange or apple falls from the tree, it becomes personal property.

52. Crops planted yearly are personal property called **emblements**. (chattel)

53. A **lease** is personal property. (**Leasehold**) It's a piece of paper that gives a lessee the right to live in a landlord's real property. You can pick up a piece of paper and move it. **Real property** is immovable. Stock is also personal. Stock is the piece of paper that gives you an interest in a corporation. Personal property is movable, real property can't be moved.

54. Fructus Industrials: crops (as wheat, corn) produced by labor on the part of man for industry.

55. A personal property loan document is called a Chattel Mortgage. (Chattel is the French word for cattle. Cattle are movable.

56. Inventory and equipment are personal property. **Personal Property** is transferred by a **"Bill of Sale**.

57. The renter is responsible for insuring his personal property. Renter's Insurance. It's personal property.

58. **Land** is not a fixture. **Land** is **real property**. **Fixtures** are attached to the land or the building attached to the land. (Trees, fences, shrubs or an attached door, doorknob, window, awning, faucet, sink.)

59. **Trade fixtures** are personal property. Trade Fixtures are a commercial tenant's personal property. A trade fixture is a renter's personal property attached to the landlord's real property. At the end of the lease, the tenant removes the trade fixture and takes it with him.

60. The most **Trade Fixture** used in a course of business is a bowling alley.

61. **Immobility** is the physical characteristic in which a city, county or state would depend upon in order to predict future tax income from property owners.

62. When the developer built two identical homes with the same material, the one that was located on the sand beach was more expensive than the one located 10 blocks inland because of situs. (area preference or location)

63. Supply and demand deals with scarcity.

64. Section 16 is set aside for schools.

65. A metes and bounds description is a story. H surveyor walks the boundaries of the property and returns to the Point of Beginning.

66. The purpose of a correction line is to offset the earth. The earth is not flat. (Rectangular survey system.)

67. 640 acres is one square mile. 640 acres is usually in a question asking which area size is smallest. One square mile or 640 acres is usually the answer.

68. The area of the country that uses metes and bounds are the original 13 colonies and the older parts of the United States and Texas. It might say the original 13 states.

69. The north south lines in a government survey are called **meridians**. **Range lines** run parallel.

70. The east west lines are **baselines**. **Township lines** run parallel.

71. A **township** contains 36 sections. Each section is one square mile.

72. An Oak Tree, rock or a man-made monument can be a landmark used in the measurement of land when using the "**metes and bounds**" approach. **Point of Beginning or POB.** The surveyor will always return to the POB. The **Metes and Bounds** question. = **"Point of Beginning"**. There's a question that will just say either "a very large oak tree" or "A large boulder. If you get that question, your answer is "metes and bounds".

73. **Easement by Necessity**– A property cannot be land locked.

74. Squatters Rights deal with adverse possession.

75. A truck driver has an **easement** over his neighbor's property in order to store his large truck when he is not working. The **easement** may be terminated if the man sells his truck and retires. **(**Or the merging of titles.)

76. Sharing a driveway is an **encumbrance**.

77. The best way to find an **encroachment** is to hire a surveyor.

78. An **easement** terminates with the **merger of titles**. (Merger of title means that one entity bought both properties.)

79. When a gas company would like to bury its pipes over the property of several homes, they will apply for an **easement in gross**. There is no dominant tenement in an Easement in Gross.

80. An **easement by necessity** is important to a land locked property.

81. Bob allowed Tom to hunt on his farm during hunting season. This is a **license**. A license is a revocable right that is temporary.

82. A **Less Than Freehold Estate** is a Leasehold. Not a life estate. **Freehold** estates involve ownership, Non-freehold estates involve tenants.

83. Mary was granted a life estate for her life. Upon her passing the property will pass to her child. The type of ownership the child has is remainder. (Remainder man)

84. **Fee simple absolute** is the highest form of ownership. (They may just call it Fee Simple or Fee Simple Estate.)

85. **Fee simple defeasible** means the highest form of ownership with a condition. An example would be a hospital that is given property to keep as long as they remain a nonprofit or a zoo that receives property by deed and is allowed to keep it as long as they don't charge an admission fee.

86. When a hospital receives a gift of ownership from an older couple which states that the hospital will get the property when the old couple dies, the hospital is the remainder man.

87. **Remainder- remainder man**- in a life estate. The person who gets the property after the life estate holder dies.

88. **Reversion** in a life estate. An example would be, "Bob gave a life estate to Sal. When Sal dies, the property will revert back to Bob."

89. **Pur Autre Vie** means "for the life of another". It's a life estate based on another's life

90. Carol had a life estate. She rented the property to Tom for five years. In year three Carol died. The lease is now void. It was only valid during the term of the life.

91. A special assessment can be charged a neighborhood to help pay for new street improvements, sewer lines or road repairs.

92. When a city builds a new cement walkway down a dirt road, the people whose homes are benefiting from the new walkway pays the special assessment.

93. A special assessment and ad valorem taxes are encumbrances.

94. Property taxes are specific liens.

95. When one co-owner wants to sell his interest in real estate and the other co-owners don't, he may bring a legal action to the courts to sell his interest. It's called a **Suit for Partition** or **Partition the Property**. His interests will be sectioned off (partitioned from the rest of the property) and can be sold.

96. **Severalty** – to own to the exclusion of anyone else. Own it by yourself.

97. When there is a **Tenants by the Entirety** ownership, a broker should get both husband and wife to sign the listing. With **Joint Tenancy** and **Tenancy in Common**, you only need one person to list a property. All owners must sign to actually sell it.

98. **JTWROS**- Joint tenancy with the right of survivorship.

When Joe inherited a piece of land from his father, he immediately began digging up the topsoil and sold it to a landscaping company. He then dug out the gravel and sold it to a cement company. He then found clay, dug it out and sold it also. He had a will giving the property to his daughter upon his passing. When he dies his daughter will inherit a big hole in the ground.

PART TWO

1. The least obvious lead product to be found on a property is a lead pipe. It's a **latent defect**. (Latent Defect is an unseen defect.)

2. **Zoning** changes require a public hearing first.

3. **UFF (UFFI) or Urea Formaldehyde Foam** is **pumped** between the walls and banned in the 70's. When you see the word "pumped" in a question, UFF is the only could be answer.

4. **PUD: Planned Unit Development,** A project or subdivision that has individually owned parcels and homes, together with stores, schools, churches, recreational or landscaping elements owned by a home-owner's association and managed for the mutual benefit of all homeowners.

5. When the developer of an apartment complex is forced into having two parking spaces for each unit, it is a building code. It is **police power**.

6. A government entity can take your property by **eminent domain**. The only person who can do **Reverse Condemnation** is the property owner.

7. **Joint and Several Liability** is when a single person and a group is held liable for damages.

8. **Retroactive Liability** is liability extending back to the previous owners of a parcel of land.

9. **Lead Poisoning** is a potential cause of mental retardation in children.

10. **Lead Based Paint Disclosure Act** is a federal law that gives the buyer 10 days after an accepted offer to inspect a home built **before 1978**.

11. **CERCLA** is associated with **Superfund** and holds the responsible polluting party for the clean-up or liability **without excuse.**

12. **SARA** expanded the innocent landowner fund.

13. **Brownfields Legislation** helps revitalize deserted, defunct and polluted areas of contamination.

14. **Strict Liability** is when the owner of a polluted property is responsible for the cleanup **Without Excuse. CERCLA**

15. **Zoning Ordinance**- Defines how property in specific geographic zones can be used. It regulates lot sizes, density, height structures and purpose. Government Law. **Police Power**.

16. **Amenities**- They enhance value by a home's proximity to amenities off the property. Examples are a bike trail, a community pool or a beautifully shaded park.

17. What should an agent tell a buyer if the buyer would like to have a test for radon done? Hire a professional because you can't smell or see radon and it causes lung cancer.

18. **Radon Gas** can be Easily Mitigated. It enters the house through the basement. It costs about $3000.

19. **Zonin**g is local government police power. States allow the cities to do their own zoning through State Enabling Acts. "**State Enabling rights**".

20. Flood insurance is required when a property is in a **SFHA**. **Special Flood Hazard Area. (FEMA flood area)**

21. When you want to extend your patio, check **setback limits** first.

22. When a commercial property is in a neighborhood that gets downzoned, the property gets **grandfathered in** and is of **non-conforming use**. If the property burns down or gets destroyed, it cannot be built back without getting a **conditional use permit**.

23. A public limitation on use would be caused by **police power. (Eminent domain – zoning)**

24. A private limitation would be a deed restriction. (I can't cut down my oak trees.)

25. An easement created by adverse use is a **Prescriptive Easement**. (Prescription)

26. Restrictive covenants and shared driveways are encumbrances on the property. (An **encumbrance** is something that bothers the property.)

27. A current lawsuit on real property is called a **Lis pendens**. (Litigation Pending)

28. Police power allows the government to place restrictions on the use of private property.

29. An owner wants to construct a fence beyond the **setback limits**. In order to do this, she must obtain a **variance**.

30. After an owner built a factory on his property, the city downzoned the neighborhood to residential. In this case, the factory will be **grand fathered in**.

31. **Compensation** usually follows the court action of **condemnation**. **(eminent domain)**

32. **Set back limits** are the difference between the lot line and the improvements.

33. The homeowners enforce the CC and Rs in a Neighborhood Association.

34. Eminent Domain, Condemnation and Just Compensation are words that go together. One will be in the question and one of the others will be in the answer.

35. A county airport took several streets of homes in order to expand its runway through the government power of eminent domain.

36. When the county took several streets through eminent domain to extend an airport runway, they left one house which is now experiencing extreme noise and shaking due to the expansion. The homeowner may be able to get the county to take the property through the use **of reverse condemnation**. Only a homeowner can apply for reverse condemnation. It's forcing the government (reverse eminent domain) entity to take your property.

37. A condominium complex cannot eminent domain the three houses adjacent to their parking lot to extend their parking.

38. **Bulk Zoning -** regulations restrict the density in a given area. Bulk Zoning include, open space requirements, floor area ratios and setback requirements.

Part Three

1. **Diminishing Returns**- The point in time when improvements can't add value to a property anymore. The property is over built or over improved for the neighborhood.

2. **Progression** - the least expensive or smallest home in the neighborhood made up of larger and more expensive homes.

3. **Regression**. The doctor suffered from regression when he built a very large home in a neighborhood of very small homes.

4. **Physical Deterioration**- a leaky roof, a cracked foundation wall, worn out window tracks. Fixable.

5. **Functional Obsolescence**- a four bedrooms two story home with one bathroom. A home with three bedrooms on the second floor and one bathroom on the first floor. Loss in value. Something on the property. Usually Fixable

6. **External Obsolescence**- Loss in value due to an airport expanding its runway and now planes fly over a neighborhood at a low altitude. A deteriorating neighborhood with buildings not being maintained. External is something outside the property. Could be a tainted water well. Could be a public dump or railroad tracks.

7. **External obsolescence** could result from a gas storage tank located near the property.

8. A single car garage could cause **functional obsolescence**.

9. A poor floor plan can cause functional obsolescence.

10. When finding the "**Highest and best use**" of a property is not concerned with the loans on the property. (Concerned with net yield, utility of neighborhood and relationship to development.)

11. The final analysis an appraiser uses for the different approaches to value is **reconciliation. Reconciliation** is the last step an appraiser takes. **Stating the problem** is the first step an appraiser takes.

12. Dry rot and termite damage are **physical deterioration**.

13. The "highest and best use property" is the one that delivers the highest net return.

14. Normal wear and tear on a building is neither external nor functional (internal) obsolescence.

15. When an appraiser is doing an appraisal, he does not use 'land depreciation'.

16. When an agent wants to do a **CMA** in a neighborhood of mostly foreclosures, he will take the actual arm's length (or more) **sales comparisons** from the bank instead of the foreclosed price

17. **Substitution** - what an appraiser uses to determine value by comparing equally desirable substitutes nearby.

18. **CMA- Comparative Market Analysis**- Benefits the Seller. It helps agents determine a price range for a property to list. It doesn't determine value. Only an appraisal can determine value.

19. The economic life of a building has come to an end when the value of the land and the building equals the value of the land only. It's a tear down.

20. The best reason for buying real estate is appreciation.

21. In a **sales comparison approach** to appraisal, you subtract or add from the comparable, not the subject property.

22. GRM - Gross Rent Multiplier. Residential homes.

23. **Comparable** - a name for sold homes used in an appraisal or a CMA. The comparable gets adjusted when comparing it to the subject property.

24. A capitalization rate incorporates return on land and building and recapture of the building.

25. **USPAP** relates to the appraisal specialty of real estate.

26. The replacement cost approach is appropriate to appraise a new home as opposed to an old home, condominium or tract home. (Imagine the home was built on a ranch or farm where there are no comparable properties.)

27. Comparison, income and replacement costs are the three best ways to determine value.

28. A post office or city hall is best appraised using the cost approach. (Special purpose buildings use the cost approach / replacement cost.)

29. When the appraiser uses the monthly rental income or total monthly income to find value, he is using the GRM (Gross Rent Multiplier)

30. When an appraiser is using the income approach to a building, he is not concerned about the price of the building next door.

31. **Capitalization** is an investor's rate of return.

Part Four

1. **Home Affordable Modification Program**: Helps homeowners avoid foreclosure by lowering their monthly payment. (Making monthly payments affordable)

2. **FHA loan** = 3.5% down. FHA is an insurance company. It insures the bank will get its money.

3. Definition of **Points**. One point equals one percent of the loan.

4. Banks sometimes will not take a **Deed in Lieu of Foreclosure** because junior liens may need to be paid off.

Following a first mortgage foreclosure, all junior liens are extinguished and the liens are removed from the property title. The second mortgage debt is no longer attached to the foreclosed property. The creditor's judgment remains with the creditor as an unsecured debt.

5. Lender can decline a loan based on the applicant's income. It would not be a violation of **Fair Lending Laws.**

6. **Usury Laws** protect the consumer.

7. A **"Purchase Money Mortgage"** is a form of Seller Financing.

8. **Equal Credit Opportunity Act** - Age is a protected class. A 93-year-old person can get a 30-year loan.

9. Equal Credit Opportunity Act does not address interest rates. Banks set their own rates.

10. **Public assistance** is considered income when deciding to rent or sell to someone.

11. Commission is not considered income when renting or applying for a loan.

12. There can be discount points on a VA and a FHA loan.

13. **ECOA – Equal Credit Opportunity Act**. Legislation preventing discrimination in lending.

14. **Trigger Terms**- The amount or percentage of any down payment, the number of payments or period of repayment, the amount of any payment and the amount of any finance charge.

15. **Annual Percentage Rate**- a Trigger term, which must be clearly stated for comparative purposes for the true the cost of loans.

16. **Regulation Z/ Truth in Lending** - Disclosure of the true cost of credit. Includes Trigger Terms and a Three-Day Right of Rescission if the home loan is based on the home you live in.

17. Federal Trade Commission- FTC the agency that enforces Regulation Z and Truth in Lending.

18. **RESPA- Real Estate Settlement Procedures Act**. Settlement of cost legislation. Prohibits undisclosed kickbacks.

19. **Private Mortgage Insurance (PMI)** is not needed when you put 20% down.

20. A bank that substitutes its judgment on behalf of another bank is a **bank intermediary**.

21. Mortgage brokers do not lend their own money.

22. Mortgage brokers have more loan products than do mortgage bankers.

23. **Regulation Z** requires that the buyer have a three day right of rescission if the loan is on his personal residence.

24. A **CMA and BPO** differ from an appraisal in that the appraisal "can determine more". An appraisal can determine value while a BPO and CMA estimates a selling range.

25. A loan that only interest is paid and at the end has a **balloon payment** is a straight loan. (term loan)

26. A loan with a partial payment is a **partially amortized loan**. There is a balloon payment.

27. The mother or father of an active military person cannot get a **DVA-VA loan**.

28. **The Truth in Lending Act (Regulation Z)** is designed to disclose the true cost of lending and advertising.

29. When a FHA or DVA-VA buyer wants to take out a loan, he must go to a qualified lender. FHA and DVA does not lend money. FHA is an insurance company and DVA-VA is a guarantee company.

30. A mortgage broker cannot take a kick back for an appraisal.

31. A **subordination agreement** is a release for a lender to take a second position. The second loan on your house is a subordinated loan to the first lien holder (loan, lender).

32. A Reverse Amortization Loan is a **reverse mortgage**. It is for older people who would like to have tax-free income. (Seniors, retired couple)

33. Each **discount point** equals 1% of the loan not the sales price.

34. The disadvantage in investing in real estate is that the money is not easily accessible. It is not easily liquid.

35. The Real Estate Settlement Procedures Act (RESPA) is designed to regulate disclosure of closing information.

36. **Leverage**- using other people's money. Financing by using borrowed funds.

37. You can have points on both FHA and VA. Both are assumable. A non-veteran can assume a VA loan.

38. A **Fully Amortized Mortgage** has the same payment each month with the amount going to interest decreasing monthly and the amount going toward principal increasing each month. No balloon payment. It reverses over time.

39. **Pre-payment penalties** or the total amount of interest paid does not have to be disclosed with Regulation Z.

40. **Novation** is the substitution of one party on a loan for another. It would be used when someone is assuming a loan regardless of the type of loan. Novation would release the seller from responsibility if the new person defaults.

41. Qualified lenders supply the funds for **FHA and VA loans**.

42. Amortization is the liquidation of a debt thru periodic payments.

43. The seller becomes the lender in a **"land contract"**, "seller carryback", **"purchase money mortgage"** and "contract for deed".

44. The buyer holds **equitable title**. The seller holds **legal title**. You can devise both titles.

45. A **sale-leaseback** is a transaction where the seller leases back the property from the new owner.

46. **Discount points** charged on a loan yield a higher return for the lender.

47. A **graduated payment mortgage** causes the payment to go up gradually.

48. A **sale-leaseback** is usually done so that the seller can write off the rental amounts paid.

49. A **mortgage broker** arranges loans between borrowers and lenders. A **mortgage banker** works for a bank.

50. The holder of a second mortgage most likely signed a **subordination agreement**.

51. A **"Mortgage Satisfaction"** document is a bank releasing a lien.

52. The borrower / mortgagor signs the mortgage.

53. A wraparound mortgage is a **junior mortgage**. It encompasses the difference between the existing mortgage and the total loan. The interest is usually lower than the prevailing rate.

54. The first mortgage recorded takes precedence unless there is a **subordination agreement**.

55. A developer would get a **blanket mortgage** on his property. He subdivides the lots and records the new legal description. A **partial release clause** allows for the payment and then release of certain parcels.

56. A **balloon payment** is the last payment that pays the unpaid balance on a mortgage at a predetermined time. It is the largest payment.

57. **Loan Originator** – meets with the borrower who fills out the loan application. He obtains all the needed documents.

58. **Loan Processor** – Orders the reports such as appraisals, title report, termite inspection and other inspections.

59. **Underwriter** – reviews and evaluates the information.

60. If the foreclosure sale proceeds are less than the amount owned, the mortgagee may obtain a **deficiency judgment** against the mortgagor for the unpaid balance.

61. Payment under an **adjustable rate mortgage** may go up and down.

62. Personal property is transferred by **Bill of Sale**.

63. Banks set their own interest rates.

64. In some cases, a seller financing a property will use a deed of trust because it's easier to foreclose on than a regular mortgage.

> **FDIC** – Federal Deposit Insurance Corporation Deposits in banks are insured up to **$250,000** per depositor.

Part Five

1. You are not a **REALTOR (Trademarked)** until you join the National Association of Realtors. It's trademarked. The National Association of Realtors subscribes to a Code of Ethics. (**Realtists** are a parallel organization who also subscribes to a code of ethic.)

2. Know at what point a broker earns his commission. When he brings **a ready willing and able buyer who can meet the terms of the listing agreement**. (They may call the listing agreement "the contract".)

3. A salesperson's death does NOT kill the deal.

4. A seller does not have to accept an offer lower than the asking price.

5. A **trust account** is a checking account. A demand Account.

6. A broker and her **unlicensed assistant** were travelling to deliver a signed counter offer to their client. On their way, they got into a terrible car crash and the broker was rushed to the hospital. What should the unlicensed assistant do? Carry the counter offer to the client before going to the hospital. Offers and counter offers need to be delivered ASAP. As long as the Broker is alive, the deal is alive. Also, an unlicensed personal assistant can "carry paper". An unlicensed personal assistant can refer buyers and sellers to the broker.

7. **Protection clause**- extends the period of time that a seller agrees to pay a commission.

8. **Commingling**- Unlawful mixing of the broker's money and his client's funds.

9. A couple made an offer on a home and before it was accepted they made another offer on another home. They can either back out of the first offer if it is not accepted or buy both. If both offers get accepted before they back out, the buyers are responsible to both contracts. Be careful on this question because one version talks about a couple that maybe they wanted to buy both houses.

10. What can cancel all contracts? Mutual consent of all parties. (Or death, insanity or bankruptcy.)

> **Delegated authority and consent to act create agency.**

11.   **Delegated authority**- the principal's act that creates agency.

12.   **Consent to act**- to create agency the principal delegates authority, and the broker must do this.

13. **Principal**- The person or entity that delegates authority in order to create an agency relationship. It's the **Client**.

14. Do not **comingle**.

15. A Buyer made an offer on Bob's house that included a contingency that he would buy Bob's home if he can sell his home first. Bob accepted. In order for Bob to protect himself, he added an escape clause so he wouldn't be caught up in a lengthy transaction. He included in the acceptance that if another ready, willing and able buyer made a genuine offer to purchase Bob's house, he would give the first purchaser a 48 hour **first right of refusal**.

16. An owner's death kills the listing. A fire to the property does not necessarily kill a listing.

17. When a seller accepts an offer from a buyer who needs to sell his or her own home first, to keep from being caught in a lengthy transaction the seller can add an escape clause to the contract.

18. A **Customer** is someone you work with. A customer is not represented.

19. A **Client** is someone you work for.

20. **Commingling** is the mixing of the broker's funds with the client trust account funds. It's illegal.

21. **Unlicensed Personal Assistant's** duties must be defined in the **broker's policy and procedures manual**. They can carry paper.

> An unlicensed personal assistant can refer buyers and seller to their broker. Many times they are receptionists and part of their job is to answer the phone. If a buyer or seller asked to speak to a salesperson, the unlicensed personal assistant can refer that person to his broker.

22. A good training program creates a high morale in the brokerage.

23. A Broker is responsible for the direct supervision of a brokerage firm. A broker is responsible for the real estate activities of his salespeople. A broker is not responsible for everything his salespeople do in their day-to-day lives.

24. Only one owner of the property needs to sign the listing agreement. If the agent brings a ready, able and willing buyer that can meet the terms of the listing agreement and the other property owners refuse to sell the property, the agent is entitled to her commission from the person who signed the listing.

25. When a salesperson had a listing with Bob but Bob died in a car accident before the salesperson could procure a buyer, the listing terminates immediately.

26. A broker can take money out of the client trust account only if the buyer and seller have given written approval.

27. The person named in a corporate resolution is the person authorized to sign a listing agreement for a corporation.

28. The type of listing in which the listing agent is least likely to know what his commission will be is a net listing.

29. The listing broker is responsible to pay the selling broker as per written agreement.

30. A listing broker has earned her commission on the sale of a property even if it's a land contract to be completed in four years and agreed upon by both buyer and seller.

31. When a seller is refusing to pay the listing broker after the transaction has closed, the listing agent still needs to turn the earnest money back to the buyer. The listing broker can then sue the seller in court for her earned commission.

32. Bob secured a six-month Exclusive Right Listing Agreement with Sam. Two months into the contract, Sam gave written notice to Bob that he no longer wanted to sell. The contract will be cancelled but Sam will be liable for any expenses incurred by agent Bob.

33. On a contingent offer from a buyer, the agent has not earned his commission until the contingency is removed. An example would be a buyer making an offer based on him securing financing.

34. The broker is not entitled to a commission if the seller sells the property one day after the expiration of the listing unless there is a protection clause in the listing and the agent was the procuring cause of the transaction.

35. A **General Agent** is a property manager. A property manager's primary responsibility is to get the highest net return for the property owner. A General Agent is hired to do general duties.

The property manager doesn't give the rent he collected to the owner of the property. All monies collected by a property manager must be given to his broker.

---

36. All money collected by sub agents must be given to the broker...

37. **Special Agent** is a listing / Seller's Agent or a Selling / Buyer's Agent. They are hired to do one specific act.

Seller = Client = Principle = Fiduciary

Seller's Agent = Listing Agent

Buyer

Selling Agent = Buyer's Agent

If a **Buyer's Agent / Selling Agent** gets a written buyer's agreement for representation, then the buyer becomes a client.

38. **Independent Contractor- vs. Employee**

39.

40.

41.

42. **Covenant of Seisin**- the grantor's expression that he or she has possession and the right to convey the property. Example: When there are three partners who own an apartment complex and one of the partners is trying to sell 100% ownership of the

property without the other two partners knowing it, he has violated the **Covenant of Seisen.** In this case the deal will fail because of **Impossibility of Performance.**

43. For an acceptance to be valid it must be **Delivered and Accepted.**

44. An Offer becomes the **Purchase Agreement/Contract** once it's accepted. It is the same document. The Purchase Agreement defines the legal rights of the seller and buyer. It is a legal document between the seller and buyer.

45. **Equitable Title** is also known as an insurable interest of real estate. It's the Buyer's interest. It can be willed.

46. **Net Listings** are prohibited in most states because of the uncertainty of the selling price. An example would be your Client says to you that he needs $500,000 from the sale and you can keep anything you above that.

47. **Exclusive Right to Sell** is a listing stating the listing agent will get paid regardless of who procures the buyer. (Procuring Cause) A broker will spend more money on advertising on this listing.

48. **An Open Listing** is hiring multiple agents. Only the real estate firm who procures the buyer gets paid by the seller. A unilateral contract.

49. **An Exclusive listing** is when the seller wants an exclusive agent but reserves the right to sell the property himself without paying a commission.

50. **Earnest Money** can be used as **liquidated damages** if it is stated in the contract. **Earnest money** is given by the buyer when he makes an offer in order to show his true intention to move forward with the transaction. Money Talks.

51. **Consideration** is not a legal requirement of agency. (cash or equivalent) You may do representation for free.

52. Undisclosed **dual agency** is an illegal form of real estate representation.

53. Delivery of the Deed gives **Legal Title** to the Buyer.

54. **Agency Disclosure** is informing clients/fiduciaries and customers of your relationships which each person.

55. The **primary duty of a property manager** is to get the highest net return for the owner.

56. Giving a seller an Estimation of Proceeds from an income property to determine their net profit before listing the building for sale in an example of **Care.**

57. **Obedience** is the type of duty required of an agent when asked by an owner not to place a "Seller Financing" sign in the yard. (Or any sign)

58. A **Subagent** is an agent's agent. The agents of the responsible broker are sub agents.

59. **The Protection Clause** in the listing extends the period of time that a seller agrees to pay a commission.

60. Representing both sides of the same transaction with written permission explaining what is due each party is **Dual Agency**.

61. A duty to a **principal** that includes **confidentiality is loyalty**.

62. To create agency the principal **Delegates Authority**, and the broker must **Consent to Act**.

63. A **Principal-Client** is the person or entity that delegates authority in order to create an agency relationship.

64. The buyer and attorney can decide and determine the method of ownership. The attorney is the **Conveyancer**. A **Conveyancer** is an attorney. Brokers and agents cannot practice law. If a Client or customer asks an agent how they should take title to a property, you tell then to ask an attorney.

65. **Caveat Emptor** means Buyer Beware. Caveat Venditor means Seller Beware.

66. When a salesperson doesn't know something, but should have, he did not practice care. **Negligent Misrepresentation**. (If an agent tells a client that her fireplace will add ambiance in winter and the client buys the property and then finds out the fireplace is actually just a fake fireplace front, it is **Negligent Misrepresentation**.) OR (A buyer tells her agent she wants to purchase a home in order to have a beauty salon in her garage. She would like to have a home-based business. The agent shows the buyer a home with the garage big enough for the home-based salon. The buyer purchases the property. When the new homeowner is moving in her salon equipment, the city code enforcer pulls up and tells her the neighborhood is not zoned for home based business). The agent did not practice care.

67. (**Negligent Misrepresentation**) The agent is responsible for actual damages. Her **E and O insurance** will help her pay for her mistake. E and O insurance will not help an agent when the agent commits fraud.

68. The agent will be responsible for **Actual Damages**. Her **E and O insurance** should help cover it.

69. The death of an associated broker does not cancel a contract. Associated brokers are broker agents (subagents). The death of the Responsible Broker kills the deal. Agents can die and the deal stills lives.

70. An agent gets to keep his commission if the seller lied about a **material fact** and the buyer finds out after the close. **The Purchase Agreement** is between the Seller and Buyer. Neither agent is a party to the Purchase Agreement.

71. An **open agreement** is when the seller hires multiple agents. The agent that gets paid is the one that procures the buyer. (The **procuring cause**)

72. A **counter offer** voids an offer.

73. A broker or agent should caution the seller not to respond to all multiple offers at the same time.

74. The phrase **"procuring cause"** is most important to the broker and seller in an open listing contract. "Procure the Buyer"

75. It is unethical for a broker representing the seller to tell the buyer the lowest price a seller will accept.

76. Offers and Counteroffers must be delivered ASAP.

77. Monies in a **trust account (escrow account)** are not assets of the broker. It is the client's funds and **accurate records** must be kept.

78. A broker's **trust account (escrow account)** is a non-interest bearing checking account.

79. If a broker would like to buy his seller's property, he should make his true intentions known.

80. A broker should tell his seller the ramifications and effects of an offer and to present all offers to the seller as soon as possible. A broker may not hold back any offers from the seller even if he believes the seller will reject them.

81. An agent may never give law advice or accounting advice.

82. When a **For Sale by Owner** sign contains the term "principals only", it is telling licensees not to bother the seller.

83. The relationship with the principal/client is one of **fiduciary**.

84. If a seller tells you that the roof was replaced 5 years ago and the patio was added without a permit, you should tell the seller to **disclose it**.

85. It is unethical for the Seller's Agent to tell the buyer the lowest price the seller will accept.

86. When selling a property with an illegal addition of 600 feet, the seller's agent should **disclose** that the buyer might be forced to remove the addition.

87. Present all offers as soon as possible. If you have more than one offer, submit them at the same time.

88. Disclose that a property has a shared driveway because a shared driveway is an encumbrance and a **material fact** that must be disclosed

89. **Fiduciary**- a type of relationship based on trust and confidence. The Listing Broker owes the Seller Fiduciary Duties.

Part Six

1. **Commission** is negotiable.

Antitrust Act (Sherman Antitrust Act)
Everything is negotiable.
The Board of Realty or similar organization cannot set commissions.
Brokers from separate companies cannot get together to stamp out competition of
other brokers. They cannot get together and boycott other brokers.
Brokers from separate companies cannot price fix.
Fines for individuals: Up to one million dollars and 10 years in jail.

---

2. **Constructive Notice**- By recording a **deed** a person has given **Constructive Notice to the world**. Once the deed is recorded everyone has been given notice whether they know about it or not. An unrecorded deed is valid only to those parties involved and to those who actually know about it.

3. **Covenant of Seisin**- the grantor's expression that he or she has possession and the right to convey the property. Example: When there are three partners who own an apartment complex and one of the partners is trying to sell 100% ownership of the property without the other two **partners knowing it, he has violated the Covenant of Seisen. In this case the deal will fail because of Impossibility of Performance**.

4. A prospective buyer has the right to demand his deposit money back before the offer is accepted. If a buyer makes an offer and on her way home she finds a property she likes better and wanted to make an offer, she can withdraw the first offer before it's accepted and purchase the other property.

5. **Liquidated Damages- Earnest Money** can become **Liquidated Damages** if the buyer **breaches** the **Purchase Contract**

6. The first person to record the deed is the owner. An **unrecorded deed** is valid only between the parties involved and to those who have been given notice.

7. A **Power of Attorney** allows someone to act for someone else. If an **unmarried minor** was given a power of attorney by his brother to sign on his behalf, only the **unmarried minor** needs to sign. The contract is also a voidable contract.

8. **Devise** is the transfer of real property by a will. (A **Codicil** is used to change a will.)

9. **Dower** is woman and **Curtsey** is man.

10. Executor is a man and executrix is a woman.

11. When an investor would like to purchase a property to build a casino in a non-casino state, the contract will fail because of **Impossibility of Performance**. When a person would like to purchase an unlicensed whiskey store in order to run a whiskey store, the contract will fail for Impossibility of Performance.

12. **A Tie In - Tying Arrangement (tie-in)**: Requiring a buyer to list his or her current home with the same agent in order to purchase the desired new home the buyer wants.

Seller

The contract between the Seller and the **Seller's Agent** is the **Listing Agreement**.

The Listing Agreement can be considered an employment contract.

Fiduciary Duties due the Client /Seller /Principal

Confidentiality

Obedience

Loyalty

Disclosure

Accountability

Care

(C O L D . A C)

The Seller's Agent has earned a commission when he brings a ready, willing and able buyer that meets the terms of the listing agreement.

Confidentiality
Obedience
Loyalty
Disclosure
Accountability
Care

C O L D
A C

Trust and Confidence refers to the Fiduciary Responsibilities of the Seller's Agent.

Part Seven

1. The agent's obligation to the seller in regards to disclosure is to have him disclose all **material defects**.

2. **Seller's Property Disclosure Act** is legislation requiring the seller to reveal the honest condition of the property whether a defect is seen or a **Latent Defect**.

3. When a town installs sidewalks, gutters and lighting down a dirt road. The added tax increase levied on the property owners in that city is called a **special assessment**.

4. A Listing agent noticed shingles that were broken on the roof. He should **disclose** that defect.

5. A **Buyer's Agent** was told a property had no defects. Upon his inspection, he found several problems. The agent should **disclose the defects** to his buyer.

6. Who keeps the **Purchase Agreement**? Both Seller and Buyer and Both Agents.

7. When an inspector asks if he can remove a piece of drywall from the basement wall, he is looking for a **latent defect**.

Part Eight

1. Title to property transfers only when the **deed** is **delivered and accepted**.

2. The "**Procuring Cause**" is the person who will get paid in an "**Open Listing**".

3. How does an owner of an apartment complex and a real estate broker enter into an agreement for the broker to manage the property? Through the use of a **Property Management Agreement**.

4. Who does the listing agent owe **fiduciary duties** to? **The Client**

5. When a tenant vacates their lease because the landlord will not fix the heat, it called **constructive eviction.**

6. Leases and agreements must be in writing to bring action. Everything in real estate has to be in writing to be enforceable in court according to the **Statue of Frauds**.

7. **Habendum clause**- "To have and to Hold" A granting clause in the deed.

465

8. **Percentage Lease**- Used for shopping centers or stores, sometimes restaurants. The rent includes a percentage of the tenant's sales receipts. An example would be "$2000 a month plus 2 percent of the store's sales total".

9. **Stature of Frauds** requires all real estate contracts regardless of what type to be in writing.

10. Violation of **Specific Performance** is when the seller took the drapes and water softener which were fixtures attached to the property. A court order requiring a promise to be carried out is a suit for **Specific Performance**.

11. An **Exclusive Agreement** does not guarantee you a commission but an **Exclusive RIGHT Agreement** does. A broker will spend more money on advertising with an **Exclusive RIGHT Agreement**. The **Exclusive Agreement** allows the seller to sell it him or herself without paying a commission. (If it doesn't RIGHT, then it's wrong for you.)

12. When a broker receives an **earnest money deposit check**, he must deliver it to the **trust account – escrow account** by the end of the next business or banking day or in a timely manner according to state laws.

13. A property manager's duties do not include investing the property owner's funds.

14. **Novation**: an agreement to replace an old debtor with another one. (Used when assuming a loan.)

15. **Subletting** is when a tenant rents his place to another tenant.

16. When an agent collects money from a tenant, the agent gives it to her broker, not the owner.

17. The term that best describes a tenant's interest in property is **Lease Hold Estate**. It is **personal property**. It's a reversionary estate since it reverts back to the owner.

18. An option contract is a **unilateral contracted**. In a "rent to own", the renter need not buy but if he chooses to buy, the seller must sell.

19. An **Option** and a **Listing** are both **Unilateral Contracts**. ("I will do something if you do something first.") Only one person is forced into doing something.

20. A contract with an **unmarried minor** is a **Voidable Contract**. At any time the minor can change his mind. An adult cannot force a minor to complete a transaction.

21. **Net lease**- when a tenant pays all or some of the landlord's operating expenses.

22. An agent does not have to disclose if a felony was committed on a property.

23. Acknowledgement is needed when parties want to record a sales contract.

24. A court order to carry out a promise is a suit for **Specific Performance.**

25. If Carol and Tom had a verbal agreement to sell property to each other and Carol backed out, Tom could not take Carol to court because there was no written contract.

26. In an option contract the seller must sell but the buyer is not forced into buying. It's a **unilateral contract**.

27. Sales contracts generally may be assigned to other people if both buyer and seller give written permission.

28. When Tom threatened to beat up Bill if Bill didn't sign a contract, Bill was under duress. The contract may be voided even if both parties sign.

29. If a buyer withdraws his offer before the seller accepts it, the buyer is entitled to his earnest money deposit.

30. When a seller rejects an offer, it should be noted on the offer and a copy sent to the offeror.

31. Earnest money deposits may serve as liquidated damages.

32. The rescission of a contract is a return to status quo.

33. The buyer takes possession at the transfer of title.

34. Liquidate damages are negotiated.

35. An earnest money deposit does not make the contract valid.

36. All grantors are required to sign the deed. Only one owner is required to sign the listing agreement. If only one seller signs and the listing agent brings a ready willing and able buyer who meets the term of the contract, the person who signed is responsible for the commission payment.

Part Nine

1. An owner's **title insurance** protects the owner from loss to a claimant with superior right of title. Title insurance insures up to the date it's issued.

2. An **abstract of title** is the history of the recorded documents on the property.

3. The attorney reads the abstract of title. **Abstract and Opinion.**

4. The **Grantor** signs the Deed.

5. Real Estate is not easily liquid. If you need money it will take some time to get the money out of real estate. (Example: re-finance or sell it or new loan.)

6. **Novation**: an agreement to replace an old debtor with another one. (Used when assuming a loan.)

7. **Title insurance** extends to unrecorded documents.

8. You are assured you are getting fee simple ownership when the seller can furnish title insurance.

9. **Seisen** is legal ownership. To be seized in property means you own it. The Covenant of Seisen.

10. When an elderly couple gifts a property to a hospital but reserve the right to have a **life estate**, the hospital is said to be the Remainder Man.

11. **General Warranty Deed = Fee Simple Absolute Title.** The deed with the highest form of protection.

12. A deed defines the covenants by which the grantor is bound.

13. Ownership by **Joint Tenancy** has an advantage because a person can avoid the expense and delay of probate. Joint Tenancy with Rights of Survivorship = JTWROS

14. **Title Insurance**- When issued, it insures that the title is free of all encumbrances, defects and liens except for those listed. It protects against loss from title defects. Title Insurance extends to unrecorded documents.

15. **Trust deed**- most often seen in seller financing situations. A way of conveying real estate by the trustor.

16. Covenant of Quiet Enjoyment- the Grantor guarantees that title is good and is insuring against other parties who might claim superior title.

17. **Quitclaim deed**- the deed that gives the least protection. A deed that offers the grantee no warranty as to the status of the property title. Quitclaim deeds are used to remove a cloud on title. (Quiet a Title)

18. **Joint Tenancy**- The last one living owns in severalty. **JTWROS**: Joint Tenancy with Rights of Survivorship

19. Trust Account– Escrow Account- A checking account (demand account), non-interest bearing. The funds deposited belong to the clients and customers. Trust Account Funds are not the assets of the broker.

20. Boot is related to a **1031 tax deferred exchange**.

21. If Al puts a deed in a box conveying his property to Tom at Al's death, the deed was not delivered to Tom. When all died, Tom had no rights to the property and the property goes to Al's heirs. A properly executed deed needs to be delivered and accepted.

22. **Involuntary alienation** is transfer of property without the owner's consent. Involuntary alienation could be a foreclosure.

23. A deed that limits liability of the grantor to the time of his ownership only is a special warranty deed. A general warranty deed extends the liability to all previous owners as well as the current owner.

24. A corporate seal on a deed indicates the property was purchased by a corporation.

25. Recording a deed is not necessary to make the transfer legal. The deed will be legal between the parties and anyone that knows about it. Recording the deed gives constructive notice to the world. The first one to record the deed will create ownership if there is a dispute.

26. A **quitclaim deed** offers the least protection to the buyer. A general warranty deed creates the most protection to the buyer.

27. An acknowledgement is the signing. A notary public will witness an acknowledgement to make sure the signing was voluntary and to witness that the person signing is who he or she say they are.

28. An acknowledgement may be called a declaration.

29. A deed must be signed by the grantor to be recorded.

30. A valid deed is least likely to be conveyed by an **unmarried minor**.

31. The deed that conveys no warranties is the quitclaim deed.

32. Lack of money in a transaction does not affect the validity of the deed. It could be a gift.

33. If Joe, Tom and Al are partners and Joe attempts to sell 100% interest in the property without the knowledge of his two partners. Joe has violated the covenant of **seisin.** The transaction will fail because of Impossibility of Performance.

34. A standard **title insurance** policy insures against forgery of a deed.

35. **An extended title insurance policy** insures against hidden risks that an inspection of the physical property could reveal such as easements, encumbrances, property lines, mechanic liens, mining rights, oil rights and rights of parties.

36. An **extended title insurance policy** (may call it an ALTA policy) does not include the disclosure of zoning or changes in zoning.

37. An **abstract of title** is a history of the recorded documents. The recorded documents can include deeds, rental agreements, mortgages, mechanic liens.

38. Tracing the conveyances and encumbrances of real property is a title search. The abstract is the actual history.

39. Both buyer and seller must consent in writing before a broker is allowed to take an advance of money out of an escrow / trust account.

40. If a buyer is purchasing property out of state and has never seen the property, he should obtain an extended coverage title insurance.

41. Title insurance is only paid once at the purchase. It extends up to the date it's issued.

42. **RESPA** is designed to disclose closing data. There cannot be an undisclosed kick back.

43. The person who receives the title by deed is the buyer. (grantee)

44. Grantor- The person who sells the property. The one conveying the property to the Grantee by deed. It's the seller. The Grantor is the only person(s) who signs the deed.

Part Ten

1. A **convicted drug dealer** is not protected under federal fair housing laws. A convicted drug user may be protected under the **American with Disabilities Act.**

2. If someone discriminates but they don't know they did because they are just basically ignorant or stupid, it is still a violation.

3. **Civil Rights Act of 1968** is also known as the Fair Housing Act.

4. An owner of a property can discriminate if he lives on his 1-4-unit property.

5. A man going door-to-door in an older neighborhood and telling the residents that children or a family from another country will be moving into their quiet neighborhood is guilty of **blockbusting/panic peddling.**

6. **Civil rights act of 1866** prohibits discrimination on race. It was the first act.

7. **ADA- American with Disability Act**- Prohibits discrimination based on disability. An office with 15 or more employees must be accessible to those with disabilities.

8. Religious organizations and private clubs may be allowed to discriminate under certain circumstances.

9. **Steering**- is when an agent shows minority buyers properties only in certain neighborhoods instead of the entire market.

10. **Steering** is when an agent shows a buyer properties only in neighborhoods where the agent believes the buyer should live.

11. **Redlining**- when a lending institution decides NOT to lend money within a specific neighborhood based on a heavy population of a protected class.

12. **Blockbusting**- Trying to induce owners to sell their property because minorities or any protected group is moving into their neighborhood. Also called **Panic Peddling**.

13. **62 years and older**- Senior Housing exempt from **familial status** discrimination.

14. **Title VIII**- The Federal Fair Housing Act of 1968.

15. **EHO Poster- the Equal Housing Opportunity Poster** must be conspicuously displayed in all real estate, appraising and lender offices. If the poster is not conspicuously displayed, it is considered, **"Prima Facie Discrimination"**.

16. **Familial Status**- A protected class that includes women who are pregnant or have children under 18. It's the status of the family. An unmarried woman with kids is protected. Children under 18 are protected.

17. An owner of an apartment complex cannot segregate families with children into certain buildings within a complex. A landlord cannot decide to NOT rent to an unmarried woman with kids or a pregnant woman based on **Familial Status** unless the landlord/owner lives in the 1-4-unit building.

18. Complexes built for a segment of the population who are 55 years of age and older may discriminate based on familiar status. A senior complex can choose not to rent to someone based on the age of the children. When the senior complex bases the decision not to rent because of familiar status, **Fair Housing Laws** protect the senior complex.

19. AIDS, HIV and a convicted drug user are protected under disability.

20. **HUD**- The enforcement agency who oversees **fair housing laws**.

21. **A Tie In - Tying Arrangement (tie-in)**: The agent tied in the sale of a listing client' home if the client also turns around and buys swamp land the agent is selling.

22. **Boycotting** is the illegal action where two or more brokers agree not to cooperate with a third broker.

23. One broker may decide on his own to not pay another agent the same commission split as he offers others. An agent acting on his own can decide to boycott another agent as long as he does not get together with other brokers to do the same.

24. **REALTORS Code of Ethics** is the standard of ethical behavior for Realtors. (*National Association of Realtors Trademark)

25. **Puffing** is an agent's exaggerated opinion. Not illegal. **Puffing** could lead to **misrepresentation**.

26. **HUD** protects people dealing with **Fair Housing** complaints. You have one year to file a complaint. Some people will take their complaint to the courts because the courts do not cap rewards.

27. A handicapped person may make **Reasonable Alterations or Accommodations** to an apartment or rental at his cost but he must return the apartment to its original condition at the end of the lease (also at his cost). The least likely thing to be brought back to its original condition is the handrail screwed into tile in the shower. (They are left because it will do more damage to remove them.)

28. Brokers cannot get together and price fix commissions, fees or boycott other agents. **(Sherman Antitrust Act)**

29. **Laches** is when you waited too long to sue someone. (Laches=locks=locked out of suing) (For instance, if you wait one year and three days to file a Fair Housing Suit, the doctrine on Laches has taken over. You are locked out of suing because you attempted your suit after the one year allowance time to sue.)

30. When a brokerage does not predominately display the **Equal Housing Opportunity (EHO) Poster**, it is called **Prima Facie** Discrimination. (Prima Facie=Prime Face=in your face.)

31. Refusing to rent to someone based on race is a violation of the **Fair Housing Act**.

32. Landlord cannot segregate all the families with children in one area of the complex.

33. When three banks independently turn down a loan for a consumer based on the property's neighborhood economic factors, it is not **redlining**. Their decisions were not based on the protected classes. They were based on economic factors

34. Agents can- not steer people into neighborhoods where they believe people should live. It's called **steering**.

35. Agents can't go around the neighborhood inducing fear to get commissions. It is called **panic peddling** and **blockbusting**.

36. Dogs are allowed to live in non-pet apartments for handicap purposes including "**comfort pets**". **Americans with Disability Act**. A landlord cannot charge an extra pet fee for a comfort dog.

Part Eleven

1. REIT: A conglomerate of investors who pool their money to buy investments such as residential income property, high rises, malls, commercial building.

2. The disadvantage of a corporation is double taxation. When a corporation owns a shopping mall or high-rise or income property, double taxation still exists.

3. A notary The MOST important thing for a notary to do is to make sure the person is who he or she says they are and that the signing is not under duress or undue influence. (Voluntary)

4. A real estate licensee with many years of practice may become a real estate counselor to help people make real estate decisions.

5. A first-year real estate agent should not take a complicated listing such as a 200-unit apartment complex.

6. Know what 1099 S and 1099 MISC.

7. E and O Insurance will not cover an agent who makes a deliberate falsehood or tries to deceive someone on purpose.

8. It is illegal for a broker to supply health insurance or a retirement plan to an independent contractor. And 90% (a high percentage) of his income has to come from sales or commission.

9. Franchises like Century 21, Tarbell and Prudential have Volume Advertising. It is an advantage.

10. Capital gains exclusion- single at 250,000 and married 500,000.

11. Co-operative owners are shareholders of the corporation. Their ownership interest is personal property.

12. Desk Cost- An office with a Desk Fee is most likely to be found in a 100% commission office.

13. Company dollar- Gross income minus all commissions. (Basically it's what's left over after the agents are paid.) After finding the Company Dollar, then the bills are paid.

14. Employee- At least 90% of his income must come from salary and wages. Can be told what to do and exactly how to do it.

15. Independent Contractor- At least 90% of his income must be made by commissions and sales. Has an agreement with his broker to produce certain results without being told how to do the job? The broker cannot offer a health insurance or a retirement plan. Will get a 1099misc from his broker yearly with the amount of commission received from the broker in order to pay his taxes.

16. 100% commission plan-is a landlord broker that makes his money on desk fees. A landlord broker is renting out the space in the office but in exchange to the agent, the agent is allowed to keep 100% of his earned commissions.

17. Franchise- Examples are Century 21, Tarbell, Keller Williams, and Prudential. Members pay a percentage of their earning to the franchise for expertise and/or advertising and branding.

18. S. Corporation- Ownership is limited to 35 shareholders. "A Pass-through Company."

19. Corporation- A legal entity that never dies. "Double Taxation."

20. General Partnership- Every partner has a personal liability.

21. Limited Partnership- The Limited Partners has limited liability in the amount of their investment. The General Partners have unlimited liability. The General Partners run the business.

22. Capital Gains-Exclusion Used for your personal residence. Must have lived there for at least two years out of the last five. Capital Gains exclusion is: $250,000 for a single person and $500,000 for a married couple. Capital Gains are computed on the difference between the net adjusted basis (cost) and the selling price.

23. UCC- Uniform Commercial Code regulates the sale of personal property apart from the real estate being sold when a business transfers ownership. Personal property should be transferred with a Bill of Sale.

24. Mission Statement- "To exceed our customer's expectations."

25. A Tie In - Tying Arrangement (tie-in): Requiring a buyer to list his or her current home with the same agent in order to purchase the desired new home the buyer really wants.

26. A beneficiary right to a property is personal property. It's a will. A will can be picked up and moved like a lease. The real estate itself is real property.

27. A building constructed off site is a modular home.

28. Standard Accounting Practices are used for keeping records.

29. Whenever money is transferred into a client's trust account, accurate records must be kept

30. A husband and wife own a property and when the husband died, one third of his interest went to each of his children and one third went to his wife. What form of ownership did he and his wife most likely have? In Common. (unequal interests)

31. A husband and wife own property as Joint Tenants. The husband's will give his interest to his property to his son. Upon his passing, how is title held? The wife owns the property In Severalty. The last surviving person owns the property by himself or herself. JTWROS (Joint Tenancy With Rights O Survivorship)

32. A husband and wife took title as joint tenants so that when one passes away the title to the real estate will avoid probate.

33. Title insurance extends to unrecorded instruments.

34. Joint tenancy: Time, title, possession and interest are the common components.

35. Tenancy in Common only has possession as the common component.

36. Spanish Common Law is usually found in the western states. They are community property states. Property a couple acquires after marriage is the property of both husband and wife. (Does not include inheritance)

37. Age 62 is the exemption age for familial status.

38. A 55+ community is excluded from the violation of familial status. A woman can be turned down on the rental because she has children younger than 18 years old.

39. Private Clubs can be excluded from Fair housing laws as long as they don't operate commercially. (They don't advertise or hire a real estate broker.)

40. Religious organizations may be excluded from fair housing rules.

41. Single family housing owned by one individual owning less than three such homes may sell or rent without being subject to the federal Fair Housing Act if no more than one such house is sold within a two-year period.

42. A one to four residential home is excluded from the federal Fair Housing Act if the owner lives on the property.

43. A single mother with two children applied to live in a singles complex. Her friend lives there and recommended the property. The single mother's rental application was rejected based on her having children. When the complex management found out her friend that lives in an apartment on the property recommended the rental, the friend got evicted. The mother's rejection and the friend's eviction violate federal fair housing laws.

44. A property management company can't demand that a person with a comfort pet pick up and carry the pet if she wants to ride in the elevator.

45. For blockbusting to exist there has to be some indication the agent is giving discounts on the listings in a particular neighbor based on the entry of a minority group in the area.

46. Redlining is when a bank refuses to give loans in a neighborhood because of a concentration of a protected class.

47. If three banks independently refuse to give a loan to person because the economic factors of the property neighborhood are deteriorating, it is not redlining. The decision was not based on a protected class.

48. Steering is directing a client into a property or neighborhood based on his belief that it is where the client belongs.

49. A landlord can discriminate if the property is a two to four-unit residential property and the landlord lives there.

50. A borrower is entitled to a three day right of rescission if his loan is on the residence where he lives.

51. Airborne asbestos is friable.

52. PCBs (polychlorinated biphenyls0 are found near electrical equipment.

53. A property manager was given permission by the owner to have an air conditioner repaired. The owner gave the property manager $1000. The repair ended up costing only $600. The property manager cannot keep the balance.

54. Fixed expenses in a property management agreement are things that occur regularly such as gas, electrical and maintenance expenses. It does not include repairs.

55. A property management agreement does not contain the legal address of the property. It contains terms and condition of employment, outline of expected duties and scope of authority.

56. Real estate agents cannot practice law. They cannot draw up legal agreements. They cannot practice accounting.

57. If rent is not paid by the due date, the property manager should first find out the problem and then if needed pursue an eviction. They shouldn't go straight to eviction.

58. During a time of inflation, a property manager would not wish to have long-term leases.

59. The landlord holds a reversionary interest when his property is rented.

60. The long-term lease of the land where the tenants expects to build an office is a ground lease.

61. When Joe rents the ski lodge from November 2nd to March 1st, it is an estate for years. It has a definite beginning and a definite end.

62. When Joe buys the commercial property with three existing leases, he has to honor those leases.

63. A renter's security deposit is to cover any repairs needed once the tenant vacates. It is not the last month's rent.

64. State laws that regulate real estate securities are called blue-sky laws.

> A blue-sky law is a state law in the United States that regulates the offering and sale of securities to protect the public from fraud.

65. A Purchase Agreement is still valid even if it doesn't contain a closing date.

66. The Buyer may rescind his offer and get his earnest money deposit back if done before the seller accepts the offer.

67. A broker must present all offers.

68. A seller is not forced to accept an offer less than asking price.

69. In an option the optionor is forced into seller the property if the optionee decides to purchase it.

70. The accepted ethical behaviors in the real estate profession are the Code of Ethics.

71. Brownfields help resurrect toxic, defunct and deserted industrial waste sites.

72. In investor will buy time in the purchase of an investment property through the use of an option contract.

73. If the bank cannot recover the amount due in a foreclosure, they may sue the mortgagor with a deficiency judgment.

74. The secondary mortgage market does not originate loans.

75. To find the medium household size or medium income, use a demographics report.

76. If a lease vacates before the end of the lease, he can be held responsible for the rents till the end of the lease.

77. The owner in a ground lease is the lessor. (or or givor)

78. Land contracts, installment contracts and purchase money mortgage are seller financing.

79. In a seller financing, the lessor will most likely use a Trust Deed because it's easier to foreclose.

80. A lender bases the amount they will loan on the appraised value.

81. The listing agent cannot tell the buyers the lowest price a seller will accept.

82. Delivery of a deed to a vendee completes the contract.

83. Bob executed a deed to Sally and then put it into a box. When he died, the property went to his heirs because the deed was not recorded.

84. A quitclaim deed gives the less protection in a deed. A General Warranty deed gives the most protection.

85. A deed that is not recorded is valid only between the parties.

86. A deed that is not dated is still valid between the parties.

87. An easement to a dominant tenement is an appurtenance.

88. An easement to a servient tenement is an encumbrance.

89. Riparian rights are found on a small waterway, creek or small stream.

90. Littoral water rights are found on navigable waterways. The Mississippi River is littoral.

91. When a person dies with no will and no heirs, the property become owned by the government. Land cannot be ownerless.

92. One cannot will a life estate.

93. Personal property is transferred by bill of sale.

94. A Chattel Mortgage is used to finance personal property.

95. Restrictions in a deed that only the grantor benefits can be removed by a quitclaim deed.

96. In a Cooperative, if one or more stockholders do not pay their mortgage, the other stockholders have to pay it for them so that the corporation does not default.

97. Owner in a cooperative own their units through stock. It is personal property because stock is a piece of paper. The amount of stock determines location and size of their units.

98. In a condominium, the owners own real estate.

99. If a broker establishes a company policy of charging a 6% commission, he is not in violation of the Sherman Antitrust Act. If that broker got together with another broker and they decided to do it together (price fix), it is illegal.

100. If a person doesn't pay their property tax, the taxing authority can foreclose.

101. It is permissible for a lending institution to refuse a loan based on income.

102. The chain of title is the history of a property's recorded ownership.

103. A landlord can refuse to rent to a person with a violent criminal history.

104. Lead abatement is not mandatory in a lead based paint disclosure.

105. Tenancy in Common allows for unequal interest in property. In Joint tenancy, ownership is always equal interests.

106. All liens are encumbrances.

107. Not all encumbrances are liens. (easements, encroachments)

108. A shared driveway is an encumbrance.

109. In a promissory note the purchase price does not appear.

110. An easement by necessity is used for a landlocked property.

111. When money is deposited into a broker's trust account, accurate records must be kept.

112. Recording a document gives constructive notice to the world.

113. If a seller changes his mind before the closing date, the broker must return the earnest money deposit to the buyer and look toward the seller for compensation.

114. A listing agreement terminates immediately upon the death of the seller or listing agent.

115. An Abstract of Title is the history of the property's recorded instruments.

116. An attorney will read the Abstract and Opinion.

117. The Purchase price is a debit to the buyer.

118. A credit score contains 3 digits.

119. A Suit to Partition can only be done in a Tenancy in Common and a Joint Tenancy.

120. Laws that prohibit monopolies are antitrust laws.

121. If a tenant in common tries to convey 100% interest in a property without the knowledge of the other investors, he has violated the Covenant of Seisen. The deal will be voided because of Impossibility of Performance.

122. A valid bill of sale does not have to include the date.

123. A mortgage banker lends his own money. He cannot prepare an appraisal for a fee.

124. VA and FHA loans are for owner occupied properties.

125. Before buying a property for a home-based business, check for zoning.

126. Before you extend a patio in the front yard, check set back limits.

127. VA is a guarantee company. They do not lend money. You need to go to a qualified lender.

128. FHA is an insurance company. They do not lend money. You need to go to a qualified lender.

129. Novation is the substitution of one party for another on a loan.

130. Pur Autrie Vie is a life estate based on the life of another.

Added: 2016

1. When a buyer pays discount points, the bank yield increases.

2. When a woman remolded her old home to look like an antebellum home, the listing agent should advertise the home as "an Antebellum Styled" home.

3. A buyer made an offer which matched the terms of the listing agreement between the seller and his agent. The seller accepted the offer but scratched out the close of escrow and extended the closing 30 extra days. The offer became voided. (A counter offer voids the original offer.)

4. An agent was sitting at a model home when after closing hours a buyer knocked on the door. The agent let the buyer in and the buyer made a written offer on a property. The agent should deliver the offer to the developer.

5. Land can never be a fixture.

6. Appurtenant easements run with the land.

7. Zoning regulations regulate and control the height of buildings, the population density and use of a building.

8. Moving a chain link fence closer to the street than is allowed by law may require a variance.

9. If a house has mold, the seller's agent must disclose it. (Seller, Seller's Agent and Buyer's Agent must disclose.)

10. Performance is not value.

11. The date of sale of a comparable property in a CMA or appraisal is very important.

12. Banks buy and sell from each other on the secondary mortgage market.

13. The change of position between two lenders requires a subordination agreement.

14. If a Special Agent becomes a property manager, she becomes a General Agent. New contracts are needed.

15. The broker must deposit an earnest money deposit into his checking account even if he receives it over the weekend.

16. The Chain of Title is the history of ownership.

17. A buyer's agent knows his buyer has bad credit. What should the agent have the buyer do before making an offer? See a loan broker or loan banker.

18. When a brokerage is advertising for "Veterans Only" because they specialize in veteran's loans, it is not discrimination.

19. When a developer finishes his subdivision plat map, he will record it.

20. When a seller built a bookcase that fit perfectly into an alcove in the home, it is considered personal property. It was not attached to the property. The seller can take it with him.

21. The seller can be held responsible to return the window boxes he removed from the home after the meeting of the minds. He can be sued for specific performance.

22. The seller may take the two oversized planters on the outside of his front door even if he needed a forklift to remove them. They were not attached to the property. They were personal property.

23. A seller and an agent discussed a contract for the agent to be the listing agent. There was no contract and the property was sold by the agent. The agent had no contract and does not have to be paid.

Know:
1031 Tax Deferred Exchange
Steering
Judicial Foreclosure
Blanket Loan
Package Loan
Title Insurance
Discount Points
Boycotting
Commingling
Unilateral option contracts
Bundle of Rights

Chapter Twenty-two

GLOSSARY – OPEN SOURCE

1031 exchange: "under Internal Revenue Code section 1031, a tax-deferred exchange of "like kind" properties."

1099-S Reporting: "a report to be submitted on IRS Form 1099-S by escrow agents to report the sale of real estate, giving the seller's name, Social Security number, and the gross sale proceeds."

abandonment: failure to occupy or use property that may result in the extinguishment of a right or interest in the property.

abatement: a legal action to remove a nuisance.

addendum clause: "a clause in a deed, usually following the granting clause and beginning with the words "to have and to hold," that describes the type of estate being transferred."

abstract of judgment: judgment that can be recorded in which the debtor owns property and to create a judgment lien against such properties.

abstract of title: summary of all grants, liens, wills, judicial proceedings, and other records that affect the property's title.

abstractor: the person who prepares an abstract of title.

acceleration clause: "a clause in either a promissory note, a security instrument, or both that states that upon default the lender has the option of declaring the entire balance of outstanding principal and interest due and payable immediately."

acceptance: consent (by an offeree) to an offer made (by an offeror) to enter into and be bound by a contract

accession: "the acquisition of additional property by the natural processes of accretion, reliction, or avulsion, or by the human processes of the addition of fixtures or improvements made in error."

accretion: a natural process by which the owner of riparian or littoral property acquires additional land by the gradual accumulation of soil through the action of water.

accrued depreciation: depreciation that has happened prior to the date of valuation.

acknowledgment: "a written declaration signed by a person before a duly authorized officer, usually a notary public, acknowledging that the signing is voluntary."

acknowledgment of satisfaction or satisfaction of mortgage: "a written declaration signed by a person before a duly authorized officer, usually a notary public, acknowledging that a lien has been paid off in full and that the signing is voluntary."

adjustable-rate mortgage (ARM): a mortgage under which interest rates applicable to the loan vary over the term of the loan.

administrator: a person appointed by a probate court to conduct the affairs and distribute the assets of a decedent's estate when there was no executor named in the will or there was no will.

ad valorem: a Latin phrase meaning "according to value." The term is usually used regarding property taxation.

advance fee: a fee charged in advance of services rendered.

adverse possession: the process by which unauthorized possession and use of another's property can ripen into ownership of that other's property without compensation.

agency: "an agency in which the agent is employed by the principal, either by express agreement, ratification, or implication."

agent: a person who represents another.

alienation clause: a due-on-sale clause

alluvium: addition to land acquired by the gradual accumulation of soil through the action of water.

Americans with Disabilities Act: "a federal act that prohibits discrimination against persons with disabilities, where "disability" is defined as "a physical or mental impairment that substantially limits a major life activity.""

amortization: "in general, the process of decreasing or recovering an amount over a period of time; as applied to real estate loans, the process of reducing the loan principal over the life of the loan."

annual percentage rate (APR): "expresses the effective annual rate of the cost of borrowing, which includes all finance charges, such as interest, prepaid finance charges, prepaid interest, and service fees."

appraisal: an estimate of the value of property resulting from an analysis and evaluation made by an appraiser of facts and data regarding the property.

appreciation: an increase in value due to any cause.

appurtenance: "an object, right or interest that is incidental to the land and goes with or pertains to the land."

asbestos: "a naturally occurring mineral composite that once was used extensively as insulation in residential and commercial buildings, in brake pads, and in fire-retardant products, such as furniture. As asbestos ages, it breaks down to small fibers that, if inhaled in sufficient quantity over sufficient time, can cause a variety of ailments, including a type of cancer known as mesothelioma."

assignment: the transfer of the rights and obligations of one party (the assignor) to a contract to another party (the assignee); a transfer of a tenant's entire interest in the tenant's leased premises.

assumption: "an adoption of an obligation that primarily rests upon another person, such as when a purchaser agrees to be primarily liable on a loan taken out by the seller."

attachment lien: "a prejudgment lien on property, obtained to ensure the availability of funds to pay a judgment if the plaintiff prevails."

attorney in fact: a holder of a power of attorney.

average price per square foot: the average price per square foot for a given set of properties is arrived at by adding the per-square-foot cost of each property in the set by the number of properties in the set.

avulsion: "a process that occurs when a river or stream suddenly carries away a part of a bank and deposits it downstream, either on the same or opposite bank."

balloon payment: "significantly greater" generally being considered as being more than twice the lowest installment payment paid over the loan term.

beam: "a horizontal member of a building attached to framing, rafters, etc., that transversely supports a load."

bearing wall: "a wall that supports structures (such as the roof or upper floors) above it. In condominiums, non-bearing walls are owned by the individual condominium owners, whereas bearing walls usually are property owned in common."

beneficiary: "(1) the lender under a deed of trust, (2) one entitled to receive property under a will, (3) one for whom a trust is created."

bilateral contract: a contract in which a promise given by one party is exchanged for a promise given by the other party.

bill of sale: a written document given by a seller to a purchaser of personal property.

blanket mortgage: a mortgage used to finance two or more parcels of real estate.

blight: "as used in real estate, the decline of a property or neighborhood as a result of adverse land use, destructive economic forces, failure to maintain the quality of older structures, failure to maintain foreclosed homes, etc."

blind ad: an advertisement that does not disclose the identity of the agent submitting the advertisement for publication.

blockbusting: "the illegal practice of representing that prices will decline, or crime increase, or other negative effects will occur because of the entrance of minorities into particular areas."

bona fide: in good faith; authentic; sincere; without intent to deceive.

boot: cash or other not like-kind property received in an exchange.

bridge loan: a short-term loan (often referred to as a swing loan) that is used by a borrower until permanent financing becomes available.

broker: "a person who, for a compensation or an expectation of compensation, represents another in the transfer of an interest in real property. "

brownfields: "as defined by the EPA, "real property, the expansion, redevelopment, or reuse of which may be complicated by the presence or potential presence of a hazardous substance, polluted, or contaminant.""

buffer zone: "in zoning, a strip of land to separate, or to ease the transition from, one use to another, such as a park separating a residential zone from a commercial zone, or a commercial or industrial zone separating residential zones from busy streets or highways."

bundle of rights: rights the law attributes to ownership of property.

buyer's agent: a real estate broker appointed by a buyer to find property for the buyer.

capital gain: the amount by which the net sale proceeds from the sale of a capital asset exceeds the adjusted cost value of the asset.

capitalization rate: The rate of return for an investor. "the annual net income of a property divided by the initial investment in, or value of, the property; the rate that an appraiser estimates is the yield rate expected by investors from comparable properties in current market conditions."

CC&Rs: often used to refer to restrictions recorded by a developer on an entire subdivision.

certificate of occupancy: "a written document issued by a local governmental agency, stating that a structure intended for occupancy has been completed, inspected, and found to be habitable."

chain of title: a complete chronological history of all of the documents affecting title to the property.

Civil Rights Act of 1866: "a federal law enacted during Reconstruction that stated that people of any race may enjoy the right to enforce contracts, to sue, be parties, and give evidence, to inherit, purchase, lease, sell, hold, and convey real and personal property, and to full and equal benefit of all laws."

Civil Rights Act of 1968: "a federal law (often referred to as the Fair Housing Act) that prohibited discrimination in housing based on race, creed, or national origin.

client: an agent's principal

closing: "in reference to an escrow, a process leading up to, and concluding with, a buyer's receiving the deed to the property and the seller's receiving the purchase money."

cloud on title: "any document, claim, lien, or other encumbrance that may impair the title to real property or cast doubt on the validity of the title."

coastal zone: a region where significant interaction of land and sea processes occurs.

Coastal Zone Management Act (CZMA): "a federal act intended to protect coastal zones, including the fish and wildlife that inhabit those zones, of the Atlantic, Pacific, and Arctic oceans, the Gulf of Mexico, Long Island Sound, and the Great Lakes from harmful effects due to residential, commercial, and industrial development."

commingling: "regarding trust fund accounts, the act of improperly segregating the funds belonging to the agent from the funds received and held on behalf of another; the mixing of separate and community property."

commission: "an agent's compensation for performance of his or her duties as an agent; in real estate, it is usually a percent of the selling price of the property or, in the case of leases, of rentals."

community property: "property owned jointly by a married couple or by registered domestic partners, as distinguished from separate property. As a general rule, property acquired by a spouse or registered domestic partner through his/her skills or personal efforts is community property."

comparable property: "a property similar to the subject property being appraised that recently sold at arm's length, where neither the buyer nor the seller was acting under significant financial pressure."

comparative market analysis (CMA): "a comparison analysis made by real estate brokers using recent sales, and current listings, of similar nearby homes to determine the list price for a subject property."

condemnation proceeding: a judicial or administrative proceeding to exercise power of eminent domain.

conditional use: "a zoning exception for special uses such as churches, schools, and hospitals that wish to locate to areas zoned exclusively for residential use."

condominium: "a residential unit owned in severalty, the boundaries of which are usually walls, floors, and ceilings, and an undivided interest in portions of the real property, such as halls, elevators, and recreational facilities."

conflict of interest: "a situation in which an individual or organization is involved in several potentially competing interests, creating a risk that one interest might unduly influence another interest."

consideration: "anything of value given or promised, such as money, property, services, or a forbearance, to another to enter into a contract."

construction mortgage: a security instrument used to secure a short-term loan to finance improvements to a property.

constructive eviction: a breach by the landlord of the covenant of habitability or quiet enjoyment.

constructive notice: "(1) notice provided by public records; (2) notice of information provided by law to a person by exercising reasonable diligence, could have discovered the information."

contingency: "an event that may, but is not certain to, happen, the occurrence upon which the happening of event is dependent."

contract: a contract is an agreement to do or to forbear from doing a certain thing.

conventional loan: a mortgage loan that is not FHA insured or VA guaranteed.

cooperating broker: a broker who attempts to find a buyer for a property listed by another broker.

cost approach: an appraisal approach that obtains the market value of the subject property by adding the value of land (unimproved) of the subject property to the depreciated value of the cost (if currently purchased new) of improvements on subject property.

counteroffer: a new offer by an offeree that acts as a rejection of an offer by an offeror.

coupled with an interest: "an aspect of an agency that refers to the agent's having a financial interest in the subject of the agency, which has the legal effect of making the appointment of the agent irrevocable."

covenant: "a contractual promise to do or not do certain acts, such as on a property, the remedy for breach there of being either monetary damages or injunctive relief, not forfeiture."

crawlspace: the space between the ground and the first floor that permits access beneath the building.

debits: "in reference to an escrow account, items payable by a party. This definition of a debit does not conform to its use in double-entry bookkeeping or accounting."

deed: a document that when signed by the grantor and legally delivered to the grantee conveys title to real property.

deed in lieu of foreclosure: a method of avoiding foreclosure by conveying to a lender title to some property lieu of the lender's foreclosing on the property.

deferred maintenance: any type of depreciation that has not been corrected by diligent maintenance.

deficiency judgment: a judgment given to a lender in an amount equal to the balance of the loan minus the net proceeds the   lender receives after a judicial foreclosure.

demand: the level of desire for a product.

deposit receipt: a written document indicating that a good-faith deposit has been received as part of an offer to purchase real property; also called a purchase and sale agreement.

depreciation: the loss in value due to any   cause.

depreciation deduction: an annual tax allowance for the depreciation of property.

490

designated agent: "an agent authorized by a real estate broker to represent a specific principal to the exclusion of all other agents in the brokerage. This designated agent owes fiduciary responsibilities to the specified principal, but other agents in the brokerage may represent other parties to the same transaction that the specified principal is a party to without creating a dual agency situation. Where this practice of designated agency is allowed, disclosure of the designated agency relationship is required."

devise: (1) (noun) a gift of real property by will; (2) (verb) to transfer real property by a will.

devisee: a recipient of real property through a will.

discounted rate: a rate (also called a teaser rate) on an adjustable-rate mortgage that is less than the fully indexed rate.

discount points: "a form of prepaid interest on a mortgage, or a fee paid to a lender to cover cost the making of a loan. The fee for one discount point is equal to 1% of the loan amount."

documentary transfer tax: a tax imposed by counties and cities on the transfer of real property within their jurisdictions.

dominant tenement: land that is benefited by an easement appurtenant.

down payment: the amount of money that a lender requires a purchaser to pay toward the purchase price.

drywall: prefabricated sheets or panels nailed to studs to form an interior wall or partition.

dual agent: a real estate broker who represents both the seller and the buyer in a real estate transaction.

due diligence: the exercise of an honest and reasonable degree of care in performing one's duties or obligations. A real estate agent's due diligence involves investigating the property to ensure that the property is as represented by the seller and to disclose accurate and complete information regarding the property.

due-on-sale clause: "a clause in the promissory note, the security instrument, or both that states that the lender has the right to accelerate the loan if the secured property is sold or some other interest in the property is transferred."

duress: unlawful force or confinement used to compel a person to enter into a contract against his or her will.

earnest money deposit: a deposit that accompanies an offer by a buyer and is generally held in the broker's trust account.

easement: "a non-possessory right to use a portion of another property owner's land for a specific purpose, as for a right-of- way, without paying rent or being considered a trespasser."

easement appurtenant: "an easement that benefits, and is appurtenant to, another's land."

easement by necessity: "easement by necessity —arises as a creation of a court of law in certain cases were justice so demands, as in the case where a buyer of a parcel of land discovers that the land he or she just purchased has no access except over the land of someone other than from the person from whom the parcel was purchased."

emblements: "growing crops, such as grapes, avocados, and apples, that are produced seasonally through a tenant farmer's labor and industry."

eminent domain: "right of the state to take, through due process proceedings (often referred to as condemnation proceedings), private property for public use upon payment of just compensation."

encroachment: "a thing affixed under, on, or above the land of another without permission."

encumber: To place a lien or other encumbrance on property.

encumbrance: "A right or interest held by someone other than the owner the property that affects or limits the ownership of the property, such as liens, easements, licenses, and encroachments."

Environmental Impact Statement (EIS): " a written document that federal agencies must prepare for any development project that a federal agency could prohibit or regulate, and any development project for which any portion is federally financed. An EIS can include comments on the expected impact of a proposed development on such things as air quality, noise, population density, energy consumption, water use, wildlife, public health and safety, and vegetation."

Equal Credit Opportunity Act (ECOA): "a federal law that prohibits a lender from discriminating against any applicant for credit on the basis of race, color, religion, national origin, sex, marital status, or age (unless a minor), or on the grounds that some of the applicant's income derives from a public assistance program."

equitable title: the right to possess or enjoy a property while the property is being paid for. An insurable interest for the buyer.

escalator clause: "a provision in a lease that provides for periodic increases in rent in an amount based on some objective criteria not in control of either the tenant or the landlord, such as the Consumer Price Index."

escheat: "a process whereby property passes to the state if the owner of the property dies intestate without heirs, or if the property becomes abandoned."

escrow: a neutral depository in which something of value is held by an impartial third party (called the escrow agent) until all conditions specified in the escrow instructions have been fully performed.

escrow agent: an impartial agent who holds possession of written instruments and deposits until all of the conditions of escrow have been fully performed.

escrow instructions: "the written instructions signed by all of the principals to the escrow (buyers, sellers, and lenders) that specify all of the conditions that must be met before the escrow agent may release whatever was deposited into escrow to the rightful parties."

estate: "the degree, quantity, nature, duration, or extent of interest one has in real property."

estate at sufferance: "a leasehold that arises when a lessee who legally obtained possession of a property remains on the property after the termination of the lease without the owner's consent. Such a holdover tenant can be evicted like a trespasser, but if the owner accepts rent, the estate automatically becomes a periodic tenancy."

estate at will: "an estate (or tenancy) in which a person occupies a property with the permission of the owner; however, the tenancy has no specified duration, and, in most states, may be terminated at any time by either the tenant or the owner of the property upon giving proper notice. "

estate for years: "a leasehold that continues for a definite fixed period of time, measured in days, months, or years."

estate from period to period: "a leasehold that continues from period to period, whether by days, months, or years, until terminated by proper notice."

estoppel: "a legal principle that bars one from alleging or denying a fact because of one's own previous actions or words to the contrary. Ostensible agency can be created by estoppel when a principal and an unauthorized agent act in a manner toward a third-party that leads the third party to rely on the actions of the unauthorized agent, believing that the actions are authorized by the principal."

exclusive agency listing: a listing agreement that gives a broker the right to sell property and receive compensation (usually a commission) if the property is sold by anyone other than the owner of the property during the term of the listing.

exclusive right to sell listing: "a listing agreement that gives a broker the exclusive right to sell property and receive compensation (usually a commission) if the property is sold by anyone, including the owner of the property, during the term of the listing."

executed contract: a contract that has been fully performed; may also refer to a contract that has been signed by all of the parties to the contract.

executor: a person named in a will to carry out the directions contained in the will.

executory contract: a contract that has not yet been fully performed by one or both parties.

express contract: "a contract stated in words, written or oral."

external obsolescence: "depreciation that results from things such as (1) changes in zoning laws or other government restrictions, (2) proximity to undesirable influences such as traffic, airport flight patterns, or power lines, and (3) general neighborhood deterioration, as might result from increased crime."

false promise: a promise made without any intention of performing it.

Fannie Mae: a U.S. government conservatorship originally created as the Federal National Mortgage Association 8 to purchase mortgages from primary lenders.

fee simple absolute estate: the greatest estate that the law permits in land. The owner of a fee simple absolute estate owns all present and future interests in the property.

fee simple defeasible estate: "a fee estate that is qualified by some condition that, if violated, may "defeat" the estate and lead to its loss and reversion to the g r a n t o r." **FHA:** "the Federal Housing Administration is a federal agency that was created by the National Housing Act of 1934 in order to make housing more affordable by increasing home construction,

FICO score: a credit score created by the Fair Isaac Corporation that ranges from 300 to 850 and is used by lenders to help evaluate the creditworthiness of a potential borrower.

fiduciary relationship: "a relationship in which one owes a duty of utmost care, integrity, honesty, and loyalty to another."

first mortgage: a security instrument that holds first-priority claim against certain property identified in the instrument.

fixture: "an object, originally personal property, that is attached to the land in such a manner as to be considered real property."

flashing: sheet metal or other material used in roof and wall construction to prevent water from entering.

flat fee listing: a listing in which the broker's compensation is a set amount rather than a percentage of the sale price.

floodplain: "an area of low, flat, periodically flooded land near streams or rivers."

flue: a channel in a chimney through which flame and smoke passes upward to the outer air.

footing: "concrete poured on solid ground that provides support for the foundation, chimney, or support columns. Footing should be placed below the frost line to prevent movement."

foreclosure: "a legal process by which a lender, in an attempt to recover the balance of a loan from a borrower who has defaulted on the loan, forces the sale of the collateral that secured the loan."

four unities in Joint tenancy: "refers to the common-law rule that a joint tenancy requires unity of possession, time, interest, and title."

Freddie Mac: a U.S. government conservatorship originally created as the Federal Home Loan Mortgage Corporation to purchase mortgages from primary lenders in the private mortgage money market.

freehold estate: an estate in land whereby the holder of the estate owns rights in the property for an indefinite duration.

fully amortized loan: a loan whereby the installment payments are sufficient to pay off the entire loan by the end of the loan term.

functional obsolescence: "depreciation that results (1) from deficiencies arising from poor architectural design, outdated style or equipment, and changes in utility demand, such as for larger houses with more garage space, or (2) from over- improvements, where the cost of the improvements was more than the addition to market value."

general agent: an agent who is authorized by a principal to act for more than a particular act or transaction. General agents are usually an integral part of an ongoing business enterprise. A property manager.

general lien: a lien that attaches to all of a person's nonexempt property.

general partnership: a partnership in which each partner has the equal right to manage the partnership and has personal liability for all of the partnership debts.

gift deed: "a deed used to convey title when no tangible consideration (other than "affection") is given. The gift deed is valid unless it was used to defraud creditors, in which case such creditors may bring an action to void the deed."

Gennie Mae: the Government National Mortgage Association is a wholly owned U.S. government corporation within HUD to guarantee pools of eligible loans that primary lenders issue as Gennie Mae mortgage-backed securities.

graduated lease: "a lease that is similar to a gross lease except that it provides for periodic increases in rent, often based on the Consumer Price Index."

grantee: one who acquires an interest in real property from another.

grantor: one who transfers an interest in real property to another.

gross income: total income from a property before any expenses are deducted.

gross income multiplier (GIM): a number equal to the estimated value of a property divided by the gross yearly income of the property.

gross lease: "a lease under which the tenant pays a fixed rental amount, and the landlord pays all of the operating expenses for the premises."

gross rent multiplier (GRM): a number equal to the estimated value of a property divided by the gross monthly rental income of the property.

ground lease: a lease under which a tenant leases land and agrees to construct a building or to make other significant improvements on the land.

group boycott: "in antitrust law, the action of two or more brokers agreeing not to deal with another broker or brokers."

heir: a person entitled to obtain property through intestate succession.

hip roof: a sloping roof that rises from all four sides of the house.

holographic will: "a will written, dated, and signed by a testator in his or her own handwriting."

home equity line of credit (HELOC): a revolving line of credit provided by a home equity mortgage.

home equity mortgage: a security instrument used to provide the borrower with a revolving line of credit based on the amount of equity in the borrower's home.

homestead: a homestead exemption that applies to a homeowner's principal residence and that provides limited protection for the homeowner's equity in that residence against a judgment lien foreclosure.

homestead exemption: the amount of a homeowner's equity that may be protected from unsecured creditors.

HUD-1 Uniform Settlement Statement: an escrow settlement form mandated by RESPA for use in all escrows pertaining to the purchase of owner-occupied residences of 1-4 dwelling units that use funds from institutional lenders regulated by the federal government.

implied contract: "a contract not expressed in words, but, through action or inaction, understood by the parties."

income approach: "an appraisal approach that estimates the value of an income-producing property as being worth the present value of the future income of the property through a three-step process: (1) determine the net annual income, (2) determine an appropriate capitalization rate, and (3) divide the net income by the capitalization rate to obtain the estimate of value."

incurable depreciation: depreciation that results from (1) physical deterioration or functional obsolescence that cannot be repaired at a cost that is less than or equal to the value added   to the property and (2) economic obsolescence (which is beyond the control of the property owner).

independent contractor: "a person who performs work for someone, but does so independently in a private trade, business, or profession, with little or no supervision from the person for whom the work is performed."

index: "under an adjustable-rate mortgage, the benchmark rate of interest that is adjusted periodically according to the going rate of T-bills, LIBOR, or the like."

innocent landowner defense: "a defense to liability for cleanup of toxic waste under CERCLA (the Superfund Law) by one who acquires contaminated property after the contamination occurred and who acquired the property by inheritance or bequest or who, prior to purchasing the property, performed "all appropriate inquiries" to determine that the property had not been contaminated."

installment note: "a promissory note in which periodic payments are made, usually consisting of interest due and some repayment of principal."

intentional misrepresentation: "the suggestion, as a fact, to a party that which is not true committed by another party who does not believe it to be true and who makes the suggestion with the intent to deceive the first party, who was deceived to his or her detriment, such as by being induced to enter into a contract."

interest: the compensation fixed by the parties for the use of money.

interest-rate cap: "interest-rate cap —under an adjustable-rate mortgage, the maximum that the interest rate can increase from one adjustment period to the next or over the life of the entire loan."

interpleader: "an action that allows for a neutral third party (such as a real estate agent) to avoid liability to two or more claimants (such as a seller and buyer) to the same money or property (such as an earnest money deposit) by forcing the claimants to litigate among themselves, letting the court determine who deserves what while not enmeshing the neutral third party in the litigation."

Interstate Land Sales Full Disclosure Act: a federal consumer protection act that requires that certain land developers register with the Consumer Financial Protection Bureau if they offer across state lines parcels in subdivisions containing 100 or more lots. Subdivisions where each lot in the subdivision contains at least 20 acres are exempt from this registration requirement. A developer must provide each prospective buyer with a Property Report that contains pertinent information about the subdivision and that discloses to the prospective buyer that he or she has a minimum of 7 days in which to rescind the purchase agreement.

intestate: "not having made, or not having disposed of by, a will."

intestate succession: transfer of the property of one who dies intestate.

inverse condemnation: a judicial or administrative action brought by a landowner to force the condemnation of the landowner's land where nearby condemned land or land used for public purposes (such as for noisy airports) severely reduces the value of the landowner's land.

involuntary lien: "a lien created by operation of law, not by the voluntary acts of the debtor."

joint tenancy: "joint tenancy —a form of joint ownership which has unity of possession, time, interest, and title."

joist: one of a series of parallel heavy horizontal timbers used to support floor or ceiling loads.

judgment: a court's final determination of the rights and duties of the parties in an action before it.

judicial foreclosure: "a foreclosure carried out not by way of a power-of-sale clause in a security instrument, but under the supervision of a court."

junior mortgage: "a mortgage that, relative to another mortgage, has a lower lien-priority position."

land installment contract: a real property sales contract. The Seller retains legal title and the buyer is given equitable title until the loan is paid in full. During the time of the contract, the buyer has possession of the property.

leasehold estate: a less-than-freehold estate.

lease-option: "a lease (also referred to as a lease with an option to purchase) that provides the tenant with the right, but not the obligation, to purchase the leased property at a specified price within a specified period of time."

lease-purchase: an agreement (also referred to as a lease with an obligation to purchase) that provides for the purchase of property preceded by a lease under which a portion of each lease payment is applied to the purchase price.

lease renewal: a continuation of tenancy under a new lease.

lessee: a person (the tenant) who leases property from another.

lessor: a person (the landlord) who leases property to another.

less-than-freehold estate: an estate in which the holder has the exclusive right to possession of land for a length of time. The holder of a less-than-freehold estate is usually referred to as a lessee or tenant.

leverage: a method of multiplying gains (or losses) on investments by using borrowed money to acquire the investments.

lien: "lien —an encumbrance against real property that is used to secure a debt and that can, in most cases, be foreclosed."

lien priority: the order in which lien holders are paid if property is sold to satisfy a debt.

lien theory: "a legal theory of mortgage: the mortgagor retains both legal and equitable title of the property, including exclusive possession and use of the property. The mortgagee simply possesses a lien against the property (usually a lien of higher priority than certain other liens, such as judgment liens). Upon default, the mortgagee must go through a formal (judicial) foreclosure proceeding to obtain legal title and possession." **life estate:** "either by the life of the person holding the estate, or by the life or lives of one or more other persons."

limited liability partnership: a partnership in which there is at least one general partner and one or more limited partners. The limited partners have no liability beyond their investment in and pledges to the partnership.

liquidated damages: "a sum of money that the parties agree, usually at the formation of a contract, will serve as the exact amount of damages that will be paid upon a breach of the contract."

lies pendent: (Latin for "action pending") a notice of Lis pendens of action.

listing agreement: "a written contract between a real estate broker and a property owner (the principal) stipulating that in exchange for the real estate broker's procuring a buyer for the principal's property, the principal will compensate the broker, usually with a percentage of the selling price."

loan modification: a restructuring or modification of a mortgage or deed of trust on terms more favorable to the buyer's ability (or desire) to continue making loan payments.

loan-to-value ratio (LTV): the amount of a first mortgage divided by the lesser of (1) the appraised value of the property or (2) the purchase price of the property.

long-term capital gain: "the capital gain on the sale of a capital asset that was held for a relatively long period of time, usually more than one year."

margin: "a number of percentage points, usually fixed over the life of the loan, that is added to the index of an adjustable-rate mortgage to arrive at the fully indexed rate."

market allocation: "in antitrust law, the process of competitors agreeing to divide up geographic areas or types of products or services they offer to customers."

market price: the price actually paid for a particular property.

market value: "as defined for appraisal purposes by HUD/FHA is: "The most probable price which a property should bring in a competitive and open market under all conditions requisite to a fair sale, the buyer and seller, each acting prudently, knowledgeably and assuming the price is not affected by undue stimulus.""

material fact: a fact that is likely to affect the decision of a party as to whether to enter into a transaction on the specified terms.

mechanics lien: a specific lien claimed by someone who furnished labor or materials for a work of improvement on real property and who has not been fully paid.

median price per square foot: the median price per square foot of a set of properties is the price per square foot of the property whose price per square foot is such that half of the properties in the set have an equal or lower price per square foot and half have an equal or higher price per square foot.

Megan's Law: an informal name for various federal and state laws that provide for the registration of sex offenders and for the making available to the public information regarding the location of these offenders.

metes and bounds land description: "a method of describing a parcel of land that uses physical features of the locale, along with directions and distances, to define the boundaries of the parcel."

moldings: "patterned strips, usually of wood, used to provide ornamental finish to cornices, bases, windows, and door jambs."

mortgage banker: a primary lender that uses its own money in creating a mortgage loan.

mortgage broker: an individual or company that finds borrowers and matches them with lenders for a fee.

mortgagee: a lender or creditor to whom a mortgagor gives a mortgage to secure a loan or performance of an obligation.

mortgage loan originator (MLO): "a person who takes, or offers to take, a residential mortgage loan application or offers or negotiates terms of a residential mortgage application for compensation or gain or in expectation of compensation or gain."

mortgagor: the borrower who gives a mortgage on his or her property to secure a loan or performance of an obligation.

multiple listing service: an organization (MLS) of real estate brokers who share their listings with other members of the organization.

mutual consent: refers to the situation in which all parties to a contract freely agree to the terms of the contract; sometimes referred to as a "meeting of the minds."

National Association of Real Estate Brokers: a real estate trade association whose members are called Realists®. They subscribe to a code of ethics.

National Association of Realtors®: "the largest real estate trade association in the United States, founded in 1908, whose members are called Realtors®." They subscribe to a code of ethics.

National "Do Not Call" Registry: a registry established by the Federal Trade Commission to protect consumers from unwanted commercial telephone solicitations.

negative amortization: a loan repayment scheme in which the outstanding principal balance of the loan increases because the installment payments do not cover the full interest due.

negative amortized loan: "the unpaid part of the interest due being tacked onto the principal, thereby causing the principal to grow as each month goes by."

negligent misrepresentation: "an assertion not warranted by the information of the party making the assertion that an important fact was true, which was not true, relied on by another party to that party's detriment."

net income: income from a property remaining after expenses are deducted from gross income.

net lease: a lease under which the tenant pays a fixed rental amount plus some of the landlord's operating expenses.

net listing: a listing agreement providing the broker with all proceeds received from the sale over a specified amount. Net listings are not legal in many states.

nonconforming loan: a loan not in conformance with FHFA guidelines.

nonconforming use: "a zoning exception for areas that are zoned for the first time or that are rezoned and where established property uses that previously were permitted to not conform to the new zoning requirements. As a general rule, such existing properties are "grandfathered in," allowing them to continue the old use but not to extend the old use to additional properties or to continue the old use after rebuilding or abandonment." **non-judicial foreclosure:** "a foreclosure process culminating in a privately conducted, publicly held trustee's sale. The right to pursue a non-judicial foreclosure is contained in the power-of- sale clause of a mortgage or deed of trust, which, upon borrower default and the beneficiary's request, empowers the trustee to sell the secured property at a public auction."

notice of completion: "a written form that notifies that a work of improvement on real property has been completed and that limits the time in which mechanic's liens may be filed against the property."

notice of default (NOD): a document prepared by a trustee at the direction of a lender to begin a non-judicial foreclosure proceeding.

notice of sale: a document prepared by a trustee at the direction of a lender that gives notice of the time and place of sale of an identified foreclosed property.

novation: "a substitution of a new obligation or contract for an old one, or the substitution of one party to a contract by another, relieving the original party of liability under the contract."

nuisance: "anything that is indecent or offensive to the senses, or an obstruction to the free use of property, so as to interfere with the comfortable enjoyment of life or property."

offer: a proposal by one person (the offeror) to enter into a contract with another (the offeree).

offeree: one to whom an offer to enter into a contract is made.

offeror: one who makes an offer to enter into a contract.

open listing: "a listing agreement that gives a broker the nonexclusive right to sell property and receive compensation (usually a commission) if, but only if, the broker is the first to procure a buyer for the property. "

opinion of title: a written rendering of an opinion on the condition of ownership of title in a real estate transaction prepared by an attorney after examination of an abstract of title.

option contract: a contract that gives the purchaser of the option the right to buy or lease a certain property at a set price any time during the option term.

origination fee: "the fee a lender charges to cover expenses of processing a loan, such as purchasing credit reports, inspection reports and appraisals, and paying office expenses and salaries of personnel who interview borrowers and analyze the reports and appraisals."

partially amortized loan: "an installment loan under which monthly payments pay all of the interest due but not enough of the principal to fully pay off the loan at the end of the loan term. In such a case, a balloon payment would be due at the end of the loan term."

partial release clause: "a clause in a blanket mortgage that allows a developer to sell off individual parcels and pay back, according to a release schedule, only a proportionate amount of the blanket loan."

partition: partition —a court-ordered or voluntary division of real property held in joint ownership into parcels owned in severalty.

passive income: "in general, income from either rental activity or from a business in which the taxpayer does not materially participate."

passive investor: an investor who does not actively contribute to the management of the business invested in.

payee: the person to whom a promissory note is made out.

payment cap: "payment cap —under an adjustable-rate mortgage, the maximum amount that installment payments may increase from one adjustment period to the next or over the life of the loan."

percentage lease: "a lease, often used in shopping centers, under which the tenant typically pays a base rent amount plus a percentage of the gross receipts of the tenant's business."

periodic tenancy: an estate from period to p e r i o d .

period of redemption: a period of time after a sheriff's sale in   a judicial foreclosure proceeding during which the borrower may redeem his or her property by paying off the entire debt plus costs.

physical deterioration: depreciation that results from wear and tear of use and from natural causes.

physical life: the period of time that the property lasts with normal maintenance.

pitch: the degree of inclination or slope of a roof.

plaintiff: the one who brings a lawsuit.

plaster: "a mixture of lime or gypsum, sand, water, and fiber that is applied to walls and ceilings and that hardens into a smooth coating."

point: "in finance, a point is equal to 1% of the loan amount. The term is used by lenders to measure discount charges and other costs such as origination fees and private mortgage insurance premiums."

point of beginning: the fixed starting point in the metes and bounds method of land description.

police power: "the power of a government to impose restrictions on private rights, including property rights, for the sake of public welfare, health, order, and security, for which no compensation need be made."

power of attorney: a special written instrument that gives authority to an agent to conduct certain business on behalf of the principal. The agent acting under such a grant is sometimes called an attorney in fact.

power-of-sale clause: "a clause contained in most trust deeds that permits the trustee to foreclose on, and sell, the secured property without going to court."

preapproval: preapproval —an evaluation of a potential borrower's ability to qualify for a loan that involves a credit check and verification of income and debt of the potential borrower.

predatory lending: "the imposition of unfair, deceptive, abusive, or fraudulent loan terms on borrowers."

prepayment penalty: a fee charged to a borrower for paying off the loan faster than scheduled payments call for.

prequalification: an initial unverified evaluation of a potential borrower's ability to qualify for a mortgage loan.

prescription: a method of acquiring an interest in property by use and enjoyment for five years.

prescriptive casement: an easement acquired by prescription.

price fixing: an agreement between competitors to set prices or price ranges. **price per square foot:** the price per square foot of a specific property is determined by dividing the price (either selling or listing) by the property's square footage. Appraisers determine the square footage of a property by using the outside measurement of the property.

primary financing: first mortgage property financing.

primary mortgage market: the market where mortgage loans are originated.

principal: the one whom an agent represents.

principle of anticipation: "principle that value is derived from a calculation of anticipated future benefits to be derived from the property, not from past benefits, though past benefits may inform as to what might be expected in the future."

principle of conformity: "principle that the maximum value of land is achieved when there is a reasonable degree of social, economic, and architectural conformity in the area. "

principle of contribution: "principle that improvements made to a property will contribute to its value or that, conversely, the lack of a needed improvement will detract from the value of the property."

principle of four-stage life cycle: "principle that property goes through a process of growth, stability, decline and revitalization."

principle of pottage: states that assembling two or more parcels of land into one parcel results in the larger parcel having a greater value than the sum of the values of the smaller parcels.

principle of progression: principle that the value of a residence of less value tends to be enhanced by proximity to residences of higher value.

principle of regression: principle that the value of a residence of higher value tends to be degraded by the proximity to residences of lower value.

principle of substitution: principle that the value of a property will tend toward the cost of an equally desirable substitute property.

principle of supply and demand: "principle that the value of property in a competitive market is influenced by the relative levels of supply and demand: the greater level of demand in relation to the level of supply, the greater the value."

principle of the highest and best use: principle that the best use of a property in terms of value is the use most likely to produce the greatest net return (in terms of money or other valued items).

private mortgage insurance (PMI): mortgage insurance that lenders often require for loans with an LTV more than 80%.

probate: a legal procedure whereby a superior court in the county where the real property is located or where the deceased resided oversees the distribution of the decedent's property.

procuring cause: "a common law legal concept developed by the courts to determine the proportioning of commissions among agents involved in a real estate transaction In general, an agent who is a procuring cause of a sale originated a chain of events that resulted in the sale and is thereby entitled to at least some part of the total commission generated by the sale."

promissory note: "a contract whereby one person unconditionally promises to pay another a certain sum of money, either at a fixed or determinable future date or on demand of the payee."

property disclosure statement: "a statement filled out by the seller of residential property consisting of 1 to 4 dwelling units, disclosing to potential purchaser's defects in the property that are known to the seller, or that should be known to the seller upon reasonable inspection."

proration: an adjustment of expenses that either have been paid or are in arrears in proportion to actual time of ownership as of the closing of escrow or other agreed-upon date.

protected class: a group of people protected from discrimination by federal or state law.

public dedication: "a gift of an interest in land to a public body for public use, such as for a street, a park, or an easement to access a beach."

public grant: "public land conveyed, usually for a small fee, to individuals or to organizations, such as to railroads or universities."

puffing: the act of expressing a positive opinion about something to induce someone to become a party to a contract.

purchase money loan: "a deed of trust or mortgage on a dwelling for not more than four families given to a lender to   secure repayment of a loan which was in fact used to pay all or part of the purchase price of that dwelling, occupied entirely or in part by the purchaser."

pyramid roof a hip roof that has no ridge.: pyramid roof a hip roof that has no ridge.

quantity survey method: " the most detailed method of estimating the replacement or reproduction cost of a structure, in which an estimate is made of the cost of all of the raw materials needed to replace the building. Such material-cost information is available in construction cost h a n d b o o k s "

quiet title action: "see, suit to quiet title"

quitclaim deed: "a deed that contains no warranties of any kind, no after-acquired title provisions, and provides the grantee with the least protection of any deed; it merely provides that any interest (if there is any) that the grantor has in the property is transferred to the grantee."

rafter: "one of a series of parallel sloping timbers that extend from the ridge board to the exterior walls, providing support for the roof."

real estate investment trust (REIT): "a company that invests in and, in most cases operates, income-producing real estate and that meets numerous criteria, such as the necessity of being jointly owned by at least 100 persons."

real estate owned (REO): property acquired by a lender through a foreclosure sale.

Real Estate Settlement Procedures Act (RESPA): "a federal law designed to prevent lenders, real estate agents, developers, title insurance companies, and other agents (such as appraisers and inspectors) who service the real estate settlement process from providing kickbacks or referral fees to each other and from facilitating bait-and-switch tactics."

real property sales contract: an agreement in which one party agrees to convey title to real property to another party upon the satisfaction of specified conditions set forth in the contract and that does not require conveyance of title within one year from the date of formation of the contract.

Realist®: a member of the National Association of Real Estate Brokers. Subscribe to a code of ethics.

Realtor®: a member of the National Association of Realtors®. Subscribe to a code of ethics.

reconciliation: the process of ascertaining value by comparing and evaluating values obtained from comparable or from different valuation approaches; the process of comparing what is in a trust fund account with what should be in the account.

conveyance deed: "a deed executed by the trustee of a deed of trust after the promissory note is paid off in full by the borrower and the lender instructs the trustee to so execute the conveyance deed, which recovers legal title to the b o r r o w e r"

recorded map or plat system: "a method of land description that states a property's lot, block, and tract number, referring to a map recorded in the county where the property is located.   "

rectangular survey system: a method of land description based on a grid system of north-south lines ("ranges") and east- west lines ("tier" or "township" lines) that divides the land into townships and sections.

red flag: "a condition that should alert a reasonably attentive person of a potential problem that warrants further investigation. Examples include stains on ceilings or walls, the smell of mold, and warped floors or walls."

redlining: the illegal practice of refusing to make loans for real property in particular areas.

Regulation Z: the set of regulations that implement the Truth- in-Lending Act (TILA).

reinforced concrete: "concrete poured around steel bars or metal netting to increase its ability to withstand tensile, shear, and compression stresses."

rejuvenation: "the phase when a property is rebuilt, remodeled, or otherwise revitalized to a new highest and best use."

reliction: a natural process by which the owner of riparian or littoral property acquires additional land that has been covered by water but has become permanently uncovered by the gradual recession of water.

remainder: "the residue of a freehold estate where, at the end of the estate, the future interest arises in a third p e r s o n."

remainder man: a person who inherits or is entitled to inherit property held as a life estate when the person whose life determines the duration of the life estate passes away.

replacement cost: "the cost of replacing improvements with those having equivalent utility, but constructed with modern materials, designs, and workmanship."

reproduction cost: the cost of replacing improvements with exact replicas at current prices.

rescission: the cancellation of a contract and the restoration of each party to the same position held before the contract was entered into.

reserve account: "in reference to loan servicing, the escrow account from which the loan servicer typically pays, on behalf of the borrower, property taxes, hazard insurance and any other charges (such as mortgage insurance) with respect to the loan."

retaliatory eviction: an eviction action brought to retaliate against a tenant for making a habitability complaint or for asserting other of the tenant's legal rights.

return on investment (ROI): an investor's cash flow (net income minus financing charges) divided by the investor's actual cash investment (as distinct from the purchase price).

reverse mortgage: "a security instrument for a loan for homeowners over the age of 62 who have a large amount of equity in their homes, usually designed to provide such homeowners with monthly payments, often over the lifetime of the last surviving homeowner who either moves out of the house or dies."

reversion: "the residue of a freehold estate where at the end of the estate, the future interest reverts to the grantor."

revocation: the withdrawal of an offer by the person who made the offer.

rezoning amendment: an amendment to a zoning ordinance that property owners may request if they feel that their area has been improperly zoned.

Ridge-board: a horizontal board placed on edge at the apex of a roof to which the upper ends of the rafters are attached.

right of first refusal: "the right to be given the first chance to purchase a property at the same price, terms, and conditions as is offered to third parties if and when the property is put up for sale."

right of survivorship: "the right to succeed to the interest of a joint tenant or, if community property with right of survivorship, to succeed to the interest of a spouse or registered domestic partner. Right of survivorship is the most important characteristic of joint tenancy."

riparian rights: "the rights of a landowner to use water from a stream or lake adjacent to his or her property, provided such use is reasonable and does not injure other riparian owners."

rob call: "a pre-recorded, auto-dialed telephone call."

R-value: "a measure of the resistance of insulation to heat transfer. The FTC requires sellers of new homes to disclose the R-value of each home's insulation. The higher the R-value, the greater is the effectiveness of the insulation."

safety clause: "a provision in a listing agreement, providing that the broker will earn the full commission if the property is sold within a specified number of days after the termination of the listing to a buyer with whom the broker has dealt in certain specified ways regarding the property."

sales comparison approach: an appraisal approach that compares recent sales of similar properties in the area to evaluate the market value of the subject property.

salesperson: a natural person who is employed by a licensed real estate broker to perform acts that require having a real estate license.

sandwich lease: a leasehold interest that lies between a primary lease and a sublease.

sash: frames that contain one or more windowpanes.

scarcity: a lack of abundance.

secondary financing: second mortgage and junior mortgage property financing

secondary mortgage market: the market where mortgages are sold by primary mortgage lenders to investors.

second mortgage: a security instrument that holds second- priority claim against certain property identified in the instrument.

secret profit: any compensation or beneficial gain realized by an agent not disclosed to the principal. Real estate agents must always disclose any interest that they or their relatives have in a transaction and obtain their principals' consent. **section:** "one square mile, containing 640 acres."

security instrument: the written instrument by which a debtor pledges property as collateral to secure a loan.

seller carry back loan: a loan or credit given by a seller of real property to the purchaser of that property.

seller's agent: a real estate broker appointed by the seller to represent the seller.

selling agent: the real estate agent who sells or finds and obtains a buyer for the property in a real estate transaction.

senior mortgage: "a mortgage that, relative to another mortgage, has a higher lien-priority position."

separate property: "property that is owned in severalty by a spouse or registered domestic partner. Separate property includes property acquired before marriage or the registering of domestic partnership, and property acquired as a gift or by inheritance during marriage or registered domestic partnership."

servient tenement: land that is burdened by an easement.

setback: "a designation of a governing body as to how far a structure must be situated from something else, such as a curb or a neighboring property."

severalty: ownership of property by one person.

severance: "the act of detaching an item of real property that changes the item to personal property, such as the cutting down of a natural tree. Also, the act of terminating a relationship, such as the act of partitioning by court order for the transfer of an interest that changes a joint tenancy into a tenancy in common."

severance damages: damages paid to an owner of land partially taken by eminent domain where the value of the remaining portion of the owner's land is severely reduced by the severance of the condemned a portion of owner's land.

Sherman Act: "the federal law passed in 1890 that prohibits agreements, verbal or written, that have the effect of restraining free trade."

short sale: a pre-foreclosure sale made by the borrower (usually with the help of a real estate agent) with lender approval of real estate for less than the balance due on the mortgage loan.

short-term capital gain: "the capital gain on the sale of a capital asset that was held for a relatively short period of time, usually one year or less."

sill: "the board or metal forming the lower side of the frame for a window or door; the lowest part of the frame of a house, resting on the foundation and providing the base for the   studs."

single agent: an agent who represents only one party in a given transaction.

situs: "the legal location of something; also refers to the preference for a particular location to live, work, or invest   in"

special agent: an agent for a particular act or transaction.

special assessment: "a tax levied against properties in a particular area that are benefited by improvements such as for streets, water, and sewers."

specific lien: a lien that attaches only to specific property.

specific performance: a court order that requires a person to perform according to the terms of a contract.

spot zoning: "spot zoning —refers to the zoning of isolated properties for use different from the uses specified by existing zoning laws. To spot zone a particular property may, in some cases, be a violation of the requirement that police power applies similarly to all property similarly situated, which in turn arises from the constitutional guarantee of equal protection under the law."

square-foot method: "the most widely used method of estimating reproduction or replacement cost of a building, involving the collection cost data on recently constructed similar buildings and dividing the total cost by the square footage to obtain cost per square f o o t "

statute of frauds: "a law that requires certain types of contracts, including most real estate contracts, to be in writing and signed by the party to be bound in order for the contract to be enforceable."

statute of limitations: a law that requires particular types of lawsuits to be brought within a specified time after the occurrence of the event giving rise to the lawsuit.

steering: "the illegal practice of directing people of protected classes away from, or toward, housing in particular areas."

stigmatized property: a property having a condition that certain persons may find materially negative in a way that does not relate to the property's actual physical condition.

stock cooperative: a corporation formed or availed of primarily for the purpose of holding title to improved real property either in fee simple or for a term of y e a r s .

straight-line depreciation: "the expensing of a property by equal amounts over the useful life of the property, determined by subtracting from the cost of the property the estimated residual value of the property and dividing that amount by the useful life of the property measured in years."

straight-line method: a method of calculating annual depreciation of an improvement by dividing the cost of the improvement by the estimated useful life of a typical such improvement.

straight note: a promissory note under which periodic payments consist of interest only.

strict foreclosure: full title simply passes to the lender.

subagent: an agent of an agent.

subject to: acquiring real property that is burdened by a mortgage without becoming personally liable for the mortgage debt.

sublease: a transfer of a tenant's right to a portion of the leased premises or to the entire premises for less than the entire remaining lease term.

subordination clause: a provision in a mortgage or deed of trust that states that the mortgage or deed of trust will have lower priority than a mortgage or deed of trust recorded later.

suit to quiet title: "a court proceeding intended to establish the true ownership of a property, thereby eliminating any cloud on title."

tax deed: "the deed given to the successful buyer at a tax sale. A tax deed conveys title free and clear from private liens, but not from certain tax liens or special assessment liens or from easements and recorded restrictions."